IaC Mastery

Infrastructure as Code

Your All-in-One Guide to Terraform, AWS, Azure, and Kubernetes

4 BOOKS IN 1

Book 1
Getting Started with IaC: A Beginner's Guide to Terraform

Book 2
Cloud Infrastructure Orchestration with AWS and IaC

Book 3
Azure IaC Mastery: Advanced Techniques and Best Practices

Book 4
Kubernetes Infrastructure as Code: Expert Strategies and Beyond

ROB BOTWRIGHT

Published by Rob Botwright
Library of Congress Cataloging-in-Publication Data
ISBN 978-1-83938-582-7
Cover design by Rizzo

Disclaimer

The contents of this book are based on extensive research and the best available historical sources. However, the author and publisher make no claims, promises, or guarantees about the accuracy, completeness, or adequacy of the information contained herein. The information in this book is provided on an "as is" basis, and the author and publisher disclaim any and all liability for any errors, omissions, or inaccuracies in the information or for any actions taken in reliance on such information.

The opinions and views expressed in this book are those of the author and do not necessarily reflect the official policy or position of any organization or individual mentioned in this book. Any reference to specific people, places, or events is intended only to provide historical context and is not intended to defame or malign any group, individual, or entity.

The information in this book is intended for educational and entertainment purposes only. It is not intended to be a substitute for professional advice or judgment. Readers are encouraged to conduct their own research and to seek professional advice where appropriate.

Every effort has been made to obtain necessary permissions and acknowledgments for all images and other copyrighted material used in this book. Any errors or omissions in this regard are unintentional, and the author and publisher will correct them in future editions.

Introduction

In a world where technology evolves at a breakneck pace, staying ahead of the curve is not just an advantage; it's a necessity. The realm of cloud infrastructure management has witnessed a seismic shift with the advent of Infrastructure as Code (IaC). To empower you on this transformative journey, we present the ultimate guide to IaC in one comprehensive book bundle.

Welcome to **"IaC Mastery: Infrastructure as Code"**, where you will embark on an educational odyssey through the core pillars of modern cloud infrastructure. Our bundle consists of four meticulously crafted volumes, each designed to elevate your skills from a beginner to an expert across Terraform, AWS, Azure, and Kubernetes.

⊡ **Book 1: Getting Started with IaC: A Beginner's Guide to Terraform** In this foundational volume, we lay the groundwork for your IaC adventure. If you're new to Terraform and IaC, fear not! We start from the basics, guiding you through Terraform's configuration, syntax, and best practices. By the end of this book, you'll have a solid understanding of how to create, manage, and scale infrastructure as code.

⊡ **Book 2: Cloud Infrastructure Orchestration with AWS and IaC** Venture into the vast expanse of Amazon Web Services (AWS) and master the art of orchestrating cloud infrastructure using IaC. From setting up your AWS environment for IaC to exploring advanced techniques, security, and compliance, this volume equips you with the skills needed to navigate the AWS cloud with confidence.

⊡ **Book 3: Azure IaC Mastery: Advanced Techniques and Best Practices** Azure is your next destination, where you'll discover the advanced intricacies of IaC tailored specifically for the Azure cloud ecosystem. Dive deep into networking, security, testing, and optimization strategies to become a true Azure IaC expert. Real-world best practices will elevate your Azure infrastructure management game.

🔲 **Book 4: Kubernetes Infrastructure as Code: Expert Strategies and Beyond** The final leg of your journey takes you to the dynamic world of Kubernetes IaC. Here, you'll unravel the intricacies, security measures, testing frameworks, and advanced strategies for managing Kubernetes infrastructure as code. By the end of this volume, you'll be equipped with expert-level skills for orchestrating containerized workloads.

Each book in this bundle is a stepping stone toward mastery, providing you with the knowledge, tools, and real-world insights needed to excel in the ever-evolving landscape of cloud infrastructure management. Whether you're just starting or looking to enhance your expertise, "IaC Mastery" offers a comprehensive roadmap to success.

Prepare to unlock the true potential of Infrastructure as Code across Terraform, AWS, Azure, and Kubernetes. Your journey to becoming an IaC master begins here, and we're thrilled to be your guide through this transformative experience. Get ready to conquer the future of cloud infrastructure management with "IaC Mastery: Infrastructure as Code." 🔲

Book 1
Getting Started with IaC
A Beginner's Guide to Terraform

ROB BOTWRIGHT

Chapter 1: Introduction to Infrastructure as Code (IaC)

Infrastructure as Code (IaC) represents a transformative approach to managing and provisioning computing infrastructure. It emerged as a response to the increasing complexity and scale of modern IT environments, enabling organizations to treat their infrastructure as software. In essence, IaC leverages the principles and practices of software development to automate and manage infrastructure deployments, configurations, and updates. By doing so, it brings agility, scalability, and consistency to the management of IT resources.

One of the core tenets of IaC is the use of code to define and provision infrastructure components. This code, often written in domain-specific languages (DSLs) or using configuration management tools, captures the desired state of the infrastructure. Through IaC, infrastructure becomes programmable and reproducible, reducing the risk of configuration drift and human errors that can lead to downtime or security vulnerabilities.

IaC tools and practices have gained immense popularity in recent years, driven by the growth of cloud computing, microservices architectures, and DevOps methodologies. Cloud platforms like AWS, Azure, and Google Cloud offer robust IaC support, enabling users to define and manage cloud resources using code.

Terraform, one of the most widely adopted IaC tools, provides a declarative approach to infrastructure provisioning. Users define their infrastructure in Terraform configuration files, specifying the desired resources, their properties, and dependencies. When applied, Terraform analyzes the current state of the infrastructure and makes the necessary changes to bring it in line with the desired state.

This declarative approach offers a significant advantage in terms of predictability and idempotence, as Terraform ensures that the infrastructure remains consistent with the code's intent, regardless of the current state. Moreover, Terraform supports a wide range of cloud providers, making it a versatile choice for multi-cloud and hybrid cloud environments.

Other IaC tools, such as AWS CloudFormation, Azure Resource Manager templates, and Google Cloud Deployment Manager, are tailored for specific cloud platforms. They offer native support for provisioning and managing resources on their respective clouds, providing deep integration and automation capabilities.

One of the key benefits of IaC is its ability to codify infrastructure best practices. Infrastructure code can be reviewed, tested, and versioned just like application code. This means that teams can apply software development practices, such as continuous integration (CI) and continuous delivery (CD), to their infrastructure code.

With CI/CD pipelines, changes to infrastructure code can be automatically built, tested, and deployed, reducing the time and risk associated with manual deployments. This approach also facilitates collaboration among teams, as code changes are tracked, reviewed, and documented through version control systems like Git.

IaC promotes infrastructure as a codebase, making it easier to manage and scale complex environments. As organizations grow, their infrastructure needs evolve, requiring the ability to scale resources up or down dynamically. With IaC, scaling becomes a matter of adjusting the code that defines the infrastructure, allowing organizations to respond quickly to changing demands.

Moreover, IaC promotes modularity and reusability. Infrastructure components can be defined as modules or templates, which can be reused across projects or shared with the wider community. This modular approach simplifies the management of complex infrastructures by breaking them down into manageable, composable pieces.

However, while IaC offers numerous benefits, it also comes with its set of challenges and considerations. Managing infrastructure through code requires a shift in mindset and skill set for IT operations teams. They must become proficient in writing and maintaining infrastructure code, which may involve learning new languages and tools.

Security is another critical aspect of IaC. With infrastructure defined as code, vulnerabilities or misconfigurations in the code can expose organizations to risks. Therefore, it's essential to incorporate security best practices into the IaC development process, such as code reviews, automated testing for security issues, and adherence to compliance standards.

IaC also requires robust testing procedures. Infrastructure code changes can have a significant impact on an organization's operations, and therefore thorough testing is crucial to ensure that changes do not lead to outages or disruptions.

Another challenge is achieving a balance between automation and control. While automation is a key driver of IaC, it's important not to automate blindly. Organizations should maintain control over their infrastructure and avoid overly complex or convoluted code that can hinder visibility and troubleshooting.

As IaC adoption continues to grow, the ecosystem of tools and best practices is constantly evolving. This book aims to provide readers with a comprehensive understanding of Infrastructure as Code, covering various aspects from fundamental concepts to advanced techniques and real-world use cases.

Throughout the chapters, you will delve into the specifics of IaC with a focus on Terraform, one of the most versatile and widely adopted IaC tools. Whether you are a beginner looking to get started with IaC or an experienced practitioner seeking advanced strategies, this book will guide you on your journey to mastering Infrastructure as Code.

Advantages of Implementing Infrastructure as Code (IaC) in modern IT environments are significant and far-reaching. First and foremost, IaC enhances agility by allowing organizations to provision and manage infrastructure resources quickly and efficiently. This agility is especially valuable in today's fast-paced business landscape, where the ability to respond to changing demands swiftly can be a competitive advantage.

IaC also promotes consistency by ensuring that infrastructure configurations are standardized and uniform across all environments. This consistency reduces the risk of configuration drift, where differences between development, testing, and production environments can lead to unexpected issues and downtime.

Another notable advantage is scalability. IaC empowers organizations to scale their infrastructure resources up or down as needed, often with a single change in the code. This dynamic scalability aligns with the principles of elasticity and cost-efficiency, allowing organizations to optimize resource allocation and minimize unnecessary expenses.

Furthermore, IaC enhances collaboration among development and operations teams. By treating infrastructure as code, these traditionally separate groups can work together seamlessly, using shared version control systems and automated deployment pipelines. This collaboration fosters a culture of DevOps, where rapid, reliable, and iterative development and deployment processes become the norm.

The ability to version and track changes to infrastructure configurations is a fundamental advantage of IaC. Organizations can maintain a history of changes, which aids in troubleshooting, rollback procedures, and auditing. This versioning also facilitates compliance with regulatory requirements, as organizations can demonstrate adherence to specific configurations over time.

Efficiency gains are another compelling reason to implement IaC. Manual infrastructure provisioning and configuration can be time-consuming and error-prone. IaC automates these tasks, reducing the reliance on manual interventions and minimizing the potential for human errors that can lead to outages or security vulnerabilities.

Moreover, IaC brings transparency to infrastructure management. All changes are documented in code, providing visibility into who made the changes, what those changes entailed, and when they were implemented. This transparency simplifies the process of tracking and auditing changes, ensuring accountability within the organization.

Security is a critical advantage of IaC. By treating infrastructure as code, organizations can apply security best practices to their infrastructure configurations. Security policies and compliance requirements can be codified and enforced, reducing the risk of misconfigurations and vulnerabilities.

Scalability is a key advantage of IaC, enabling organizations to scale their infrastructure resources in response to varying workloads and demands. This scalability supports the dynamic nature of modern applications, ensuring that infrastructure resources can grow or shrink as needed to maintain optimal performance. IaC also promotes cost optimization. By automating resource provisioning and decommissioning, organizations can allocate resources more efficiently, reducing unnecessary spending on idle or underutilized resources. This cost optimization aligns with the cloud's pay-as-you-go pricing model, helping organizations maximize the value of their cloud investments.

Flexibility is another advantage of IaC. Infrastructure configurations can be modified easily by changing the code, allowing organizations to adapt to evolving requirements and respond to market changes rapidly. This flexibility enhances the organization's ability to innovate and stay competitive. Reliability and repeatability are essential advantages of IaC. Infrastructure deployments become highly predictable and consistent when managed through code. Organizations can trust that the infrastructure will match the desired state defined in the code, reducing the likelihood of unexpected issues or failures.

Disaster recovery and resilience are improved through IaC. Infrastructure configurations can be versioned and backed up, making it easier to recreate infrastructure in the event of a disaster or failure. This capability enhances an organization's ability to maintain business continuity.

Furthermore, IaC fosters a culture of automation, which is essential in modern IT operations. Automation not only streamlines routine tasks but also reduces the need for manual intervention, resulting in improved efficiency, reduced operational costs, and fewer human errors.

IaC's advantages extend to testing and validation. Infrastructure changes can be tested in a controlled environment before being applied to production, reducing the risk of disruptions and ensuring the stability of critical systems.

Finally, IaC promotes the sharing of best practices and code reuse within and across organizations. Infrastructure code can be modularized and shared as reusable templates or modules, facilitating collaboration and knowledge transfer.

In summary, the advantages of implementing Infrastructure as Code (IaC) are multifaceted, encompassing agility, consistency, scalability, collaboration, versioning, efficiency, transparency, security, cost optimization, flexibility, reliability, disaster recovery, automation, testing, and code reuse. These benefits make IaC a compelling approach for modernizing IT operations and meeting the challenges of today's dynamic and fast-paced business environments.

Chapter 2: Understanding the Basics of Terraform

Deconstructing Terraform begins with understanding its core principles and components. At its essence, Terraform is an Infrastructure as Code (IaC) tool that allows users to define and provision infrastructure resources declaratively. Declarative provisioning means that users specify the desired state of their infrastructure, and Terraform is responsible for making the necessary changes to align the actual state with the desired state.

A fundamental concept in Terraform is the use of configuration files written in HashiCorp Configuration Language (HCL). These configuration files serve as the blueprints for defining infrastructure resources. In HCL, users describe the resources they want to create, their attributes, dependencies, and any other necessary configurations.

Terraform configurations are organized into modules, which are reusable units of configuration. Modules enable users to encapsulate and share infrastructure components, making it easier to maintain and scale infrastructure as projects grow in complexity.

Terraform configurations consist of resource blocks that define the various infrastructure components. Each resource block corresponds to a specific resource type, such as virtual machines, networks, or databases, and includes attributes that specify the resource's configuration.

Dependency management is a critical aspect of Terraform. Resource dependencies are explicitly defined in the configuration, ensuring that resources are provisioned in the correct order. Terraform uses this dependency information to create a directed acyclic graph (DAG) of resources, allowing it to determine the provisioning order automatically.

Terraform's command-line interface (CLI) is the primary tool for interacting with and managing infrastructure. Users run Terraform commands to initialize a working directory, plan changes to the infrastructure, apply those changes, and manage the state of the infrastructure.

The Terraform CLI communicates with various providers, such as cloud platforms like AWS, Azure, and Google Cloud, to create, update, or delete resources. Terraform providers are responsible for translating the declarative configuration into specific API calls to the respective cloud platforms.

One of Terraform's distinguishing features is its support for multiple providers within a single configuration. This means users can define resources from different cloud providers or other infrastructure platforms within the same Terraform configuration, enabling multi-cloud and hybrid cloud deployments.

Terraform state is a crucial aspect of managing infrastructure. State files store the current state of the provisioned resources and are used to track changes over time. Terraform uses the state file to determine what actions need to be taken to bring the infrastructure into the desired state.

To ensure collaboration and versioning, Terraform configurations are often stored in version control systems (VCS) like Git. This allows teams to work on infrastructure code collaboratively, track changes, and maintain a history of modifications.

Terraform's configuration files can be parameterized using variables. Variables enable users to define dynamic values that can be passed into the configuration during deployment. This parameterization enhances the flexibility and reusability of Terraform configurations.

Outputs are another essential feature of Terraform configurations. Outputs allow users to expose specific values from the infrastructure, such as IP addresses or resource IDs, for further use or reference by other parts of the configuration or external systems.

Terraform supports remote backends, which are storage locations for Terraform state files. Remote backends enable teams to share and collaborate on infrastructure across different environments while maintaining a consistent and centralized state.

Terraform's plan command is a critical step in the provisioning process. It generates an execution plan that outlines the changes

Terraform will make to the infrastructure to achieve the desired state. This plan is essential for reviewing and validating changes before they are applied.

Terraform apply is the command used to execute the changes specified in the execution plan. It provisions or modifies the infrastructure resources based on the desired state defined in the configuration. Terraform apply is a potentially destructive operation, making it essential to review and confirm the changes before proceeding.

Terraform's state management is a key aspect of its reliability. The state file is typically stored remotely, allowing for safe and centralized management. This approach prevents conflicts and ensures that the state remains consistent across team members and environments.

Terraform supports a rich ecosystem of community-contributed modules and providers. Modules provide reusable configurations for common infrastructure patterns, while providers extend Terraform's capabilities to work with various services and platforms beyond its core functionality.

In summary, Terraform is a powerful Infrastructure as Code tool that enables users to define and provision infrastructure resources declaratively using HashiCorp Configuration Language (HCL). Terraform configurations consist of resource blocks that specify the desired infrastructure components, and dependencies are managed explicitly. The Terraform CLI interacts with providers to create, update, or delete resources, and state management ensures the infrastructure's desired state is maintained accurately. Terraform configurations can be parameterized using variables and expose values through outputs, enhancing flexibility and reusability. Collaboration is facilitated through version control systems and remote backends, while the plan and apply commands provide essential control over infrastructure changes. Terraform's reliability is bolstered by its state management and support for a wide range of modules and providers, making it a valuable tool for managing and provisioning infrastructure at scale.

Key Components of Terraform are central to understanding how the Infrastructure as Code (IaC) tool operates and manages infrastructure. At the heart of Terraform is the configuration file, which serves as the blueprint for defining and provisioning infrastructure resources. These configuration files are written in HashiCorp Configuration Language (HCL), providing a clear and human-readable syntax for describing infrastructure components.

Within Terraform configurations, one of the primary elements is the resource block. Resource blocks are used to define specific infrastructure resources, such as virtual machines, networks, databases, and more. Each resource block corresponds to a particular resource type and includes attributes that specify the resource's configuration, properties, and dependencies.

Resource dependencies are explicitly declared in the configuration to ensure that resources are provisioned in the correct order. Terraform uses this dependency information to build a directed acyclic graph (DAG) that represents the order in which resources should be created or updated. This automated dependency resolution is a critical aspect of Terraform's functionality.

Terraform configurations can be modularized using modules, which are reusable units of configuration. Modules allow users to encapsulate and share infrastructure components, making it easier to manage and scale infrastructure as projects grow in complexity. Modules can be reused across different projects and even shared with the broader community, promoting collaboration and code reuse.

Dependency management in Terraform is essential for ensuring that resources are created, updated, or destroyed in the correct order. By explicitly declaring dependencies between resources, Terraform can determine the optimal provisioning sequence and avoid potential issues related to resource interdependencies.

The Terraform command-line interface (CLI) serves as the primary tool for interacting with Terraform and managing infrastructure. Users run various Terraform commands to initialize a working directory, plan changes to the infrastructure, apply those changes, and manage the state of the infrastructure. The CLI is the gateway to Terraform's functionality and provides a robust set of commands for infrastructure management.

Terraform communicates with infrastructure providers, such as cloud platforms (e.g., AWS, Azure, Google Cloud), to create, update, or delete resources. These providers are responsible for translating the declarative Terraform configuration into specific API calls and actions within the respective cloud platforms. Terraform's ability to support multiple providers within a single configuration enables users to define resources from different providers, facilitating multi-cloud and hybrid cloud deployments.

Terraform state is a critical component for managing infrastructure. State files store the current state of provisioned resources and are used to track changes over time. Terraform relies on the state file to understand the differences between the actual infrastructure state and the desired state specified in the configuration. Proper state management is essential for Terraform to determine what actions need to be taken to bring the infrastructure into the desired state.

To facilitate collaboration and versioning, Terraform configurations are often stored in version control systems (VCS), such as Git. Storing configurations in VCS enables teams to work on infrastructure code collaboratively, track changes, and maintain a history of modifications. This approach aligns with modern software development practices and promotes code sharing and review.

Terraform configurations can be parameterized using variables. Variables allow users to define dynamic values that can be passed into the configuration during deployment. This parameterization enhances the flexibility and reusability of Terraform configurations, as users can customize configurations for different environments or scenarios by providing different variable values.

Outputs are another key feature of Terraform configurations. Outputs allow users to expose specific values from the infrastructure, such as IP addresses, DNS names, or resource IDs. These values can be used for further reference or passed to other parts of the configuration or external systems, enhancing the configurability and integration of Terraform-managed infrastructure.

Terraform supports remote backends, which are storage locations for Terraform state files. Remote backends provide several advantages, including centralized state management, collaboration across different environments, and improved security. By storing the state file remotely, organizations can ensure consistency and prevent conflicts when multiple team members work on the same infrastructure.

The Terraform plan command plays a crucial role in the infrastructure provisioning process. It generates an execution plan that outlines the changes Terraform will make to the infrastructure to achieve the desired state. This plan is essential for reviewing and validating changes before they are applied, helping users understand the impact of proposed changes.

The Terraform apply command is used to execute the changes specified in the execution plan. It provisions or modifies the infrastructure resources based on the desired state defined in the configuration. Terraform apply is a potentially destructive operation, making it essential to review and confirm the changes before proceeding to avoid unintended consequences.

State management in Terraform is critical for ensuring the reliability and consistency of infrastructure. The state file is typically stored remotely, allowing for centralized management and preventing issues related to multiple team members modifying the state simultaneously. This remote state management ensures that the infrastructure's desired state remains consistent across environments and team members.

Terraform boasts a rich ecosystem of community-contributed modules and providers. Modules provide reusable configurations for common infrastructure patterns, while providers extend Terraform's capabilities to work with various services and platforms beyond its core functionality. These modules and providers simplify the configuration and provisioning of infrastructure resources, allowing users to leverage pre-built solutions and integrate with a wide range of services.

In summary, the key components of Terraform include configuration files written in HCL, resource blocks for defining infrastructure resources, explicit dependency management, modularization through modules, a powerful command-line interface (CLI), support for multiple infrastructure providers, state management, version control integration, parameterization using variables, outputs for exposing values, remote backends for state storage, the plan command for change validation, and the apply command for executing changes. These components work together to provide a robust and versatile Infrastructure as Code (IaC) solution for managing and provisioning infrastructure.

Chapter 3: Setting Up Your Development Environment

Preparing your development environment is a crucial step in getting started with Infrastructure as Code (IaC) and tools like Terraform. It lays the foundation for creating, managing, and deploying infrastructure resources effectively. A well-configured development environment provides the necessary tools, dependencies, and settings to support your IaC workflow.

Before you begin, ensure that your system meets the prerequisites for running Terraform. These prerequisites typically include a compatible operating system, a working installation of Terraform, and access to a version control system (VCS) like Git. Terraform supports various operating systems, including Linux, macOS, and Windows, so choose the one that suits your development environment.

Next, consider the text editor or integrated development environment (IDE) you will use for writing Terraform configurations. Terraform configuration files are written in HashiCorp Configuration Language (HCL), a human-readable language designed for defining infrastructure. Popular text editors and IDEs for HCL include Visual Studio Code, Sublime Text, and JetBrains' IDEs like IntelliJ IDEA with the HCL plugin.

To enhance your development experience, consider installing plugins or extensions for your chosen text editor or IDE. These extensions often provide syntax highlighting, code formatting, and other features that make working with HCL easier and more efficient.

Managing dependencies is another essential aspect of preparing your development environment. Terraform may require external plugins or providers to interact with specific infrastructure platforms or services. It's essential to install these dependencies before you start working on your configurations.

Using version control is a best practice for managing and tracking changes to your Terraform configurations. Git is one of the most widely used version control systems and integrates seamlessly with Terraform. Ensure you have Git installed on your system and configure it with your name and email address.

Consider creating a Git repository to store your Terraform configurations. A well-organized repository structure can help you manage multiple projects and environments effectively. It's common to have separate directories or submodules for different projects, making it easier to maintain and share configurations.

When using version control, remember to add a .gitignore file to exclude sensitive or unnecessary files from being committed to the repository. Common entries in a .gitignore file for Terraform projects include .terraform, .tfstate, and .tfvars files, as well as any local cache or log directories.

To collaborate with team members or share your Terraform configurations, you may want to choose a remote version control platform, such as GitHub, GitLab, or Bitbucket. Create a repository on your chosen platform and configure the remote repository URL in your local Git configuration.

Terraform relies on environment variables for sensitive information, such as API keys, authentication tokens, or secrets. When preparing your development environment, consider how you will manage these variables. You can set environment variables directly in your shell or use tools like Vault or AWS Secrets Manager to store and retrieve sensitive information securely.

As part of your development environment setup, ensure that you have access to the cloud or infrastructure platforms you intend to manage with Terraform. This typically involves creating accounts, obtaining API credentials, and configuring access permissions. Cloud providers like AWS, Azure, and Google Cloud offer documentation and guides to help you set up your accounts and obtain the necessary credentials.

When working with Terraform configurations, it's essential to follow best practices for code organization and directory structure. A well-organized project structure can improve code readability and maintainability. Consider creating separate directories for your Terraform configurations, modules, and other resources.

As part of your development environment setup, consider how you will manage and store Terraform state files. Terraform state is a crucial aspect of tracking the actual state of your infrastructure. You can configure Terraform to store state locally or remotely. Remote state storage options include Amazon S3, Azure Blob Storage, Google Cloud Storage, and HashiCorp Terraform Cloud. Choose the storage solution that best fits your requirements and configure Terraform accordingly.

To streamline the process of initializing your Terraform working directory, create a script or automation tool that sets up the necessary dependencies and configurations. This can help standardize your development environment across team members and reduce the chances of configuration errors.

As you prepare your development environment, consider integrating Terraform into your continuous integration/continuous deployment (CI/CD) pipeline. CI/CD practices help automate the testing and deployment of your infrastructure configurations, ensuring that changes are validated and applied consistently.

In summary, preparing your development environment for Terraform involves several key steps, including meeting system prerequisites, choosing a text editor or IDE, managing dependencies, using version control, setting up a Git repository, configuring environment variables, obtaining access to cloud platforms, organizing your project structure, managing Terraform state, and integrating Terraform into your CI/CD pipeline. A well-prepared development environment sets the stage for efficient and effective Infrastructure as Code (IaC) workflows using Terraform.

Configuration and tooling setup are foundational steps in your journey to mastering Infrastructure as Code (IaC) with Terraform. These steps lay the groundwork for creating, managing, and provisioning infrastructure resources efficiently and effectively.

One of the first considerations in your configuration and tooling setup is the choice of a suitable development environment. This environment includes your local workstation or a designated development server, depending on your organization's practices and requirements. Ensure that your development environment meets the necessary hardware and software prerequisites for running Terraform.

Before you begin working with Terraform, you'll need to install the Terraform binary on your local system. Terraform provides installation packages for various operating systems, including Linux, macOS, and Windows. It's essential to choose the version of Terraform that aligns with your project's requirements and dependencies.

Text editors or integrated development environments (IDEs) play a pivotal role in your Terraform workflow. You'll be writing Terraform configuration files in HashiCorp Configuration Language (HCL), so selecting a text editor or IDE that supports HCL syntax highlighting and code formatting can significantly enhance your productivity and code quality.

Extensions or plugins for your chosen text editor or IDE can further streamline your Terraform development experience. These extensions often provide features like autocompletion, code snippets, and real-time validation, making it easier to write error-free Terraform code.

While you're setting up your development environment, consider configuring a version control system (VCS) like Git. VCS is an integral part of modern software development and provides a structured approach to managing changes to your Terraform configurations. Initialize a Git repository in your project directory and commit your initial Terraform files.

Organizing your Terraform codebase effectively is essential for maintainability. Consider adopting a directory structure that separates Terraform configurations, modules, and other resources. This separation helps you manage and scale your Terraform project as it grows in complexity.

Managing dependencies in your Terraform project involves handling external providers and modules. Terraform providers are used to interact with specific infrastructure platforms, such as AWS, Azure, or Google Cloud. Depending on your project's requirements, you may need to install and configure providers to support your chosen infrastructure.

Terraform modules are reusable units of configuration that encapsulate infrastructure components. When organizing your Terraform codebase, consider creating a separate directory for modules. This directory structure allows you to store and share modules across different projects and promotes code reuse.

Managing sensitive data and credentials is a critical aspect of configuration and tooling setup. Terraform configurations often require access tokens, API keys, or other sensitive information to interact with cloud providers and services. Ensure that you have a secure mechanism in place for managing these credentials, such as environment variables or a dedicated secrets management solution.

Another consideration in your configuration setup is the choice of a state management strategy. Terraform uses state files to track the current state of your infrastructure. You can configure Terraform to store state locally or remotely, depending on your project's requirements and collaboration needs.

Remote state storage options include cloud object storage services like Amazon S3, Azure Blob Storage, or Google Cloud Storage. Additionally, Terraform Cloud offers a managed state storage solution with advanced features like state locking and collaboration features for teams.

As part of your tooling setup, consider integrating Terraform with continuous integration/continuous deployment (CI/CD) pipelines. CI/CD practices automate the testing and deployment of your Terraform configurations, ensuring that changes are validated and applied consistently across various environments.

Furthermore, implement a testing framework or approach that suits your project's needs. Automated testing helps catch issues in your Terraform configurations early in the development process. Consider using tools like Terratest or Kitchen-Terraform for writing and running tests against your infrastructure code.

Documentation is a crucial aspect of your configuration and tooling setup. Ensure that you have a clear and comprehensive documentation strategy for your Terraform project. Document your Terraform configurations, modules, and any custom scripts or processes you use in your infrastructure provisioning workflow.

Security should be a top priority in your configuration and tooling setup. Adopt security best practices for your Terraform codebase, such as using least privilege principles, encrypting sensitive data, and regularly auditing and reviewing configurations for potential vulnerabilities.

As part of your tooling setup, select a monitoring and observability solution that allows you to track the state and performance of your infrastructure resources. Tools like Prometheus, Grafana, or cloud-native monitoring services can help you gain insights into your Terraform-managed infrastructure.

Finally, as you complete your configuration and tooling setup, consider the ongoing maintenance and evolution of your Terraform environment. Stay informed about updates and new features in Terraform and related tools, and be prepared to adapt your setup to accommodate changes in your project's requirements.

In summary, configuration and tooling setup are critical steps in your journey to mastering Infrastructure as Code (IaC) with Terraform. These steps encompass choosing a development environment, installing Terraform, configuring a text editor or IDE, setting up a version control system, organizing your codebase, managing dependencies, handling sensitive data, selecting a state management strategy, integrating with CI/CD pipelines, implementing testing, documenting your project, prioritizing security, and planning for monitoring and maintenance. A well-prepared and well-maintained development environment and tooling setup form the foundation for efficient and effective Terraform-based infrastructure management.

Chapter 4: Terraform Configuration and Syntax

Diving into Terraform configuration is a journey that takes you deep into the heart of Infrastructure as Code (IaC), where you'll learn to define, manage, and provision infrastructure resources with precision and control. At the core of Terraform's power lies the HashiCorp Configuration Language (HCL), a versatile and human-readable language designed explicitly for expressing infrastructure as code.

Terraform configurations are written in HCL, which combines declarative and imperative elements, allowing you to describe what you want your infrastructure to look like and how it should be configured. This unique blend of declarative and imperative paradigms enables you to define infrastructure resources with clarity and flexibility.

The basic building block of Terraform configuration is the resource block. Resource blocks define specific infrastructure resources you want to create, configure, or manage. Each resource block corresponds to a particular resource type, such as virtual machines, databases, networks, and more. Within a resource block, you'll specify attributes that define the resource's configuration, properties, and dependencies.

Dependency management is a key aspect of Terraform configuration. You explicitly declare dependencies between resources to ensure they are provisioned in the correct order. Terraform uses this dependency information to build a directed acyclic graph (DAG) that represents the order in which resources should be created or updated. This automated dependency resolution is a crucial part of Terraform's functionality.

Terraform configurations are organized into modules, which are reusable units of configuration. Modules allow you to encapsulate and share infrastructure components, making it easier to manage and scale your Terraform project as it grows. Modules can be reused across different projects, fostering code reuse and consistency.

Variables play a significant role in Terraform configuration. They enable you to parameterize your configurations, making them more flexible and adaptable to various environments or scenarios. Variables can be defined and used within your configurations, allowing you to customize the behavior of your infrastructure code.

Outputs are another essential feature of Terraform configurations. Outputs allow you to expose specific values from your infrastructure for further reference or use. For example, you can use outputs to retrieve the IP address of a provisioned virtual machine or the DNS name of a load balancer. These values can be leveraged by other parts of your configuration or external systems.

Terraform configurations can become complex as your infrastructure needs grow. To address this complexity, Terraform provides the ability to break configurations into multiple files, helping you maintain clarity and organization. Modularization and the use of separate configuration files can greatly improve code readability and maintainability.

Providers are a fundamental part of Terraform configuration. They are responsible for translating your declarative configuration into specific API calls and actions within infrastructure platforms or services. Terraform supports various providers, including those for popular cloud platforms like AWS, Azure, Google Cloud, and many others. This extensibility allows you to manage resources across diverse environments and providers.

Terraform supports the use of external data sources within your configurations. These data sources enable you to retrieve information from external systems or APIs and use it in your Terraform configurations. Data sources are particularly useful for dynamically configuring resources based on information from external sources.

To manage sensitive data and credentials, Terraform provides the concept of sensitive data handling. You can mark variables or attributes as sensitive, ensuring that their values are treated with care. This is essential when working with secrets or API keys that should not be exposed in logs or other outputs.

As you delve deeper into Terraform configuration, you'll likely encounter complex use cases that require advanced techniques. These can include conditional resource creation, dynamic block generation, and advanced variable manipulation. Terraform's rich set of functions, expressions, and conditional constructs empowers you to tackle these advanced scenarios with confidence.

One of the most valuable aspects of Terraform configuration is its ability to promote infrastructure as code best practices. These practices include using version control to track changes, documenting your configurations, adhering to coding standards, and implementing automated testing. By incorporating these best practices into your workflow, you can ensure the reliability, consistency, and maintainability of your infrastructure code.

Testing is a critical component of Terraform configuration. Automated tests can help catch issues early in the development process and ensure that your infrastructure code behaves as expected. Tools like Terratest and Kitchen-Terraform provide frameworks for writing and running tests against your Terraform code.

The Terraform plan command is a vital tool in your configuration workflow. It generates an execution plan that outlines the changes Terraform will make to your infrastructure to achieve the desired state. This plan is invaluable for reviewing and validating changes before they are applied, providing a clear understanding of the impact of proposed changes.

Once you are satisfied with the plan, you can apply your Terraform configuration changes using the Terraform apply command. This command provisions or modifies the infrastructure resources based on the desired state defined in your configuration. Terraform apply is a potentially destructive operation, so careful review and confirmation of changes are essential to avoid unintended consequences.

Documentation remains a crucial aspect of Terraform configuration. Clear and comprehensive documentation helps you and your team understand the purpose, usage, and behavior of your configurations. Well-documented configurations are easier to maintain and troubleshoot.

Security is a top priority when working with Terraform configuration. Implement security best practices, such as using least privilege principles, encrypting sensitive data, and regularly auditing and reviewing configurations for potential vulnerabilities. Protecting your infrastructure code and sensitive information is paramount.

In summary, diving into Terraform configuration is a journey of mastering Infrastructure as Code (IaC) that involves understanding HCL, resource blocks, dependency management, modules, variables, outputs, providers, data sources, sensitive data handling, advanced techniques, best practices, testing, planning, application, documentation, and security. As you explore these aspects of Terraform configuration, you gain the skills and knowledge needed to define and manage infrastructure resources effectively and efficiently.

Understanding the syntax and structure of Terraform files is fundamental to working effectively with Infrastructure as Code (IaC) and managing infrastructure resources using Terraform. Terraform employs a clear and structured approach to defining configurations, ensuring consistency and readability.

At the heart of Terraform configurations are HashiCorp Configuration Language (HCL) files. HCL is a purpose-built language designed for expressing infrastructure as code in a human-readable and maintainable format. HCL combines declarative and imperative elements, allowing you to specify both the desired state of your infrastructure and the steps to achieve it.

Terraform configurations typically consist of one or more .tf files. These files contain the actual infrastructure code and are written in HCL. A .tf file can represent a complete configuration or a module—a reusable unit of configuration. Modules enable you to encapsulate and share infrastructure components, promoting code reuse and maintainability.

A Terraform configuration file often begins with a provider block, which specifies the infrastructure platform or service you intend to interact with. The provider block defines the provider's name and any required configuration settings, such as authentication credentials or region.

After the provider block, you define resources using resource blocks. Resource blocks are the core building blocks of Terraform configurations, representing the infrastructure resources you want to create, configure, or manage. Each resource block corresponds to a specific resource type, such as virtual machines, networks, or databases, and includes attributes that specify the resource's configuration.

Resource blocks have a structured syntax that starts with the resource keyword followed by the resource type and a resource name. The resource type corresponds to the type of resource you are creating, and the resource name is a user-defined label for that resource instance.

Inside a resource block, you specify the resource's configuration attributes. These attributes define the resource's settings, such as its size, region, or access controls. The attributes follow a key-value syntax, where the attribute name is on the left side of an equals sign (=), and the attribute value is on the right side.

HCL supports string interpolation, allowing you to reference variables or other expressions within attribute values using the ${} syntax. This feature enhances the flexibility of Terraform configurations and enables dynamic values based on variables or computed expressions.

Comments can be added to Terraform files using the # symbol. Comments are a useful way to document your configurations, explain the purpose of specific resource blocks or attributes, or provide context to other team members.

Terraform allows you to group related resource blocks together using block syntax. Block syntax provides a way to define multiple resource blocks of the same type with different configurations in a more concise and organized manner. Block syntax uses curly braces ({}) to enclose multiple resource blocks of the same type.

Variables are an essential part of Terraform configurations, allowing you to parameterize your configurations and make them more flexible. Variables are defined in separate .tf files called variable files. These files typically have a .tfvars extension and contain variable definitions.

To use variables in your Terraform configuration, you declare them using the variable keyword in your variable files. Variable definitions include a name and an optional type constraint, which specifies the expected data type for the variable.

In your main Terraform configuration files, you can reference variables using the var. syntax followed by the variable name. Terraform automatically resolves variable references and substitutes them with their values during configuration evaluation.

Terraform provides input variables and output variables. Input variables are used to parameterize your configurations and allow users to provide values when running Terraform commands. Output variables, on the other hand, allow you to expose specific values from your infrastructure for further reference or use in other parts of your configuration.

Input variables are defined using the variable keyword in your variable files, just like regular variables. However, input variables often include additional properties, such as descriptions and default values, to enhance user-friendliness and provide sensible defaults.

Output variables are defined using the output keyword in your Terraform configuration files. Output variable definitions include a name and an expression that calculates the value of the output variable based on other attributes or values in your configuration.

Terraform uses state files to keep track of the current state of your infrastructure resources. State files are crucial for understanding the differences between the desired state defined in your configurations and the actual state of the resources.

By default, Terraform stores state files locally on your machine. However, for collaboration and consistency, it is recommended to use remote state storage, which can be set up using services like Amazon S3, Azure Blob Storage, Google Cloud Storage, or HashiCorp Terraform Cloud.

Remote state storage ensures that the state files are centralized, accessible to the entire team, and protected against conflicts when multiple team members work on the same infrastructure. Terraform supports various backends for remote state storage, allowing you to choose the one that best fits your needs.

Terraform configurations can be organized into modules to promote code reuse and maintainability. A module is a self-contained collection of Terraform configuration files that define a set of related resources. Modules allow you to encapsulate infrastructure components, making them easier to manage, share, and reuse across different projects.

To use a module in your Terraform configuration, you can reference it using a module block. The module block specifies the source of the module, which can be a local file path or a remote source from a version control repository. Terraform fetches the module and includes it in your configuration, allowing you to use its resources.

Terraform's syntax and structure are designed to promote readability, maintainability, and collaboration among team members. With clear resource definitions, variable usage, and module organization, Terraform configurations become powerful and expressive representations of your infrastructure.

In summary, understanding the syntax and structure of Terraform files is crucial for effective Infrastructure as Code (IaC) and infrastructure management. Terraform uses HashiCorp Configuration Language (HCL) files with provider, resource, variable, and output blocks. Resource blocks define infrastructure resources and their configurations, while variables and output variables provide flexibility and expose values. Remote state storage is recommended for managing state files, and modules enable code reuse and organization. By mastering Terraform's syntax and structure, you gain the ability to define and manage infrastructure resources efficiently and with precision.

Chapter 5: Managing Infrastructure with Terraform

Infrastructure management with Terraform is a dynamic and essential aspect of modern cloud computing and DevOps practices, enabling organizations to define, provision, and maintain their infrastructure as code. As you embark on your journey to master Terraform, you'll explore the intricacies of managing infrastructure resources across diverse cloud platforms and services, ensuring they align with your organization's goals and requirements.

At its core, Terraform is a tool for defining infrastructure as code, which means expressing your infrastructure in a declarative and version-controlled manner. This approach offers several advantages, including repeatability, consistency, and the ability to treat infrastructure like software.

Terraform configurations, written in the HashiCorp Configuration Language (HCL), serve as the blueprints for your infrastructure. These configurations define the desired state of your infrastructure resources, such as virtual machines, networks, databases, and more. By specifying what you want your infrastructure to look like, you establish a clear and consistent foundation.

Infrastructure as code (IaC) with Terraform is not limited to a single cloud provider. Terraform's extensive provider ecosystem supports various cloud platforms, including Amazon Web Services (AWS), Microsoft Azure, Google Cloud Platform (GCP), and many others. This multi-cloud capability empowers organizations to adopt a hybrid or multi-cloud strategy that suits their needs.

Terraform's provider-based architecture allows you to interact with specific cloud services, platforms, or on-premises infrastructure components using provider plugins. Each provider defines a set of resources and data sources that correspond to the services it supports. This versatility enables you to manage a wide range of resources across different providers within a single Terraform configuration.

To manage your infrastructure resources effectively, you'll often organize your Terraform configurations into projects or workspaces. A workspace is a separate environment where you maintain a distinct set of configurations and state files. Workspaces enable you to manage multiple infrastructure environments, such as development, staging, and production, within the same Terraform configuration repository.

Terraform state is a vital concept in infrastructure management. State files, generated and managed by Terraform, store the current state of your infrastructure. These state files track the mapping between the resources defined in your configurations and the corresponding resources in the real-world infrastructure.

State files are crucial for Terraform's plan and apply workflow. When you run the Terraform plan command, Terraform analyzes the differences between the desired state defined in your configurations and the actual state recorded in the state files. The resulting execution plan outlines the actions Terraform will take to reconcile the two states.

Once you review and approve the plan, you can apply it using the Terraform apply command. This command instructs Terraform to make the necessary changes to your infrastructure to bring it in line with the desired state. Terraform evaluates the dependencies between resources and ensures that changes are applied in the correct order, minimizing disruptions to your infrastructure.

While Terraform's core functionality is essential for infrastructure management, it also offers advanced features and capabilities to streamline and enhance your workflows. For example, Terraform provides remote state storage options, such as Amazon S3, Azure Blob Storage, and Google Cloud Storage, allowing you to centralize state management, facilitate collaboration, and prevent conflicts.

Terraform's support for modules is another powerful feature. Modules enable you to encapsulate and reuse infrastructure components, promoting code modularity and maintainability. You can create your own modules or leverage community-contributed modules to speed up the development of common infrastructure patterns.

Variables and outputs in Terraform configurations enhance configurability and integration. Variables allow you to parameterize your configurations, making them more adaptable to different environments or scenarios. Outputs expose specific values from your infrastructure that can be used for further reference or integrated with external systems.

Security is a paramount concern in infrastructure management. Terraform provides mechanisms for managing sensitive data, such as credentials and secrets, in a secure and compliant manner. You can use environment variables, external secrets management tools, or Terraform Cloud's secure variable storage to protect sensitive information.

As your infrastructure grows and evolves, Terraform offers tools and practices to ensure that your configurations remain maintainable and scalable. Adopting a modular and organized code structure, implementing naming conventions, and documenting your configurations are all essential practices for long-term success.

Infrastructure testing and validation are integral parts of infrastructure management with Terraform. Automated testing tools like Terratest and Kitchen-Terraform enable you to write and run tests against your Terraform code, ensuring that your configurations behave as expected and meet your requirements.

Integrating Terraform into your continuous integration/continuous deployment (CI/CD) pipeline further streamlines your infrastructure management process. CI/CD practices automate the testing and deployment of your Terraform configurations, providing a consistent and repeatable approach to infrastructure changes.

Monitoring and observability are critical aspects of infrastructure management. By implementing monitoring solutions like Prometheus, Grafana, or cloud-native monitoring services, you gain insights into the state and performance of your Terraform-managed infrastructure, enabling you to proactively address issues and optimize resource utilization.

Real-world infrastructure management with Terraform involves collaboration, version control, and best practices. Collaborative development allows teams to work together on infrastructure code, leveraging version control systems like Git to track changes and facilitate code review. Best practices encompass coding standards, security considerations, and compliance requirements that ensure the reliability and integrity of your infrastructure.

In summary, infrastructure management with Terraform empowers organizations to define, provision, and maintain their infrastructure as code. Terraform's declarative approach, multi-cloud support, and advanced features make it a valuable tool for modern cloud computing and DevOps practices. By mastering Terraform, you gain the skills and knowledge needed to manage infrastructure resources effectively and efficiently, aligning your infrastructure with your organization's goals and requirements.

Resource creation and deletion are fundamental operations in Terraform's Infrastructure as Code (IaC) workflow, enabling you to define, provision, and manage infrastructure resources efficiently and with precision.

Creating resources with Terraform begins by defining the desired state of the infrastructure in your Terraform configurations. These configurations specify the resources you want to create, their properties, and dependencies.

Once you've defined your configurations, you can use the **terraform init** command to initialize your Terraform working directory. This command downloads the necessary provider plugins and sets up the environment for managing your infrastructure.

The **terraform plan** command plays a pivotal role in the resource creation process. It generates an execution plan that outlines the changes Terraform will make to your infrastructure to bring it in line with the desired state defined in your configurations.

The execution plan includes details about the resources that will be created, modified, or destroyed. By reviewing the plan, you can assess the impact of the changes and ensure they align with your intentions.

After reviewing and approving the plan, you can proceed with the resource creation using the **terraform apply** command. This command instructs Terraform to make the necessary changes to your infrastructure to achieve the desired state.

Terraform evaluates the dependencies between resources and ensures that changes are applied in the correct order to maintain consistency and avoid conflicts. The apply process may involve creating new resources, updating existing ones, and destroying resources that are no longer needed.

During resource creation, Terraform communicates with the infrastructure provider's APIs to provision the resources according to your specifications. This interaction is managed by Terraform's provider plugins, which translate your declarative configuration into concrete API calls.

Terraform's declarative approach to resource creation means that you specify the "what" rather than the "how." You define the desired state of your infrastructure, and Terraform takes care of the implementation details, making resource provisioning consistent and repeatable.

Resource deletion is another critical aspect of infrastructure management with Terraform. Over time, you may need to remove resources that are no longer necessary or have become obsolete.

To initiate resource deletion, you simply remove the corresponding resource blocks from your Terraform configurations. When you run **terraform plan** and **terraform apply** after making this change, Terraform will detect that the resources are no longer defined and will generate a plan to destroy them.

The **terraform destroy** command provides a convenient way to destroy all resources defined in your configurations. While **terraform apply** applies changes incrementally, **terraform destroy** operates on the entire set of resources, removing them in reverse dependency order.

Resource deletion in Terraform is a controlled process that considers resource dependencies and ensures that resources are deleted in the correct order to prevent conflicts and maintain consistency.

Terraform also provides a **-target** flag that allows you to specify a specific resource to be targeted for deletion. This feature can be useful when you want to delete a single resource or a subset of resources without affecting the entire infrastructure.

It's important to exercise caution when using **terraform destroy** or **-target** because these commands can lead to the permanent deletion of resources. Always review the execution plan generated by Terraform to understand the scope and impact of the deletion before confirming the operation.

Resource deletion in Terraform respects the dependencies and relationships defined in your configurations. Terraform determines the correct order in which resources should be deleted to avoid breaking dependencies and ensure the integrity of your infrastructure.

In addition to resource deletion, Terraform also supports resource modification. When you update the configuration of a resource, Terraform generates a plan that outlines the changes needed to bring the resource in line with the updated configuration.

Resource modification can involve changes to resource properties, attributes, or other configuration settings. Terraform calculates the minimal set of changes required to achieve the desired state while preserving the existing resource's identity and dependencies.

Resource modification is a key feature of Terraform's declarative approach to infrastructure management. You express your desired state in your configurations, and Terraform takes care of calculating and applying the necessary changes to reach that state.

Terraform's resource management capabilities extend beyond simple creation, modification, and deletion. It also provides features for resource importing and resource state management.

Resource importing allows you to import existing resources into your Terraform state. This is particularly useful when you have pre-existing infrastructure resources that you want to manage with Terraform. By importing resources, you can bring them under Terraform's control and manage them using your Terraform configurations.

Resource state management is a critical aspect of Terraform's functionality. Terraform keeps track of the current state of your infrastructure resources using state files. These state files record the mapping between the resources defined in your configurations and the actual resources in your infrastructure.

State files serve as the source of truth for Terraform. They are essential for generating execution plans, detecting changes, and ensuring the desired state is maintained. It's crucial to manage state files carefully and securely to prevent conflicts and maintain the integrity of your infrastructure. In distributed or collaborative environments, Terraform offers remote state storage options, such as Amazon S3, Azure Blob Storage, Google Cloud Storage, or HashiCorp Terraform Cloud. These remote backends provide centralized and secure state storage, making it easier to collaborate and manage state files.

Resource creation and deletion in Terraform are core operations that enable you to define and manage your infrastructure with precision and control. Terraform's declarative approach, execution plans, dependency resolution, and state management ensure that resource changes are applied consistently and safely.

Mastering resource creation and deletion in Terraform is essential for effective Infrastructure as Code (IaC) and infrastructure management. With Terraform, you gain the ability to define, provision, modify, and delete resources across various cloud providers and platforms, aligning your infrastructure with your organization's evolving needs and objectives.

Chapter 6: Terraform State and Data Sources

Understanding Terraform state is fundamental to effectively managing infrastructure as code (IaC) and ensuring the consistency and accuracy of your infrastructure resources.

Terraform state refers to the information and data that Terraform uses to keep track of the current state of your infrastructure. This state includes details about the resources managed by Terraform, such as their attributes, dependencies, and relationships.

The Terraform state is stored in state files, which are JSON-formatted files by default, though other formats like HCL (HashiCorp Configuration Language) and more are also supported. These state files serve as the source of truth for Terraform, providing a record of the mapping between the resources defined in your configurations and the actual resources in your infrastructure.

Each Terraform project or workspace has its own separate state file. This isolation ensures that different environments, such as development, staging, and production, have independent state files and do not interfere with each other.

Terraform state files contain resource definitions, including the resource type, name, and attributes. These definitions allow Terraform to understand the current state of your infrastructure and determine what changes, if any, are needed to bring the infrastructure in line with your desired state.

One important aspect of Terraform state is resource addressing. Resources are uniquely identified by their type and name. This unique identification allows Terraform to distinguish between different resources of the same type and manage them independently.

Resource addressing is a critical feature when it comes to understanding and managing Terraform state. It ensures that Terraform can correctly identify and manage resources, even when resource names are reused across different environments or workspaces.

Terraform state is essential for Terraform's core functionality, including the **terraform plan** and **terraform apply** commands. When you run **terraform plan**, Terraform reads the current state from the state files to determine the differences between the desired state defined in your configurations and the actual state of the infrastructure.

The **terraform plan** command generates an execution plan that outlines the actions Terraform will take to reconcile the two states. It provides details about resource creation, modification, or deletion based on the changes in your configurations.

Terraform's ability to generate accurate execution plans relies on the accuracy and completeness of the state files. If the state files become outdated or inconsistent with the actual infrastructure, it can lead to incorrect or unexpected behavior during resource management.

To apply changes to your infrastructure, you use the **terraform apply** command. This command reads the state files, compares the desired state to the actual state, and performs the necessary actions to bring the infrastructure into alignment with the configurations.

Terraform also uses state locking mechanisms to prevent concurrent modifications to the same state file. When you run Terraform commands that modify the state, such as **terraform apply**, Terraform acquires a lock on the state file to ensure that only one process can make changes at a time.

State locking is crucial for preventing conflicts and data corruption when multiple team members or automation processes are working with the same Terraform configuration simultaneously.

In distributed or collaborative environments, it's often advisable to use remote state storage, such as Amazon S3, Azure Blob Storage, Google Cloud Storage, or HashiCorp Terraform Cloud, for managing Terraform state.

Remote state storage provides centralized and secure storage for state files, making it easier to collaborate and coordinate changes in a team setting. It also eliminates the need to manage state files locally, reducing the risk of data loss or inconsistencies.

Remote state storage is configured in your Terraform backend settings, and each workspace or environment can have its own backend configuration. This flexibility allows you to choose the remote backend that best fits your needs and integrates with your infrastructure management workflow.

Terraform state management extends beyond simple resource creation and modification. It also encompasses resource deletion, resource importing, and state migration.

Resource deletion in Terraform involves removing resource blocks from your Terraform configurations. When you run **terraform plan** and **terraform apply** after making this change, Terraform detects that the resources are no longer defined and generates a plan to destroy them.

Resource deletion plans ensure that resources are deleted in the correct order, respecting dependencies and preventing conflicts. Deleting resources also updates the state files to reflect the removal of the resources from the managed infrastructure.

Resource importing allows you to import existing resources into your Terraform state. This is useful when you have pre-existing infrastructure resources that you want to manage with Terraform. By importing resources, you can bring them under Terraform's control and manage them using your Terraform configurations. Resource importing involves specifying the resource type, name, and any required attributes to map the existing resources to your configurations.

State migration may be necessary when you need to reorganize your Terraform configurations or transition from local state to remote state storage. Terraform provides tools and commands to facilitate state migration, ensuring that state files are moved, updated, and consolidated as needed.

As your infrastructure grows and evolves, managing Terraform state becomes increasingly important for maintaining consistency and integrity. It's essential to adopt best practices for state management, including regular backups of state files, state locking, remote state storage, and version control.

In summary, understanding Terraform state is crucial for effective Infrastructure as Code (IaC) and infrastructure management.

Terraform state files serve as the source of truth for tracking and managing the current state of your infrastructure resources.

With accurate and well-managed state files, Terraform can generate precise execution plans, ensure resource consistency, and enable safe and controlled resource creation, modification, and deletion. By mastering Terraform state, you gain the ability to manage your infrastructure resources with confidence and precision, aligning your infrastructure with your organization's evolving needs and objectives.

Leveraging data sources in Terraform is a powerful technique that allows you to retrieve and incorporate external information and existing resources into your Infrastructure as Code (IaC) configurations.

Data sources in Terraform serve as a bridge between your IaC code and real-world infrastructure, cloud providers, and external systems.

Data sources enable you to query information that already exists in your environment and use it within your Terraform configurations, enhancing the flexibility and extensibility of your IaC code.

Data sources are defined in your Terraform configurations using the **data** block syntax, and they provide a way to retrieve data from various external sources and services.

The most common use case for data sources is retrieving information about existing resources, such as virtual machines, networks, databases, or security groups, from your cloud provider.

Data sources allow you to reference these existing resources and use their attributes within your Terraform configurations, which is especially useful when you need to integrate new resources with pre-existing ones.

Data sources can also fetch data from external systems and APIs, such as DNS records, API endpoints, or third-party services, enabling you to incorporate external information into your Terraform configurations.

To use a data source in your Terraform configuration, you specify its type, configuration, and any required query parameters in a **data** block.

The **data** block defines a resource of type **data**, followed by the data source type and a name for the data source instance. You can also provide configuration settings and query parameters as needed to retrieve the desired data.

Once you've defined a data source in your configuration, you can reference its attributes using interpolation syntax, such as **${data.data_source_type.data_source_name.attribute}**.

Interpolation allows you to include the data retrieved from the data source in your configuration expressions, resource definitions, or other parts of your IaC code.

Data sources provide a way to access information that is not directly managed by Terraform but is essential for defining your infrastructure. For example, you can use data sources to retrieve information about a virtual network in your cloud provider's environment and then create resources like virtual machines or load balancers that are connected to that network.

One common scenario for using data sources is retrieving information about existing Virtual Private Cloud (VPC) resources in cloud providers like AWS, Azure, or GCP.

By querying data sources, you can determine the VPC ID, subnet IDs, security group IDs, or other attributes of existing VPC resources. This information can then be used to configure new resources that need to be deployed within the same VPC.

Data sources can also be used to access data that is not directly related to infrastructure provisioning. For instance, you can use data sources to fetch external IP addresses, DNS records, or information from external databases to configure resources or perform conditional logic within your Terraform configurations.

Data sources in Terraform are dynamic, meaning that they are only queried when needed. Terraform evaluates data sources during the planning phase (e.g., when running **terraform plan**) to determine the current values of the data retrieved from external sources.

This dynamic behavior ensures that your Terraform configurations remain up-to-date and adaptable to changes in external data. When the external data changes, Terraform automatically reevaluates the data source during planning, reflecting the updated information in your execution plan. One of the key benefits of using data sources is maintaining separation between your Terraform configurations and external data. Data sources allow you to keep your infrastructure code clean and focused on defining and managing resources, while external data is queried as needed and integrated into your configurations. Data sources are also helpful for minimizing manual data entry in your configurations. Instead of hardcoding information about existing resources, you can use data sources to retrieve it dynamically, reducing the potential for errors and making your configurations more robust and maintainable.

Data sources in Terraform can be particularly valuable when working in environments where external systems and services play a significant role in infrastructure provisioning and configuration.

For example, in a scenario where you need to retrieve the public IP address of a load balancer to configure DNS records or update firewall rules, data sources provide a straightforward way to obtain this information without manual intervention.

Terraform's provider ecosystem offers a wide range of data sources tailored to different cloud providers and services. For example, AWS provides data sources for querying information about EC2 instances, S3 buckets, and more. Azure offers data sources for retrieving details about virtual machines, storage accounts, and other Azure resources.

The Terraform registry is a valuable resource for discovering and using data sources contributed by the Terraform community and providers. You can browse the registry to find data sources for specific cloud providers, services, or external systems.

In summary, leveraging data sources in Terraform is a valuable technique for integrating external information and existing resources into your Infrastructure as Code (IaC) configurations.

Data sources provide a dynamic and flexible way to query data from various sources, such as cloud providers, external systems, and APIs, and incorporate that data into your Terraform configurations.

By using data sources, you can create more adaptable and robust infrastructure code, reduce manual data entry, and ensure that your configurations remain up-to-date and aligned with external information and resources.

Mastering data sources in Terraform enhances your ability to manage complex infrastructure environments efficiently and makes your IaC code more powerful and responsive to changes in the real-world infrastructure landscape.

Chapter 7: Variables, Outputs, and Modules

Working with variables in Terraform is a fundamental aspect of creating flexible and reusable Infrastructure as Code (IaC) configurations.

Variables in Terraform allow you to parameterize your configurations, making them adaptable to different environments, use cases, or scenarios.

Terraform variables provide a way to input values into your configurations, and they can be used to customize resource settings, manage secrets, and define configuration parameters.

To define a variable in Terraform, you use the **variable** block syntax within your configuration files. In this block, you specify the variable name, type, and an optional default value.

Variables can have various data types, including strings, numbers, lists, maps, and more, allowing you to capture a wide range of input values.

Once you've defined a variable, you can reference it in your configuration using interpolation syntax, such as **${var.variable_name}**.

Interpolation allows you to use the value of the variable within resource definitions, expressions, and other parts of your IaC code.

Variables can also be assigned values dynamically by reading them from files, environment variables, or other external sources, providing flexibility in how you manage and use variables.

One of the primary use cases for variables in Terraform is to customize resource configurations. By defining variables for resource settings, you can create reusable configurations that adapt to different environments or requirements.

For example, you can define a variable to specify the number of instances in an auto-scaling group, allowing you to create different auto-scaling groups with varying sizes based on the value of the variable.

Variables also enable you to manage secrets and sensitive information in your Terraform configurations securely. Instead of hardcoding sensitive values directly into your code, you can define variables for secret inputs and then provide the actual values using Terraform's input mechanisms, such as environment variables or secret management tools.

Using variables for secrets helps protect sensitive data and simplifies the process of rotating or updating secret values without modifying your configurations.

Terraform's input mechanisms allow you to provide values for variables when you run Terraform commands, such as **terraform apply** or **terraform plan**. You can pass variable values directly on the command line, store them in environment variables, or use variable definition files.

Variable definition files are plain text files that associate variable names with values. These files are convenient for managing and sharing sets of variable values for different environments or scenarios.

Terraform also supports variable interpolation, allowing you to use the value of one variable to compute the value of another variable or resource attribute.

Interpolated variables are enclosed in ${} and can reference other variables or resource attributes, enabling you to create dynamic configurations that depend on the values of other variables or resources.

When defining variables in Terraform, you can set default values to provide a fallback value when a variable is not explicitly assigned a value. Default values make variables more flexible and resilient, ensuring that your configurations work even when specific values are not provided.

For example, you can define a variable for the instance type of a virtual machine with a default value of "t2.micro." If you don't specify a different instance type when running Terraform commands, the default value is used.

Terraform also allows you to specify descriptions for variables, helping document their purpose and usage within your configurations. Descriptive variable documentation makes it easier for team members to understand the intended use of variables and their expected values.

To provide values for variables when running Terraform commands, you can use the **-var** flag followed by the variable name and the desired value. For example, **terraform apply -var="instance_type=t2.large"** sets the value of the "instance_type" variable to "t2.large" during the execution of the apply command.

Environment variables provide another way to input values for variables. You can prefix variable names with **TF_VAR_** to indicate that they are environment variables.

For instance, setting the environment variable **TF_VAR_instance_type** to "t2.large" is equivalent to passing **-var="instance_type=t2.large"** on the command line.

Variable files, also known as variable definition files, allow you to store variable values in separate text files. Each variable definition file associates variable names with values, making it easy to manage sets of variable values for different environments or scenarios.

Variable files have a **.tfvars** or **.tfvars.json** file extension, depending on whether they are written in HashiCorp Configuration Language (HCL) or JSON format. You can specify variable files using the **-var-file** flag when running Terraform commands.

For example, **terraform apply -var-file="dev.tfvars"** reads variable values from the "dev.tfvars" file and uses them in the configuration.

Variables in Terraform can be classified into two main categories: input variables and output variables.

Input variables are defined in your Terraform configurations and serve as parameters that allow you to customize resource configurations and behavior. You specify input variables using the **variable** block within your configuration files.

Output variables, on the other hand, are used to export values from your Terraform configurations for external use. You define output variables using the **output** block within your configuration files.

Output variables provide a way to expose selected values generated during Terraform execution, such as resource attributes or computed values, to be used by other Terraform configurations, scripts, or external systems.

When defining output variables, you specify the variable name and the value you want to export, often referencing resource attributes or other variables.

Output variables can be queried using the **terraform output** command, which displays the values of all defined output variables. You can also access specific output variable values programmatically using Terraform's command-line interfaces or APIs.

In summary, working with variables in Terraform is a key aspect of creating flexible, reusable, and adaptable Infrastructure as Code (IaC) configurations.

Variables allow you to parameterize your Terraform configurations, customize resource settings, manage secrets securely, and create dynamic configurations that adapt to different environments or scenarios.

By defining variables, setting default values, and using Terraform's input mechanisms, you can make your configurations more versatile and maintainable, ensuring that your IaC code remains effective and responsive to changes in your infrastructure needs.

Creating modular and reusable code in Terraform is a fundamental practice that enhances the maintainability, scalability, and efficiency of your Infrastructure as Code (IaC) projects.

Modularity in Terraform involves breaking down your IaC code into smaller, self-contained modules that represent logical components of your infrastructure.

Each module encapsulates a specific set of resources, configurations, or functionality, making it easier to manage, test, and reuse across different projects.

Modular code promotes code organization and separation of concerns, enabling teams to work collaboratively on different parts of the infrastructure without causing conflicts or bottlenecks.

In Terraform, modules are defined as separate directories containing Terraform configuration files (**.tf** files) that represent a specific component or piece of infrastructure.

Modules can be used to create higher-level abstractions, such as applications, environments, or infrastructure patterns, allowing you to model your infrastructure in a more abstract and reusable way.

To create a module, you start by organizing your Terraform code into directories and defining variables and outputs that allow for parameterization and data exchange between modules.

Variables in modules serve as input parameters, allowing you to customize the behavior and configuration of the module for different use cases.

Outputs in modules enable you to expose specific values or resources from the module, making them accessible to the parent configuration or other modules that depend on it.

Once you've defined a module, you can reuse it across different Terraform configurations by calling it as a child module within your parent configuration.

Child modules are referenced using the **module** block, where you specify the source location of the module, along with any required input variables.

By modularizing your code and using child modules, you can create a library of reusable infrastructure components that can be shared and applied to various projects.

Modularization simplifies code maintenance by allowing you to focus on specific parts of the infrastructure, test modules in isolation, and make changes without affecting other parts of the codebase.

Modular code also promotes consistency across projects by providing a standardized way to configure and deploy common infrastructure components.

One of the primary benefits of modular code in Terraform is the ability to abstract and encapsulate complex infrastructure patterns and best practices.

For example, you can create a reusable module for deploying a web application that includes configurations for load balancers, auto-scaling groups, databases, and security groups.

This module can be parameterized to customize settings such as the application name, instance type, and database engine, making it adaptable to different application deployments.

By abstracting complex infrastructure patterns into modules, you reduce the risk of configuration errors, improve code readability, and ensure that best practices are consistently applied.

Another advantage of modular code is the ability to version and share modules with your team or the broader Terraform community.

Modules can be published to the Terraform Module Registry or other version-controlled repositories, making them accessible to other developers and teams.

This sharing of modules encourages collaboration, accelerates project development, and helps maintain a library of reusable infrastructure code that evolves and improves over time.

Terraform's module versioning and dependency management features allow you to specify the version of a module to use in your configurations, ensuring that your infrastructure code remains stable and predictable.

When you use modules from the Terraform Module Registry or other version-controlled sources, you can trust that the code has been tested and reviewed by the community, reducing the risk of errors and security vulnerabilities.

In addition to reusability and abstraction, modular code also supports the concept of composition, where you can build complex infrastructure configurations by composing smaller, modular components.

Composition allows you to combine modules like building blocks to create higher-level infrastructure patterns, such as multi-tier web applications, microservices architectures, or entire cloud environments.

For example, you can create a composition that deploys a three-tier web application consisting of a front-end module, an application module, and a database module, each representing a distinct layer of the application stack.

By composing these modules together and passing the necessary input variables, you can define and deploy a complete application architecture with ease.

Composition also promotes code readability and maintainability by providing a high-level view of the infrastructure's architecture and relationships between components.

Terraform's support for remote backends, such as Amazon S3, Azure Blob Storage, Google Cloud Storage, or HashiCorp Terraform Cloud, enhances the modularity of your code by allowing you to store and share modules centrally.

Remote backends provide a centralized location for storing Terraform configurations and modules, making it easier to collaborate with team members and manage modules across multiple projects.

Remote backends also offer version control and access control features, ensuring that modules and configurations are stored securely and are accessible to authorized users only.

When working with remote modules, Terraform can automatically download and use the latest version of a module, simplifying the process of keeping modules up-to-date across different projects.

To publish and share your own modules, you can create a Terraform Module Registry namespace, organize your modules into namespaces, and publish them for others to discover and use.

By following best practices for module naming, documentation, and versioning, you can make your modules more user-friendly and accessible to the Terraform community.

In summary, creating modular and reusable code in Terraform is a foundational practice for effective Infrastructure as Code (IaC) development.

Modularization enhances code organization, promotes separation of concerns, and simplifies code maintenance, testing, and sharing.

By abstracting complex infrastructure patterns into modules, you improve code quality, reduce the risk of errors, and accelerate project development.

Composition allows you to build higher-level infrastructure architectures by combining modular components, making it easier to define and deploy complex systems.

Terraform's support for remote backends and the Terraform Module Registry streamlines the sharing and management of modules, fostering collaboration and community-driven development.

Mastering modular and reusable code in Terraform is a key step toward building scalable, maintainable, and collaborative infrastructure projects that adapt to changing requirements and best practices.

Chapter 8: Best Practices for Terraform Projects

Terraform Project Best Practices are essential guidelines and principles that help you design, implement, and manage Infrastructure as Code (IaC) projects effectively.

These best practices are crucial for creating robust, maintainable, and scalable infrastructure configurations with Terraform.

Modularization: One of the core principles of Terraform best practices is to modularize your code. Break down your infrastructure code into reusable, self-contained modules that represent distinct components or resources.

Separation of Concerns: Keep your modules focused on specific concerns, such as networking, compute, or security. Avoid mixing unrelated configurations within a single module to maintain clarity and modularity.

Parameterization: Use input variables in your modules to make them configurable. Parameterization allows you to customize module behavior and adapt it to various use cases.

Output Values: Define output values in your modules to expose specific information or resources that may be useful to other parts of your infrastructure or external systems.

Standardized Naming Conventions: Adopt consistent naming conventions for resources, variables, and outputs. This makes your code more readable and manageable, especially in larger projects.

Documentation: Thoroughly document your Terraform code, including variables, outputs, and module usage. Documentation helps team members understand the purpose and usage of different components.

Version Control: Use version control systems like Git to track changes to your Terraform configurations. Commit frequently and maintain a clean commit history.

Branching Strategy: Implement a branching strategy in your version control system to manage different environments (e.g., development, staging, production) and feature branches.

Code Review: Conduct code reviews to ensure code quality, adherence to best practices, and catch potential issues before applying changes to your infrastructure.

Testing: Implement automated testing for your Terraform configurations. Tools like Terratest can help you write unit and integration tests to validate your code.

State Management: Store Terraform state files in a secure, centralized location, such as remote backends (e.g., S3, Azure Blob Storage, Terraform Cloud). Implement state locking to prevent conflicts.

Secret Management: Safeguard sensitive information, such as API keys or passwords, by using environment variables, secret management tools, or parameterized variables.

Continuous Integration (CI) and Continuous Deployment (CD): Integrate Terraform with your CI/CD pipelines to automate testing and deployment. Ensure that code is automatically applied to the appropriate environments upon successful tests.

Variable Files: Use variable files (**.tfvars**) to manage environment-specific variable values and keep them separate from your configuration code.

Terraform Workspaces: Leverage Terraform workspaces to manage multiple environments within a single configuration, allowing you to switch between environments easily.

Logging and Monitoring: Implement logging and monitoring for your infrastructure to track changes, detect issues, and ensure the health of your resources.

Backups and Disaster Recovery: Define backup and disaster recovery strategies for critical infrastructure components to minimize downtime and data loss.

Resource Tagging: Tag resources with metadata to categorize and organize them. Tags can be useful for cost allocation, security, and resource management.

Security and Compliance: Follow security best practices for your cloud provider and adhere to compliance standards relevant to your industry.

Immutable Infrastructure: Consider adopting an immutable infrastructure approach, where infrastructure is replaced with new versions rather than modified in place. This can enhance reliability and predictability.

Documentation as Code: Treat documentation as code by versioning it alongside your infrastructure code. Tools like Markdown and documentation generators can help maintain documentation efficiently.

Collaboration and Communication: Foster collaboration and communication among team members by using collaboration platforms and tools. Discuss changes, share knowledge, and document decisions.

Infrastructure as Code Policy: Establish and enforce policies for how infrastructure should be managed using Terraform, including naming conventions, security measures, and deployment processes.

Cost Management: Implement cost management practices to monitor and optimize your cloud expenses, such as using cloud cost analysis tools and setting up budget alerts.

Education and Training: Invest in education and training for your team to keep them updated with Terraform best practices and new features.

Community Involvement: Engage with the Terraform community by participating in forums, attending conferences, and contributing to open-source projects to learn from and share with others.

Continuous Improvement: Continuously review and improve your Terraform configurations and processes to adapt to changing requirements and best practices.

By following these Terraform Project Best Practices, you can build and manage infrastructure configurations that are not only efficient and reliable but also scalable and maintainable, ensuring the long-term success of your IaC projects.

Code organization and quality standards are essential aspects of any successful Infrastructure as Code (IaC) project, ensuring that your Terraform code is structured, readable, and maintainable.

A well-organized codebase is easier to work with, understand, and troubleshoot, making it crucial for efficient IaC development.

Organizing your Terraform code begins with the directory structure of your project.

A common approach is to create a directory for each environment, such as "dev," "staging," and "production," to separate configurations for different deployment targets.

Inside each environment directory, you can further organize your code into subdirectories based on resource types, modules, or functional areas, like "networking," "compute," or "security."

Having a clear and consistent directory structure helps team members locate specific configurations and understand the project's layout.

Within each directory, you should maintain a naming convention for Terraform configuration files (**.tf** files) and other associated files.

For example, you might name configuration files according to the resource they define, such as "vpc.tf" for a Virtual Private Cloud configuration or "autoscaling.tf" for an auto-scaling group configuration.

Consistent file naming fosters predictability and makes it easier to identify the purpose of each file.

In addition to organizing your code into directories, you should establish a convention for variable and output file naming.

Use meaningful and descriptive names for variables and outputs to provide clarity about their purpose and usage.

Comment your code liberally to provide explanations, document decisions, and add context to your configurations.

Clear comments help team members understand the rationale behind specific settings or resource configurations.

For example, you might include comments to explain why a particular security group rule is necessary or to provide insights into the expected behavior of an auto-scaling group.

While comments are valuable for documenting intent, you should aim for code that is self-explanatory.

Avoid overly complex configurations that require excessive comments to make sense.

Instead, use descriptive variable and resource names to make the code more readable and self-documenting.

Variable and output definitions are integral parts of your Terraform configurations, and maintaining a standardized approach to naming, formatting, and organizing them is crucial for code quality.

Use the **variable** block to define input variables at the top of your configuration files, grouped by their relevance to specific resources or modules.

Order variables logically to make it easier for others to find and understand them.

Additionally, document each variable with a meaningful description that explains its purpose, allowed values, and any constraints.

Follow a consistent naming convention for your variables, such as using lowercase letters with underscores to separate words (e.g., **instance_type** or **subnet_ids**).

Similarly, organize output values using the **output** block within your Terraform configurations.

Outputs should provide valuable information about the resources being created, making them accessible to other parts of your infrastructure code or external systems.

Assign meaningful names to outputs and include descriptions that clarify the significance of each value.

When it comes to defining resources in your Terraform configurations, maintain a clear and consistent structure.

Group related resources together within the same configuration file to facilitate understanding and reduce complexity.

For example, if you're defining a Virtual Private Cloud (VPC) and its associated subnets, security groups, and routing tables, consider placing them in the same configuration file dedicated to networking resources.

Adhere to the following best practices when defining resources:

Keep resource definitions concise and focused on their core attributes, avoiding excessive duplication or complexity.

Use interpolation to reference variables, outputs, or other resource attributes to enhance configurability and maintainability.

Leverage modules to encapsulate resource configurations for reuse across different environments or projects.

Apply consistent naming conventions for resource identifiers and labels, such as prefixing resources with environment-specific tags (e.g., "dev_" or "prod_").

Organize resources logically within a configuration file, following a clear order that reflects their dependencies or relationships.

Include comments or annotations within the configuration file to provide context and explanations for specific resource configurations.

Verify that your configurations conform to best practices recommended by your cloud provider, especially regarding security, compliance, and performance.

While Terraform's HashiCorp Configuration Language (HCL) provides flexibility in defining resource configurations, it's essential to maintain code quality by adhering to a consistent coding style.

Consistency in coding style promotes readability and reduces the likelihood of errors.

Follow these coding style guidelines for your Terraform configurations:

Indentation: Use consistent indentation (e.g., two or four spaces) to align blocks and maintain code readability.

Line Length: Limit line length to a reasonable number of characters (e.g., 80 or 120) to ensure code remains readable without excessive scrolling.

Formatting: Apply consistent formatting for HCL constructs, such as resource blocks, variable definitions, and function calls.

Align Attributes: Align attribute values within resource blocks or variable definitions to improve code organization.

Spacing: Use consistent spacing around operators, delimiters, and braces to enhance code readability.

Quotes: Prefer double quotes (") for string values, especially when defining variables or outputs, and use single quotes (') sparingly.

Line Breaks: Break long lines into multiple lines to maintain readability and avoid excessive horizontal scrolling.

Capitalization: Use lowercase letters for resource types, attributes, variable names, and output names, following a consistent naming convention.

Consistent Syntax: Apply a consistent style for HCL constructs, such as function calls, conditional statements, and loops.

Remove Unused Code: Regularly review your configurations and remove any unused variables, outputs, or resources to reduce clutter.

Following coding style guidelines ensures that your Terraform code remains clean, readable, and consistent, making it easier for team members to collaborate and maintain the codebase.

Code quality in Terraform extends beyond syntax and style; it encompasses practices that promote reliability, performance, and security.

To maintain high code quality, consider the following best practices:

Version Control: Use a version control system (e.g., Git) to track changes to your Terraform configurations, collaborate with team members, and manage code versions.

Code Review: Implement a code review process to ensure that configurations adhere to best practices, security guidelines, and coding standards.

Testing: Write and run tests for your Terraform code using tools like Terratest to validate the behavior and correctness of your configurations.

State Management: Store Terraform state files securely in a centralized location, and implement state locking mechanisms to prevent conflicts.

Secret Management: Safeguard sensitive information, such as API keys and passwords, using encryption, environment variables, or dedicated secret management tools.

Compliance and Security: Align your Terraform configurations with compliance requirements and security best practices specific to your industry and cloud provider.

Documentation: Maintain thorough documentation for your Terraform code, including variable descriptions, module usage instructions, and resource configuration details.

Error Handling: Implement error handling and graceful degradation mechanisms in your code to handle unexpected situations or resource failures.

Monitoring and Logging: Set up monitoring and logging for your infrastructure to detect and respond to issues promptly.

Backup and Recovery: Establish backup and recovery strategies for critical resources to ensure business continuity.

Immutable Infrastructure: Consider adopting an immutable infrastructure approach, where infrastructure changes are achieved by replacing resources rather than modifying them in place.

Infrastructure as Code Policy: Define and enforce policies for managing infrastructure through Terraform, covering naming conventions, security measures, and deployment processes.

Performance Optimization: Continuously optimize your Terraform configurations for performance and cost efficiency, reviewing resource sizing and provisioning.

Environment Isolation: Isolate development, staging, and production environments to minimize risks and prevent unintended changes.

Continuous Integration and Deployment (CI/CD): Integrate Terraform into your CI/CD pipeline to automate testing, validation, and deployment processes.

Collaboration and Communication: Foster collaboration and communication within your team by using collaboration platforms, code comments, and documentation.

Education and Training: Invest in ongoing education and training for your team to keep them updated with Terraform best practices and new features.

Maintaining code organization and quality standards is an ongoing process that requires continuous attention and improvement.

By following these practices, you can ensure that your Terraform configurations remain robust, reliable, and adaptable to changing requirements and best practices in the world of Infrastructure as Code.

Chapter 9: Version Control and Collaboration

Version control for Infrastructure as Code (IaC) projects is a fundamental practice that provides numerous benefits, including improved collaboration, code history tracking, and the ability to manage changes systematically.

Version control systems (VCS), such as Git, enable IaC practitioners to track and manage changes to their codebase efficiently.

In an IaC context, version control is particularly crucial because it allows teams to treat infrastructure configurations as code and apply software development best practices to their infrastructure.

One of the primary reasons to use version control for IaC is the ability to track changes over time.

In Git, for example, every change to the codebase is recorded as a commit, which includes a timestamp, author, and a summary of the changes made.

This detailed history of changes provides transparency into who made changes, when they were made, and what specifically was modified.

Having a comprehensive history of changes is invaluable when troubleshooting issues, auditing changes, or understanding the evolution of your infrastructure.

Additionally, version control systems like Git allow you to create branches for different development purposes.

Branches provide isolation for developing new features, fixing bugs, or making other changes without affecting the main codebase.

In an IaC project, you might have branches for different environments (e.g., development, staging, production) or for distinct infrastructure components.

Branches make it easy to work on multiple aspects of your infrastructure concurrently, and they enable teams to collaborate effectively by allowing team members to work independently on different branches.

Once changes are complete and tested in a branch, they can be merged back into the main branch or another target branch, ensuring that changes are integrated seamlessly.

One of the key advantages of using version control in IaC is the ability to roll back changes if issues or errors arise.

If a change causes unexpected problems in your infrastructure, you can revert to a previous, known-working state by checking out a specific commit or branch.

This rollback capability provides a safety net for IaC practitioners, allowing them to quickly recover from issues and restore the desired state of the infrastructure.

Another benefit of version control is the ability to collaborate effectively in distributed teams.

With Git and other distributed version control systems, team members can work on their local copies of the codebase, making changes independently.

Changes can then be shared and merged seamlessly when ready, promoting concurrent development and reducing conflicts.

In addition to collaboration, version control enhances the traceability of changes and fosters accountability.

Every change made to the codebase is associated with an author, and changes are tracked at a granular level.

This level of detail ensures that you can trace any change back to its source, which is essential for understanding the context and reasoning behind changes.

When working on IaC projects, version control also plays a critical role in managing the complexity of infrastructure configurations.

As infrastructure code grows, it can become challenging to maintain a clear understanding of the entire configuration.

Version control systems help by providing tools for comparing different versions of the codebase and highlighting the differences.

This "diffing" capability makes it easy to see what has changed between commits or branches, aiding in code review and troubleshooting.

Moreover, version control systems offer mechanisms for resolving conflicts when multiple team members make changes to the same part of the codebase simultaneously.

Conflict resolution tools allow teams to merge changes intelligently, ensuring that the final codebase is coherent and functional.

In addition to tracking changes to the codebase, version control systems also provide a way to manage infrastructure configurations and variables.

IaC practitioners can store configuration files, variable definitions, and other related files in version control repositories.

This practice ensures that infrastructure configurations are versioned alongside the code that deploys them, leading to consistent and reproducible deployments.

Furthermore, by storing variable definitions and secrets securely in version control, teams can maintain a centralized record of configuration parameters and ensure that they are protected according to security best practices.

For IaC projects that involve collaboration between different teams or organizations, version control systems facilitate code sharing and integration.

Teams can create public or private repositories, granting access to authorized individuals or groups.

This controlled access allows for secure sharing of infrastructure code while maintaining governance and access controls.

Furthermore, version control systems can integrate with continuous integration and continuous deployment (CI/CD) pipelines.

By connecting version control repositories to CI/CD systems, you can automate the testing and deployment of infrastructure changes.

This automation reduces the risk of human error, accelerates the delivery of changes, and ensures that infrastructure remains consistent across different environments.

In summary, version control is a critical practice for managing Infrastructure as Code (IaC) projects effectively.

Version control systems, such as Git, enable teams to track changes, collaborate efficiently, manage complexity, and ensure the reproducibility of infrastructure deployments.

By implementing version control, IaC practitioners can maintain a clear history of changes, roll back to previous states, resolve conflicts, and promote best practices in code management and collaboration.

In the evolving landscape of IaC, version control is an indispensable tool for achieving consistency, reliability, and agility in managing infrastructure configurations as code.

Collaborative development approaches play a pivotal role in the successful implementation and management of Infrastructure as Code (IaC) projects.

In the world of IaC, where infrastructure configurations are treated as code and frequently undergo changes, effective collaboration is essential for achieving desired outcomes.

Collaborative development encompasses various practices, tools, and workflows that enable multiple team members to work together seamlessly on IaC projects.

One of the foundational elements of collaborative development in IaC is version control, as it provides a shared repository where infrastructure code is stored and managed.

With a version control system like Git, team members can clone a centralized repository to their local development environments, work on code changes independently, and then merge their changes back into the central repository.

The distributed nature of Git allows team members to work offline, making it conducive to both centralized and distributed teams.

Branching is a fundamental concept in collaborative development, allowing team members to create isolated workspaces for implementing new features, fixing bugs, or making changes to infrastructure configurations.

Branches provide a way to parallelize development efforts without interfering with each other's work.

Once changes are complete and tested within a branch, they can be merged into the main codebase, ensuring a systematic integration of new features and bug fixes.

Collaboration is further facilitated by code review processes, where team members review each other's code changes for quality, correctness, and adherence to best practices.

Code reviews provide an opportunity for knowledge sharing, mentorship, and ensuring that code changes align with the project's goals and standards.

In the context of IaC, code reviews also help identify potential risks, security issues, or misconfigurations early in the development cycle.

To streamline code reviews and collaboration, many teams use code review tools and platforms that provide features like commenting, code highlighting, and history tracking.

Continuous Integration (CI) and Continuous Deployment (CD) pipelines are integral to collaborative development in IaC.

CI/CD pipelines automate the build, test, and deployment processes, allowing infrastructure changes to be automatically tested and deployed to various environments.

When a team member pushes code changes to the version control repository, the CI/CD pipeline can trigger automated tests to ensure that the changes do not introduce regressions or errors.

Successful builds and passing tests can then trigger automatic deployments to development, staging, or production environments, depending on the project's configuration.

CI/CD pipelines promote collaboration by reducing the manual effort required for testing and deployment, ensuring that code changes are consistently validated and deployed in a controlled manner.

Infrastructure as Code also benefits from Infrastructure as Documentation, where code serves as a form of documentation.

Collaborative development approaches emphasize the importance of clear and well-documented code to ensure that team members can understand and modify infrastructure configurations effectively.

Documentation within the code includes comments, explanations, and annotations that provide context, usage instructions, and explanations for specific configurations.

Such documentation ensures that team members can understand the rationale behind decisions, the purpose of specific resources, and how to make changes without causing unintended consequences.

Effective documentation promotes collaboration by reducing the learning curve for team members who join the project and by facilitating knowledge sharing.

Additionally, infrastructure code can be supplemented with external documentation that describes overall project architecture, deployment procedures, and operational guidelines.

Another crucial aspect of collaborative development is role-based access control and permission management.

In IaC projects, different team members may have varying levels of access and responsibilities.

Role-based access control allows project administrators to define who can create, modify, or delete infrastructure configurations and who can perform deployments.

These access controls ensure that only authorized team members can make critical changes to the Infrastructure, reducing the risk of unauthorized modifications.

Collaborative development also extends to the practice of Pair Programming, where two developers work together at the same workstation.

In the context of IaC, pair programming can enhance code quality and knowledge sharing by allowing team members to review each other's code in real-time, brainstorm solutions, and catch issues early in the development process.

Pair programming promotes collaboration and can lead to more robust and efficient infrastructure configurations.

Within collaborative development, it is essential to maintain effective communication channels among team members.

Communication tools, such as chat platforms, video conferencing, and issue tracking systems, enable team members to discuss changes, report issues, and coordinate efforts seamlessly.

These tools also serve as a means of recording discussions and decisions, providing a historical record of project-related conversations.

In large or distributed teams, effective communication ensures that team members are aligned on project goals, timelines, and priorities.

Additionally, collaboration often involves cross-functional teams with members from various disciplines, including development, operations, security, and compliance.

These teams must collaborate closely to address infrastructure requirements comprehensively.

Collaborative development approaches encourage cross-functional collaboration by fostering a shared understanding of infrastructure needs and requirements across different teams.

Moreover, collaborative development emphasizes the importance of documentation and knowledge sharing.

Documentation efforts extend beyond code comments to encompass broader project documentation.

This documentation includes architectural diagrams, design decisions, security policies, and operational procedures.

By documenting key aspects of the infrastructure, teams ensure that knowledge is accessible to all team members and is not confined to individual expertise.

Documentation also helps teams anticipate and plan for changes and improvements to the infrastructure.

Another collaborative development practice is to maintain a clear separation of concerns in IaC configurations.

By breaking down infrastructure code into reusable modules, each responsible for a specific aspect of the infrastructure, teams can collaborate more effectively.

Separation of concerns allows team members to work on different modules independently, reducing the risk of conflicts and enabling teams to iterate on individual components without affecting the entire project.

Collaborative development is an iterative process that benefits from regular retrospectives and feedback loops.

Teams can conduct retrospectives to reflect on their collaborative practices, identify areas for improvement, and adjust their workflows accordingly.

Feedback loops, both formal and informal, allow team members to provide input, share insights, and suggest enhancements to the collaborative development process.

In summary, collaborative development approaches are essential for successful Infrastructure as Code (IaC) projects.

Collaboration is facilitated by version control, code reviews, CI/CD pipelines, documentation, access controls, and communication tools.

These practices ensure that team members can work together efficiently, share knowledge, and produce high-quality infrastructure configurations that meet project goals and standards.

By embracing collaborative development, teams can harness the full potential of IaC to build, deploy, and manage infrastructure configurations effectively.

Chapter 10: Deploying Your First Terraform Project

Project deployment is a critical phase in the life cycle of an Infrastructure as Code (IaC) project, where infrastructure configurations are applied to create, update, or manage the desired infrastructure.

This phase involves translating the codebase, which represents infrastructure as code, into tangible resources and services within a cloud or on-premises environment.

Project deployment is the culmination of development efforts, where the infrastructure code is transformed into a running infrastructure that serves the intended purpose.

Before diving into the specifics of the deployment process, it's crucial to understand the overall deployment overview, which includes key considerations, prerequisites, and best practices.

Project deployment begins with careful planning and preparation, often involving collaboration among developers, operations teams, and other stakeholders.

It is essential to define the target environment or cloud platform where the infrastructure will be deployed, such as Amazon Web Services (AWS), Microsoft Azure, Google Cloud Platform (GCP), or an on-premises data center.

The choice of the deployment environment depends on project requirements, cost considerations, and existing infrastructure.

Once the deployment environment is established, it's essential to configure access credentials and permissions, ensuring that the deployment process can interact with the target environment.

These credentials typically include access keys, tokens, or certificates required to authenticate with the cloud provider or infrastructure management platform.

Security best practices dictate that these credentials should be stored securely and managed using dedicated credential management tools or secrets management systems.

Project deployment also relies on the concept of Infrastructure as Code (IaC) scripts, which are the code representations of infrastructure configurations.

IaC scripts, written in languages like HashiCorp Configuration Language (HCL) for Terraform, CloudFormation for AWS, or ARM templates for Azure, describe the desired state of the infrastructure.

Developers define resources, their properties, relationships, and configurations within these scripts.

The IaC scripts act as blueprints, specifying the infrastructure's architecture and dependencies in a human-readable format.

Once the IaC scripts are ready, they need to be organized and structured within the codebase.

This organization ensures that resources are logically grouped, variables are defined, and modules (if used) are configured effectively.

It's crucial to maintain code quality and readability, which simplifies the deployment process and facilitates troubleshooting.

The deployment process also involves defining input variables, which allow for customization of the infrastructure configurations.

Variables enable the same IaC scripts to be used across multiple environments, such as development, staging, and production, by adjusting variable values to match each environment's specific requirements.

Variable files, often in the form of **.tfvars** or **.json** files, are used to provide input values during deployment.

An essential consideration during project deployment is the use of a version control system (VCS) like Git.

VCS ensures that the IaC scripts remain versioned and allows for tracking changes, auditing modifications, and collaboration among team members.

Using branches in VCS facilitates the development of new features or changes to infrastructure configurations in isolation, reducing the risk of conflicts during deployment.

Additionally, VCS enables the management of configuration changes across different environments, ensuring consistency and reproducibility.

Project deployment typically involves the use of Continuous Integration (CI) and Continuous Deployment (CD) pipelines.

These pipelines automate the process of building, testing, and deploying infrastructure code.

CI/CD pipelines integrate with version control repositories and trigger actions based on code changes.

For instance, when developers push code changes to a specific branch, the CI/CD pipeline can automatically initiate testing and deployment procedures.

This automation reduces manual intervention, minimizes the potential for human error, and ensures that infrastructure changes are tested thoroughly before reaching the target environment.

Testing is a crucial part of project deployment.

It involves validating that the infrastructure code behaves as expected, adheres to best practices, and meets defined requirements.

Testing can encompass unit testing, integration testing, and end-to-end testing of the infrastructure configurations.

Various testing frameworks and tools are available to support these activities, depending on the chosen IaC platform.

Additionally, comprehensive testing helps identify potential issues, security vulnerabilities, or misconfigurations early in the deployment process.

Security considerations are paramount during project deployment.

It is crucial to adhere to security best practices, including least privilege access, encryption, and network security configurations.

Sensitive information, such as credentials and API keys, should be managed securely and protected from unauthorized access.

Access controls should be established to limit access to infrastructure resources and prevent unauthorized modifications.

Project deployment also involves the creation and management of infrastructure resources.

This includes provisioning virtual machines, networking components, storage, databases, and any other resources defined in the IaC scripts.

Resource creation is executed by the IaC platform, which interacts with the cloud provider's API or the infrastructure management platform to instantiate the resources.

The IaC platform ensures that resources are created according to the specifications provided in the IaC scripts, including resource properties, dependencies, and configurations.

Resource creation is typically orchestrated by applying the IaC scripts using the chosen IaC tool.

The IaC tool translates the code into API calls or platform-specific commands to create and configure the resources.

Resource dependencies are automatically resolved, ensuring that resources are created in the correct order to meet dependencies defined in the IaC scripts.

Once resources are created, it's important to validate the infrastructure's correctness and functionality.

This validation process involves testing the infrastructure configurations against defined criteria, which may include connectivity tests, application deployment, and integration with other services.

Validation ensures that the deployed infrastructure operates as expected and meets the project's requirements.

Monitoring and observability are essential aspects of project deployment.

Monitoring tools and practices should be in place to track the health, performance, and availability of the deployed infrastructure.

Logs, metrics, and alerts enable the proactive detection and resolution of issues that may arise during deployment or while the infrastructure is in operation.

Continuous monitoring and observability help maintain the reliability and stability of the deployed infrastructure.

Documentation plays a critical role in project deployment.

Detailed documentation should be available to describe the deployment process, including instructions for setting up the deployment environment, executing deployment procedures, and troubleshooting common issues.

Documentation ensures that deployment procedures can be followed consistently, even by team members who may not have been involved in the development process.

Furthermore, documentation assists in knowledge transfer and serves as a valuable resource for future maintenance and updates.

Project deployment is a dynamic and iterative process.

As infrastructure requirements evolve, new features are developed, and changes are introduced, the deployment process needs to adapt accordingly.

Regularly reviewing and optimizing deployment procedures is essential to ensure efficiency, security, and reliability.

In summary, project deployment is a multifaceted process that involves careful planning, code organization, testing, security considerations, and the use of automation tools.

Collaboration, continuous integration, and documentation are integral to the successful deployment of Infrastructure as Code (IaC) projects.

With proper practices and attention to detail, project deployment can yield reliable, scalable, and maintainable infrastructure that meets the needs of the project and its stakeholders.

Monitoring and validation of deployments are critical aspects of managing infrastructure in a dynamic and ever-changing environment.

Once infrastructure changes are deployed, it is essential to continuously monitor their performance and health to ensure that they meet the expected standards and deliver reliable services.

Monitoring involves the collection of data and metrics related to the deployed infrastructure, applications, and services.

These metrics can include CPU utilization, memory usage, network traffic, latency, error rates, and more, depending on the specific requirements of the project.

Effective monitoring allows teams to gain insights into the behavior of the infrastructure, identify anomalies or issues, and make data-driven decisions for optimization and troubleshooting.

Monitoring can be performed using a variety of tools and solutions, including open-source monitoring platforms like

Prometheus, commercial monitoring services, and cloud provider-specific monitoring solutions.

In addition to infrastructure metrics, application-level monitoring is crucial for assessing the performance and availability of applications running on the infrastructure.

Application monitoring tools can capture information about application response times, error rates, user interactions, and other relevant data.

These insights help teams understand how applications are performing in real-time and enable them to proactively address issues that may impact user experience.

Effective monitoring often involves setting up alerting mechanisms that notify the team when predefined thresholds or conditions are met.

Alerts can be triggered based on specific metrics, such as when CPU usage exceeds a certain threshold or when an application error rate surpasses an acceptable level.

Alerting helps teams respond promptly to critical issues, minimizing downtime and ensuring the continuity of services.

Continuous validation is another essential aspect of managing deployments.

Validation involves verifying that the deployed infrastructure and applications meet the desired state and adhere to defined standards and policies.

Validation can encompass various checks and tests, including functional testing, security scanning, compliance assessments, and more.

One common approach to validation is the use of automated testing frameworks and scripts that execute predefined tests on the deployed infrastructure.

These tests can include checks for resource provisioning, configuration correctness, and application functionality.

Automated validation helps teams ensure that deployments are consistent, reliable, and conform to the expected specifications.

Security validation is of paramount importance, particularly in today's threat landscape.

Teams should implement security scans and assessments to identify vulnerabilities and misconfigurations in the deployed infrastructure.

These scans can check for common security issues, such as open ports, weak authentication, and known vulnerabilities in software components.

Addressing security findings promptly is critical to maintaining a secure deployment.

Compliance validation ensures that the deployed infrastructure aligns with industry-specific regulations, internal policies, and best practices.

For example, organizations in highly regulated industries may need to adhere to specific compliance standards, such as HIPAA or PCI DSS.

Validation checks can confirm that the infrastructure complies with these standards and that appropriate safeguards are in place.

Performance validation assesses the performance characteristics of the deployed infrastructure under various conditions.

Teams can simulate different loads and scenarios to evaluate how the infrastructure behaves and performs.

Performance testing can help identify bottlenecks, scalability limitations, and opportunities for optimization.

Validation should be an integral part of the deployment pipeline, with automated tests and checks executed at different stages, including during development, pre-deployment, and post-deployment.

Validation results should be recorded and analyzed to provide insights into the overall health and quality of the deployment.

Teams should also establish clear criteria for passing validation, defining what constitutes a successful deployment.

In cases where validation checks fail, teams should have well-defined processes for addressing and resolving issues.

Validation feedback should be integrated into the continuous improvement cycle, driving enhancements to the deployment process and infrastructure configurations.

Logging and auditing are essential components of monitoring and validation.

Logs capture a detailed record of events and activities within the infrastructure, including changes, errors, and user interactions.

By analyzing logs, teams can gain visibility into what happened during deployments and diagnose issues effectively.

Audit trails provide a historical record of actions taken within the infrastructure, including who made changes, when they occurred, and what changes were made.

Auditing helps maintain accountability, track changes, and support compliance requirements.

Continuous validation is particularly important in environments where deployments are frequent and dynamic, such as those following DevOps or continuous delivery practices.

In these environments, changes can be introduced rapidly, and automated validation serves as a safety net to catch potential issues before they impact users.

Continuous validation promotes a culture of transparency, collaboration, and continuous improvement within the deployment team.

It encourages regular feedback and communication among team members, helping to identify areas for enhancement and optimization.

Teams should establish key performance indicators (KPIs) and service level objectives (SLOs) to measure the effectiveness of monitoring and validation efforts.

These metrics can include mean time to detect and mean time to resolve issues, the percentage of successful deployments, and the availability and performance of services.

KPIs and SLOs provide quantifiable goals and benchmarks that guide teams in continuously improving their monitoring and validation practices.

Additionally, teams should adopt a proactive approach to monitoring and validation by considering predictive analytics and anomaly detection.

By analyzing historical data and patterns, teams can identify potential issues or trends that may lead to future problems.

Predictive analytics can help teams take preemptive actions to mitigate risks and ensure the stability and reliability of the deployment.

In summary, monitoring and validation are essential components of managing deployments in dynamic and complex environments.

Effective monitoring provides insights into infrastructure performance, while continuous validation ensures that deployments meet the desired state, security standards, compliance requirements, and performance expectations.

Automated testing, security scanning, compliance checks, and performance assessments play a pivotal role in maintaining the reliability and integrity of the deployed infrastructure.

By embracing a culture of continuous monitoring and validation, teams can proactively identify and address issues, optimize performance, and deliver a seamless experience to users.

Book 2
Cloud Infrastructure Orchestration with AWS and IaC

ROB BOTWRIGHT

Chapter 1: Introduction to AWS and Infrastructure as Code (IaC)

Exploring the AWS ecosystem offers a comprehensive view of Amazon Web Services, one of the world's leading cloud computing platforms.

AWS, established by Amazon in 2006, has grown into a vast and diverse ecosystem that provides a wide range of cloud services and solutions.

At the core of the AWS ecosystem is the AWS Global Infrastructure, a network of data centers and regions strategically located around the world.

AWS regions consist of multiple availability zones, each with its own set of data centers, providing redundancy and high availability.

This global reach enables AWS to deliver services and resources to customers with low-latency access, disaster recovery options, and data sovereignty compliance.

One of the foundational services in the AWS ecosystem is Amazon Elastic Compute Cloud (EC2), which offers resizable compute capacity in the cloud.

EC2 instances are virtual machines that can run various operating systems and applications, making them suitable for a wide range of use cases, from web hosting to data processing.

Amazon Simple Storage Service (S3) is another core AWS service, providing scalable object storage for data, files, and backups.

S3 offers high durability, availability, and the capability to host static websites and distribute content through a content delivery network (CDN).

AWS provides a multitude of services for building, deploying, and managing containerized applications, such as Amazon Elastic Container Service (ECS) and Amazon Elastic Kubernetes Service (EKS).

These services simplify container orchestration, scaling, and management, making it easier to adopt container technology in the cloud.

AWS Lambda is a serverless computing service that allows developers to run code in response to events without provisioning or managing servers.

It is well-suited for building event-driven and highly scalable applications.

Amazon RDS (Relational Database Service) offers managed database solutions, including PostgreSQL, MySQL, MariaDB, Oracle, and SQL Server, simplifying database administration tasks such as patching, backup, and scaling.

Amazon DynamoDB is a managed NoSQL database service that provides seamless scalability and low-latency access for applications that require high throughput and low response times.

AWS offers a wide range of developer tools and services, including AWS CodeBuild, AWS CodeDeploy, and AWS CodePipeline, which help automate and streamline the software development and deployment process.

Amazon Elastic Beanstalk simplifies application deployment and management by abstracting the infrastructure and allowing developers to focus on code.

AWS Amplify provides a set of tools and services for building modern web and mobile applications, including authentication, data storage, and backend services.

The AWS ecosystem includes a comprehensive suite of AI and machine learning services, such as Amazon SageMaker for building, training, and deploying machine learning models, and Amazon Rekognition for image and video analysis.

Amazon Polly offers text-to-speech capabilities, while Amazon Lex provides natural language understanding for building conversational interfaces.

AWS IoT services enable the development of Internet of Things (IoT) applications, with offerings like AWS IoT Core for connecting devices to the cloud and AWS IoT Greengrass for edge computing.

AWS also offers a range of analytics and big data services, including Amazon EMR (Elastic MapReduce) for processing large datasets, Amazon Redshift for data warehousing, and Amazon Kinesis for real-time data streaming.

Data scientists can leverage Amazon SageMaker for machine learning model training and deployment, and QuickSight for business intelligence and data visualization.

The AWS ecosystem includes security and compliance services like AWS Identity and Access Management (IAM) for managing user and resource access, AWS Key Management Service (KMS) for encryption key management, and AWS Organizations for multi-account management.

AWS also provides services like AWS Shield for DDoS protection, AWS WAF (Web Application Firewall) for web application security, and AWS Config for tracking resource configurations and compliance.

Networking services in the AWS ecosystem include Amazon VPC (Virtual Private Cloud) for network isolation, Amazon Route 53 for domain name system (DNS) management, and AWS Direct Connect for dedicated network connections to AWS data centers.

AWS offers a variety of storage solutions, including Amazon EBS (Elastic Block Store) for block storage, Amazon EFS (Elastic File System) for scalable file storage, and AWS Storage Gateway for hybrid cloud storage integration.

The AWS Marketplace is a digital catalog of software and services from third-party vendors that can be easily deployed on AWS.

Customers can find and purchase a wide range of solutions, from security and monitoring tools to analytics and machine learning applications.

AWS also provides management and governance services, such as AWS CloudWatch for monitoring, AWS CloudTrail for auditing, and AWS Systems Manager for system management tasks.

Infrastructure as Code (IaC) is a fundamental concept in the AWS ecosystem, allowing users to define and provision infrastructure using code.

AWS CloudFormation is a service that enables the creation and management of AWS resources through templates, while AWS CDK (Cloud Development Kit) offers a developer-friendly way to define infrastructure using programming languages.

AWS offers a variety of deployment and container orchestration solutions, including AWS Elastic Beanstalk for platform-as-a-service (PaaS) deployments, AWS App Runner for containerized web applications, and Amazon ECS and Amazon EKS for container orchestration.

For organizations looking to adopt serverless computing, AWS Lambda and AWS Step Functions provide serverless execution and workflow orchestration capabilities.

AWS provides a wide range of databases and data storage solutions, from traditional relational databases like Amazon RDS and Amazon Aurora to NoSQL databases like Amazon DynamoDB and key-value stores like Amazon ElastiCache.

Data lakes can be built using Amazon S3 and services like AWS Glue for data ingestion and transformation.

AWS also offers a variety of migration and transfer services to help organizations move their existing workloads to the cloud, including AWS Database Migration Service (DMS) and AWS Server Migration Service (SMS).

In the realm of DevOps, AWS provides a set of tools for continuous integration and continuous delivery (CI/CD), such as AWS CodePipeline and AWS CodeBuild.

AWS CodeDeploy automates application deployments to instances or containerized environments.

For monitoring and observability, AWS offers services like Amazon CloudWatch for metrics and logs, AWS X-Ray for tracing, and AWS App Runner for application insights.

Security in the AWS ecosystem is a top priority, with services like AWS Identity and Access Management (IAM) for access control, AWS Key Management Service (KMS) for encryption, and AWS Security Hub for security monitoring and compliance.

AWS also offers solutions like AWS Config for resource tracking, AWS Secrets Manager for managing sensitive information, and AWS Firewall Manager for centralizing firewall rules.

To ensure high availability and fault tolerance, AWS provides services like Amazon Route 53 for DNS and AWS Elastic Load Balancing (ELB) for distributing incoming traffic.

AWS also offers disaster recovery solutions, including AWS Backup and AWS Disaster Recovery.

The AWS ecosystem includes specialized industry solutions, such as AWS GovCloud for government organizations, AWS Health for healthcare, and AWS Educate for educational institutions.

AWS also supports edge computing with AWS Outposts, which extends the AWS infrastructure to on-premises data centers.

The AWS ecosystem is continuously evolving, with new services and features regularly added to meet the evolving needs of customers.

In addition to the services mentioned, AWS also provides extensive documentation, training resources, and a global network of partners and certified professionals to support users in their cloud journey.

Exploring the AWS ecosystem offers organizations the flexibility and scalability needed to build, deploy, and manage a wide range of applications and workloads in the cloud.

With its extensive portfolio of services, security features, and global reach, AWS remains a leading choice for businesses and developers seeking a reliable and innovative cloud platform.

Understanding the principles of Infrastructure as Code (IaC) is essential for modernizing and optimizing the management of IT infrastructure.

At its core, IaC is a software engineering approach that treats infrastructure as code, allowing organizations to define and provision their infrastructure using code and automation tools.

This concept represents a fundamental shift from traditional manual infrastructure management to a more agile, scalable, and efficient approach.

One of the key principles of IaC is the idea of declaring infrastructure configurations in code, often referred to as infrastructure code or configuration code.

Infrastructure code is typically written using a domain-specific language (DSL) or a general-purpose programming language, depending on the IaC tool or framework being used.

By representing infrastructure as code, organizations can version control their infrastructure configurations, track changes, and collaborate more effectively among development and operations teams.

Version controlling infrastructure code brings many advantages, including the ability to roll back to previous configurations in case of issues or to replicate infrastructure in different environments accurately.

Another principle of IaC is the concept of idempotency, which means that applying the same infrastructure code multiple times should result in the same desired state, regardless of the initial state.

In practical terms, idempotency ensures that infrastructure can be safely and predictably updated or recreated without causing unintended side effects.

This is achieved through IaC tools that are designed to detect and apply only the necessary changes to align the infrastructure with the desired configuration.

Infrastructure as Code encourages a shift towards declarative definitions, where the focus is on specifying what the infrastructure should look like rather than specifying how to achieve that state.

In a declarative approach, the IaC code describes the desired end state of the infrastructure, and the IaC tool takes care of determining the steps needed to achieve that state.

This declarative nature simplifies the management of complex infrastructure and reduces the risk of configuration drift.

IaC emphasizes automation as a core principle, aiming to eliminate manual and error-prone processes in infrastructure management.

Automation allows organizations to provision, configure, and manage infrastructure resources efficiently and consistently.

By automating repetitive tasks, IaC reduces the likelihood of human errors, improves operational efficiency, and enables faster and more reliable deployments.

Another essential principle of IaC is the use of modularity and reusability in infrastructure code.

Modularity involves breaking down infrastructure code into reusable components or modules, each responsible for a specific aspect of the infrastructure.

This approach encourages a more structured and maintainable codebase and enables teams to share and reuse infrastructure components across different projects.

Reusability promotes consistency in configurations and reduces the effort required to define and manage infrastructure resources.

The principle of testing and validation is integral to IaC, ensuring that infrastructure code is reliable and functions as intended.

IaC tools often provide testing frameworks and mechanisms to validate infrastructure configurations before deployment.

Testing can include unit testing of individual modules, integration testing to verify the interactions between components, and validation of the entire infrastructure.

By incorporating testing into the IaC workflow, organizations can catch errors early in the development process, improve code quality, and reduce the risk of issues in production.

Another important principle of IaC is the use of version control systems (VCS) to manage infrastructure code.

VCS, such as Git, enable teams to track changes, collaborate on infrastructure code, and maintain a history of revisions.

Version control ensures that changes are well-documented, allows for easy rollback to previous states, and facilitates collaboration among team members.

Additionally, VCS helps enforce best practices for code review and change management.

Security is a fundamental consideration in IaC, with the principle of security by design at its core.

Organizations should embed security practices into their IaC workflows from the outset.

This includes implementing access controls, secrets management, encryption, and vulnerability scanning as part of the infrastructure code.

Security checks and audits should be integrated into the deployment pipeline to ensure that security requirements are met throughout the development and deployment process.

Scalability is another key principle of IaC, enabling organizations to adapt their infrastructure to changing workloads and requirements.

IaC allows for the easy replication of infrastructure configurations, making it possible to scale resources horizontally or vertically as needed.

By automating the scaling process, IaC ensures that infrastructure can grow or shrink dynamically based on demand, optimizing cost efficiency.

Documentation plays a crucial role in IaC, with the principle of comprehensive documentation ensuring that infrastructure code is well-documented and easy to understand.

Documentation should describe the purpose of infrastructure components, their dependencies, and how to use them.

Clear and up-to-date documentation enhances collaboration, supports troubleshooting, and facilitates knowledge sharing among team members.

The final principle of IaC is continuous improvement, which encourages organizations to regularly review and enhance their infrastructure code and processes.

This iterative approach involves collecting feedback, identifying areas for optimization, and incorporating lessons learned into future infrastructure code iterations.

Continuous improvement leads to more efficient and reliable infrastructure management over time.

In summary, understanding the principles of Infrastructure as Code (IaC) is crucial for organizations looking to modernize their infrastructure management practices.

IaC principles encompass the declaration of infrastructure configurations as code, idempotency, automation, declarative definitions, modularity, testing, version control, security, scalability, documentation, and continuous improvement.

By embracing these principles, organizations can leverage IaC to achieve greater efficiency, agility, and reliability in managing their IT infrastructure.

Chapter 2: Setting Up Your AWS Environment for IaC

Setting up and configuring an AWS account is the first step on the journey to leveraging the power of Amazon Web Services.

Creating an AWS account is a straightforward process, but it involves several essential considerations to ensure that the account is properly configured to meet your specific needs.

Before you begin, it's crucial to decide on the purpose of your AWS account.

AWS offers different types of accounts, including individual accounts for personal use, business accounts for organizations, and specialized accounts for specific purposes like education and government.

Choosing the right type of account ensures that you have the appropriate access and features to align with your goals.

Once you've determined the account type, you can proceed to create your AWS account through the AWS Management Console.

During the account creation process, you will need to provide your contact information, payment details, and verification information.

AWS may require identity verification to ensure the security of your account and adhere to regulatory requirements.

After successfully creating your AWS account, you'll gain access to the AWS Management Console, a web-based interface for managing AWS resources and services.

At this point, it's essential to configure your account settings to align with your security and billing preferences.

One critical aspect of account configuration is setting up billing alerts and budget notifications.

AWS allows you to configure billing alerts that notify you when your usage and spending exceed predefined thresholds.

These alerts are valuable for cost control and can help you avoid unexpected charges.

To gain better visibility into your AWS spending, you can set up detailed billing reports that provide granular information about your resource usage and costs.

Additionally, AWS provides a Cost Explorer tool that enables you to visualize and analyze your spending patterns.

To enhance security, AWS offers various identity and access management (IAM) features that allow you to control who can access your AWS resources and what actions they can perform.

IAM allows you to create users, groups, and roles, each with specific permissions and policies.

By following the principle of least privilege, you can ensure that users have the minimum permissions required to perform their tasks.

IAM also supports multi-factor authentication (MFA) to add an extra layer of security to your AWS account.

Enabling MFA helps protect against unauthorized access to your account, especially for actions that involve sensitive operations.

Another critical aspect of AWS account configuration is organizing and structuring your resources effectively.

AWS provides a hierarchical structure for managing resources called an AWS organization.

Organizations help you centralize billing, consolidate accounts, and define resource-sharing relationships.

By using AWS organizations, you can establish a clear and manageable structure for your AWS resources, particularly in a multi-account environment.

Configuring regions and availability zones is another consideration when setting up your AWS account.

AWS operates in multiple geographic regions worldwide, each consisting of one or more availability zones.

Availability zones are physically separate data centers with redundant power, networking, and cooling.

Selecting the appropriate region and availability zone for your resources depends on factors like latency requirements, data residency, and disaster recovery planning.

AWS provides tools like AWS Global Accelerator and Amazon Route 53 for global load balancing and routing to optimize resource distribution across regions.

To ensure the security of your AWS account, it's crucial to configure security settings and practices.

AWS offers security best practices guidelines and provides a range of security services and features.

For example, AWS Identity and Access Management (IAM) enables you to control access to your resources by defining user roles, policies, and permissions.

AWS Key Management Service (KMS) allows you to create and manage encryption keys to protect your data at rest and in transit.

Additionally, AWS offers security services like AWS GuardDuty for threat detection, AWS Inspector for vulnerability assessment, and AWS WAF (Web Application Firewall) for web application protection.

Security groups and network access control lists (ACLs) help you control inbound and outbound traffic to your AWS resources, ensuring that only authorized communication occurs.

Security monitoring and auditing are essential aspects of AWS account configuration.

AWS provides services like AWS CloudTrail to capture and log all API activity in your AWS account.

CloudTrail records API calls, user identity, resource information, and action taken, providing a comprehensive audit trail for security and compliance purposes.

AWS Config allows you to assess, audit, and evaluate the configurations of your AWS resources continuously.

Using Config rules, you can define desired configurations and receive notifications when resources deviate from those standards.

VPC (Virtual Private Cloud) configuration is crucial for network isolation and security.

AWS allows you to create and configure VPCs, subnets, route tables, and peering connections to design your network architecture securely.

By configuring VPC peering or VPN connections, you can securely connect your on-premises data center to your AWS resources.

Elastic Load Balancing (ELB) and Auto Scaling configuration are essential for achieving high availability and scalability for your applications.

AWS provides load balancing solutions like Application Load Balancer (ALB) and Network Load Balancer (NLB) to distribute incoming traffic across multiple instances.

Auto Scaling allows you to automatically adjust the number of instances based on demand, ensuring that your applications remain responsive and available.

Storage configuration in AWS involves selecting the appropriate storage services and options for your data and application needs.

AWS offers a variety of storage services, including Amazon S3 for object storage, Amazon EBS for block storage, and Amazon EFS for file storage.

Configuration options like data replication, encryption, and access control are available to protect and optimize your storage resources.

Database configuration is a critical consideration for data management.

AWS offers managed database services like Amazon RDS, Amazon DynamoDB, and Amazon Redshift for various database workloads.

Configuring database backups, replication, and scaling options ensures the reliability and performance of your data infrastructure.

Backup and disaster recovery planning should be part of your account configuration.

AWS provides backup and recovery solutions like AWS Backup and AWS Disaster Recovery to protect your data and applications from unexpected failures or disasters.

Backup policies and retention settings can be configured to meet your data protection requirements.

Monitoring and alerting configuration is essential for maintaining the health and performance of your AWS resources.

AWS CloudWatch allows you to collect and monitor metrics, set up alarms, and gain insights into the behavior of your resources.

Alert notifications can be configured to notify you of performance anomalies or issues that require attention.

Configuration management and automation are fundamental for efficiently managing your AWS resources.

AWS offers services like AWS Systems Manager and AWS OpsWorks for automating tasks like patch management, configuration drift remediation, and application deployment.

Infrastructure as Code (IaC) tools such as AWS CloudFormation and AWS CDK enable you to define and provision infrastructure resources using code.

These tools help you automate resource deployment, maintain consistency, and version control your infrastructure configurations.

In summary, AWS account setup and configuration involve a series of important steps and considerations to ensure that your account is secure, well-organized, and aligned with your business goals.

From account type selection and billing configuration to security, networking, storage, and automation, properly configuring your AWS account is essential for a successful and efficient cloud journey.

Tooling and SDK installation is a crucial step in the process of setting up your development environment for working with cloud platforms like Amazon Web Services (AWS).

The choice of tools and software development kits (SDKs) you install depends on the cloud provider you're working with and your specific development needs.

For AWS development, the AWS Command Line Interface (CLI) is an essential tool that provides a command-line interface for interacting with AWS services and resources.

Installing the AWS CLI is typically straightforward, as it's available for various operating systems, including Windows, macOS, and Linux.

Once installed, you can configure the AWS CLI with your AWS credentials, allowing you to execute commands to manage your AWS resources securely.

In addition to the AWS CLI, you may need to install SDKs for your preferred programming languages.

AWS provides SDKs for languages such as Python, Java, JavaScript, Ruby, and more, making it convenient to develop applications using your language of choice.

These SDKs allow you to interact with AWS services programmatically, enabling you to integrate AWS functionality into your applications seamlessly.

Depending on your programming language, installation may involve using package managers like pip for Python, npm for JavaScript, or Maven for Java.

AWS also offers the AWS Toolkit for popular integrated development environments (IDEs) such as Visual Studio Code, IntelliJ IDEA, and PyCharm.

The AWS Toolkit provides extensions and tools that enhance your development experience by offering features like code completion, resource management, and debugging support.

In addition to the AWS CLI and SDKs, you may need to install other development tools and utilities that are specific to your project requirements.

For example, if you're developing web applications or microservices, you might need web server software like Apache or Nginx.

If you're working with databases, you may need to install database management systems like MySQL, PostgreSQL, or NoSQL databases like MongoDB.

Docker is another tool commonly used in cloud development that allows you to containerize your applications and dependencies, ensuring consistent deployment across environments.

To install Docker, you can follow the installation instructions provided for your operating system on the Docker website.

Container orchestration tools like Kubernetes are also essential for managing containerized applications at scale.

Kubernetes can be installed using various methods, including popular distributions like Minikube for local development and managed Kubernetes services offered by cloud providers.

To streamline development workflows, it's advisable to set up a version control system (VCS) like Git.

Git allows you to track changes to your codebase, collaborate with team members, and manage different versions of your application.

Installing Git is relatively straightforward, and you can find installation instructions for various operating systems on the Git website.

Once Git is installed, you can configure it with your name and email address, and you're ready to start using version control for your projects.

Text editors or integrated development environments (IDEs) are essential for writing, editing, and managing your code.

The choice of text editor or IDE depends on your personal preference and the programming languages you work with.

Some popular text editors include Visual Studio Code, Sublime Text, and Atom, while IDEs like IntelliJ IDEA, Eclipse, and PyCharm are widely used for specific programming languages.

Installing these tools is usually straightforward, and they often provide extensions or plugins that enhance their functionality for cloud development.

To facilitate collaborative development, consider setting up a code repository on a platform like GitHub, GitLab, or Bitbucket.

These platforms offer hosting for your Git repositories, issue tracking, and collaboration features like pull requests and code reviews.

You can create a new repository on these platforms and clone it to your local development environment using Git.

Cloud-specific tools and utilities may also be required depending on the cloud provider you're working with.

For example, if you're developing for AWS, you can install the AWS SAM CLI (Serverless Application Model Command Line Interface) to build and deploy serverless applications using AWS Lambda and API Gateway.

For Azure development, the Azure CLI provides a similar command-line interface for managing Azure resources, and the Azure Functions Core Tools enable you to develop and test Azure Functions locally.

Google Cloud Platform (GCP) offers the Google Cloud SDK, which includes tools for interacting with GCP services, and the Google Cloud Functions Framework for building serverless functions.

In addition to cloud-specific tools, consider installing development plugins or extensions that are relevant to your project.

For example, if you're building web applications, you might need browser developer tools for debugging and testing.

Browser extensions like Postman or REST Client can help you interact with RESTful APIs and test HTTP requests and responses.

Continuous integration and continuous deployment (CI/CD) tools are essential for automating the build, test, and deployment processes.

Popular CI/CD platforms include Jenkins, Travis CI, CircleCI, and GitHub Actions.

You can install and configure these tools to automate tasks such as running tests, building Docker containers, and deploying your applications to the cloud.

It's essential to set up and configure your development environment consistently across your team to ensure that everyone can work efficiently and collaborate effectively.

Consider using Infrastructure as code (IaC) tools like AWS CloudFormation, Terraform, or Azure Resource Manager to define and provision the infrastructure for your development environments.

IaC allows you to create reproducible and version-controlled infrastructure configurations, ensuring that development, testing, and production environments are consistent.

To manage your development environment dependencies, consider using package managers like npm for JavaScript, pip for Python, or Maven for Java.

Package managers simplify the installation and management of libraries, frameworks, and dependencies required for your projects.

In addition to installing tools and SDKs, you should regularly update them to benefit from the latest features, security updates, and bug fixes.

Most tools and SDKs provide instructions for updating to newer versions, ensuring that your development environment remains up to date.

To facilitate collaboration and knowledge sharing within your team, document the setup and configuration steps for your development environment.

Create documentation that outlines the installation procedures, required tools, configuration settings, and any best practices specific to your projects.

This documentation will be valuable for onboarding new team members and troubleshooting issues that may arise during development.

In summary, tooling and SDK installation is a fundamental aspect of setting up your development environment for cloud development.

Choosing the right tools, SDKs, and utilities, configuring them correctly, and documenting the setup process are essential steps to ensure a smooth and productive development experience.

By investing time in properly configuring your development environment, you'll be well-equipped to build, test, and deploy cloud applications efficiently and effectively.

Chapter 3: AWS Cloud Resources and Services Overview

An overview of AWS services is essential for understanding the breadth and depth of the Amazon Web Services cloud platform.

AWS offers a vast array of services designed to meet the diverse needs of businesses and developers, enabling them to build, deploy, and manage applications and infrastructure at scale.

At the core of AWS is its compute services, which provide the foundation for running applications and workloads.

Amazon Elastic Compute Cloud (EC2) is a widely used service that offers virtual servers, known as instances, with various configurations to suit different use cases.

EC2 instances can be customized in terms of CPU, memory, storage, and networking, allowing users to choose the best fit for their applications.

AWS Lambda, on the other hand, is a serverless computing service that allows developers to run code in response to events without the need to manage servers.

Lambda functions can be triggered by events such as changes in data stored in Amazon S3, updates to a database, or HTTP requests.

For containerized applications, AWS offers Amazon Elastic Container Service (ECS) and Amazon Elastic Kubernetes Service (EKS) to orchestrate and manage container deployments.

These services simplify container management, scaling, and load balancing, making it easier to run microservices-based applications.

In addition to compute services, AWS provides a wide range of storage options to meet different data storage needs.

Amazon Simple Storage Service (S3) is a highly scalable and durable object storage service that can store and retrieve data of any size.

S3 is often used for data backup, data lakes, website hosting, and content distribution.

Amazon Elastic Block Store (EBS) offers block-level storage for EC2 instances, providing persistent and reliable storage volumes that can be attached and detached from instances as needed.

For file storage, AWS offers Amazon Elastic File System (EFS), a managed network file system that can be shared across multiple EC2 instances.

AWS also provides specialized storage solutions like Amazon Glacier for long-term archival storage and AWS Storage Gateway for hybrid cloud storage integration.

Databases are a critical component of many applications, and AWS offers a variety of database services to meet different requirements.

Amazon Relational Database Service (RDS) provides managed database instances for popular relational database engines like MySQL, PostgreSQL, Oracle, and Microsoft SQL Server.

RDS simplifies database administration tasks such as patching, backups, and high availability.

Amazon DynamoDB is a managed NoSQL database service designed for high-performance and scalability, making it ideal for applications with variable and unpredictable workloads.

AWS also offers Amazon Redshift, a fully managed data warehousing service for analytics and reporting, and Amazon Aurora, a high-performance and MySQL-compatible relational database.

AWS provides a comprehensive set of networking services to build and manage network infrastructure in the cloud.

Amazon Virtual Private Cloud (VPC) allows users to create isolated network environments with control over IP addressing, routing, and security settings.

VPC enables the creation of private and public subnets, network access control lists (NACLs), and security groups to control traffic flow and access to resources.

For global content delivery and low-latency access to applications, AWS offers Amazon CloudFront, a content delivery network (CDN) service that caches and distributes content from edge locations around the world.

AWS Direct Connect provides dedicated network connections between on-premises data centers and AWS regions, ensuring reliable and low-latency connectivity.

For DNS management, Amazon Route 53 is a scalable and highly available domain name system (DNS) web service that enables domain registration and routing traffic to AWS resources.

Security is a top priority for AWS, and the platform offers a robust set of security services and features to protect data and resources.

AWS Identity and Access Management (IAM) allows users to control access to AWS resources by defining roles, policies, and permissions for users and services.

IAM supports multi-factor authentication (MFA) and integrates with AWS Single Sign-On (SSO) for centralized identity management.

Amazon Cognito is an identity and user management service that simplifies user authentication and authorization for applications, including social sign-in and user pool management.

AWS Key Management Service (KMS) provides encryption and key management for data at rest and in transit, ensuring data security and compliance.

For threat detection and security monitoring, AWS offers Amazon GuardDuty, a managed threat detection service that analyzes logs and network traffic for suspicious activity.

AWS Web Application Firewall (WAF) helps protect web applications from common web exploits and attacks by filtering and inspecting incoming traffic.

Additionally, AWS provides compliance certifications, security best practices, and tools like AWS Config and AWS Trusted Advisor to help users maintain a secure environment.

AWS offers a range of developer tools and services to streamline application development and deployment.

AWS CodeBuild provides fully managed build environments for compiling and testing code, while AWS CodeDeploy automates application deployments to instances or containerized environments.

AWS CodePipeline is a continuous integration and continuous delivery (CI/CD) service that orchestrates and automates the release process.

For code version control and collaboration, AWS supports integration with Git repositories, and it offers services like AWS CodeCommit for managed Git repositories.

To enable serverless application development, AWS Lambda allows developers to run code in response to events without the need to manage servers.

AWS also offers a wide range of analytics and machine learning services to gain insights from data and build intelligent applications.

Amazon SageMaker is a fully managed machine learning service that simplifies the process of building, training, and deploying machine learning models at scale.

AWS Glue is a fully managed extract, transform, and load (ETL) service that automates data preparation and integration for analytics.

Amazon QuickSight is a business intelligence service that allows users to create interactive dashboards and perform data visualization.

For big data processing and analytics, AWS provides Amazon EMR (Elastic MapReduce), a managed big data platform that simplifies the deployment of Apache Hadoop and Apache Spark clusters.

AWS offers a wide range of specialized services for internet of things (IoT) applications, including AWS IoT Core for connecting and managing IoT devices, AWS IoT Greengrass for edge computing, and AWS IoT Analytics for data analysis.

For real-time data streaming and processing, Amazon Kinesis provides a set of services for ingesting, storing, and analyzing streaming data.

AWS offers several tools and services for application monitoring, management, and automation.

Amazon CloudWatch is a monitoring service that collects and tracks metrics, logs, and events for AWS resources, allowing users to gain visibility into the performance and health of their applications and infrastructure.

AWS CloudTrail captures and logs API activity, providing an audit trail for compliance and security analysis.

AWS Systems Manager offers a unified interface for managing resources, automating tasks, and configuring instances at scale.

AWS Step Functions allows users to coordinate distributed applications and microservices using visual workflows.

To simplify the deployment of infrastructure and applications, AWS provides AWS CloudFormation, an infrastructure as code (IaC) service that allows users to define and provision resources using templates.

AWS Elastic Beanstalk is a platform as a service (PaaS) that simplifies application deployment and management, allowing users to focus on code development.

AWS OpsWorks provides configuration management and automation for applications and infrastructure using Chef and Puppet.

AWS provides a range of migration and transfer services to help organizations move their existing workloads to the cloud.

AWS Database Migration Service (DMS) enables users to migrate databases to AWS with minimal downtime and data loss.

AWS Server Migration Service (SMS) simplifies the migration of on-premises virtual machines to AWS.

AWS Snowball is a physical data transport service that allows users to transfer large amounts of data to and from AWS using secure appliances.

For hybrid cloud deployments, AWS offers AWS Outposts, which allows users to run AWS infrastructure on-premises.

Additionally, AWS provides solutions for backup and disaster recovery, including AWS Backup and AWS Disaster Recovery.

AWS offers a wide range of application integration services to connect and extend applications across different environments and platforms.

Amazon Simple Queue Service (SQS) and Amazon Simple Notification Service (SNS) are messaging services that enable reliable communication between distributed applications.

AWS Step Functions provides workflow orchestration to coordinate the execution of microservices and serverless functions.

For event-driven architectures, AWS EventBridge allows users to build event-driven applications using events from AWS services, integrated software as a service (SaaS) applications, and custom sources.

AWS App Runner is a fully managed service that simplifies containerized application deployment and scaling, making it easier to build and run web applications and APIs.

AWS offers a variety of artificial intelligence (AI) and machine learning (ML) services to build intelligent applications and automate processes.

Amazon SageMaker is a fully managed machine learning service that provides tools and infrastructure for building, training, and deploying ML models.

AWS offers pre-trained AI models through Amazon Rekognition for image and video analysis, Amazon Polly for text-to-speech conversion, and Amazon Comprehend for natural language processing.

Amazon Lex enables developers to build conversational interfaces using voice and text, while Amazon Translate provides language translation capabilities.

AWS also offers specialized services for robotics, autonomous vehicles, and deep learning, such as AWS RoboMaker and AWS Deep Learning AMIs.

In the realm of IoT, AWS provides services like AWS IoT Core for device connectivity, AWS IoT Greengrass for edge computing, and AWS IoT Analytics for data analysis.

To summarize, AWS offers a comprehensive and diverse set of services that cater to a wide range of cloud computing needs.

From computing, storage, and databases to networking, security, and developer tools, AWS provides the building blocks and tools necessary to design, deploy, and manage modern applications in the cloud.

With its global reach, reliability, and innovation, AWS has become a leading choice for organizations and developers looking to harness the power of the cloud for their projects and businesses.

Understanding AWS resource types is essential for effectively using and managing the diverse set of services and infrastructure components that Amazon Web Services (AWS) offers.

AWS resources can be categorized into various types, each serving specific purposes and functions within the AWS ecosystem.

One of the most fundamental resource types in AWS is compute resources, which provide the processing power and capacity to run applications and workloads.

Amazon Elastic Compute Cloud (EC2) instances are virtual machines (VMs) that can be categorized into various instance types, each with different combinations of CPU, memory, storage, and network performance characteristics.

EC2 instances can be used for a wide range of applications, from hosting web servers and databases to running machine learning workloads.

Another important compute resource is AWS Lambda, which allows you to run code in response to events without the need to manage servers.

Lambda functions are ideal for event-driven and serverless architectures and can be triggered by events such as changes in Amazon S3 buckets, updates to DynamoDB tables, or HTTP requests.

Elastic Load Balancing (ELB) is another resource type that helps distribute incoming traffic across multiple EC2 instances or containers, ensuring high availability and fault tolerance for applications.

Amazon Elastic Container Service (ECS) and Amazon Elastic Kubernetes Service (EKS) are services that provide orchestration and management of containers, allowing you to deploy and scale containerized applications easily.

Storage resources are critical for data persistence and management, and AWS offers a variety of storage resource types to meet different needs.

Amazon Simple Storage Service (S3) is an object storage service that provides scalable and durable storage for objects, making it suitable for data backup, data lakes, and static website hosting.

Amazon Elastic Block Store (EBS) offers block-level storage volumes that can be attached to EC2 instances, providing persistent storage for databases and applications.

Amazon Elastic File System (EFS) provides scalable and shared file storage that can be used by multiple EC2 instances, making it suitable for network-attached storage (NAS) use cases.

In the database category, Amazon Relational Database Service (RDS) offers managed database instances for popular relational database engines like MySQL, PostgreSQL, Oracle, and Microsoft SQL Server.

Amazon DynamoDB is a managed NoSQL database service designed for high-performance and scalability, while Amazon Redshift is a fully managed data warehousing service for analytics.

AWS provides networking resources that help you connect, isolate, and optimize the flow of traffic within your AWS environment.

Amazon Virtual Private Cloud (VPC) is a networking service that allows you to create isolated network environments with control over IP addressing, routing, and security settings.

VPC enables you to define private and public subnets, network access control lists (NACLs), and security groups to control traffic and access to resources.

Amazon Route 53 is a scalable and highly available domain name system (DNS) web service that enables domain registration and routing traffic to AWS resources.

AWS Direct Connect provides dedicated network connections between on-premises data centers and AWS regions, ensuring reliable and low-latency connectivity.

For global content delivery and low-latency access to applications, Amazon CloudFront is a content delivery network (CDN) service that caches and distributes content from edge locations around the world.

Security is a top priority in AWS, and the platform offers a range of security resource types and features to protect data and resources.

AWS Identity and Access Management (IAM) is a critical security resource that allows you to control access to AWS resources by defining roles, policies, and permissions for users and services.

IAM supports multi-factor authentication (MFA) and integrates with AWS Single Sign-On (SSO) for centralized identity management.

Amazon Cognito is another security resource that simplifies user authentication and authorization for applications, including social sign-in and user pool management.

AWS Key Management Service (KMS) provides encryption and key management for data at rest and in transit, ensuring data security and compliance.

For threat detection and security monitoring, AWS offers Amazon GuardDuty, a managed threat detection service that analyzes logs and network traffic for suspicious activity.

AWS Web Application Firewall (WAF) helps protect web applications from common web exploits and attacks by filtering and inspecting incoming traffic.

Additionally, AWS provides compliance certifications, security best practices, and tools like AWS Config and AWS Trusted Advisor to help users maintain a secure environment.

Developer tools and services are essential for building and managing applications in AWS.

AWS CodeBuild provides fully managed build environments for compiling and testing code, while AWS CodeDeploy automates application deployments to instances or containerized environments.

AWS CodePipeline is a continuous integration and continuous delivery (CI/CD) service that orchestrates and automates the release process.

For code version control and collaboration, AWS supports integration with Git repositories and provides services like AWS CodeCommit for managed Git repositories.

Infrastructure as code (IaC) tools such as AWS CloudFormation and AWS CDK allow users to define and provision infrastructure resources using code, enabling automation and version control of infrastructure configurations.

To simplify serverless application development, AWS Lambda allows developers to run code in response to events without managing servers, making it a valuable resource for event-driven and serverless architectures.

AWS also offers a wide range of analytics and machine learning (ML) resources to gain insights from data and build intelligent applications.

Amazon SageMaker is a fully managed machine learning service that simplifies the process of building, training, and deploying ML models at scale.

AWS Glue is a fully managed extract, transform, and load (ETL) service that automates data preparation and integration for analytics.

Amazon QuickSight is a business intelligence service that enables users to create interactive dashboards and perform data visualization.

For big data processing and analytics, AWS provides Amazon EMR (Elastic MapReduce), a managed big data platform that simplifies the deployment of Apache Hadoop and Apache Spark clusters.

AWS offers a wide range of specialized services for internet of things (IoT) applications, including AWS IoT Core for connecting and managing IoT devices, AWS IoT Greengrass for edge computing, and AWS IoT Analytics for data analysis.

Amazon Kinesis provides services for real-time data streaming and processing, making it suitable for applications that require fast data ingestion and analysis.

Application integration resources help you connect and extend applications across different environments and platforms.

Amazon Simple Queue Service (SQS) and Amazon Simple Notification Service (SNS) are messaging services that enable reliable communication between distributed applications.

AWS Step Functions provides workflow orchestration to coordinate the execution of microservices and serverless functions.

For event-driven architectures, AWS EventBridge allows users to build event-driven applications using events from AWS services, integrated software as a service (SaaS) applications, and custom sources.

AWS App Runner is a fully managed service that simplifies containerized application deployment and scaling, making it easier to build and run web applications and APIs.

AWS offers a variety of artificial intelligence (AI) and machine learning (ML) resources to build intelligent applications and automate processes.

Amazon SageMaker is a fully managed machine learning service that provides tools and infrastructure for building, training, and deploying ML models.

AWS offers pre-trained AI models through services like Amazon Rekognition for image and video analysis, Amazon Polly for text-to-speech conversion, and Amazon Comprehend for natural language processing.

Amazon Lex enables developers to build conversational interfaces using voice and text, while Amazon Translate provides language translation capabilities.

AWS also offers specialized services for robotics, autonomous vehicles, and deep learning, such as AWS RoboMaker and AWS Deep Learning AMIs.

In the realm of IoT, AWS provides services like AWS IoT Core for device connectivity, AWS IoT Greengrass for edge computing, and AWS IoT Analytics for data analysis.

These resource types collectively form the building blocks for designing, deploying, and managing applications and infrastructure in the AWS cloud.

By understanding the capabilities and use cases of these resource types, users can make informed decisions about which AWS services and resources to leverage for their specific needs and requirements.

Chapter 4: Building AWS Infrastructure with IaC

Getting started with AWS Infrastructure as Code (IaC) is an essential step for organizations and developers looking to automate and manage their AWS resources efficiently.

IaC is a practice that allows you to define and provision infrastructure resources using code, making it easier to scale and manage your AWS environment.

AWS provides several tools and services that facilitate IaC, such as AWS CloudFormation, AWS CDK, and Terraform, each offering different approaches to defining and managing infrastructure.

AWS CloudFormation is a native IaC service that enables you to create and provision AWS resources using templates written in JSON or YAML.

These templates describe the desired state of your infrastructure, including EC2 instances, S3 buckets, VPCs, and more, and CloudFormation takes care of creating and managing those resources.

AWS CDK, or Cloud Development Kit, is a higher-level abstraction that allows developers to define infrastructure using familiar programming languages like TypeScript, Python, and Java.

With CDK, you can create reusable constructs and define complex infrastructure as code using object-oriented programming principles.

Terraform, on the other hand, is an open-source IaC tool that supports multiple cloud providers, including AWS.

It uses HashiCorp Configuration Language (HCL) to define infrastructure as code and offers a wide range of providers and modules to manage AWS resources.

To get started with AWS IaC, you'll first need to choose the tool or service that best aligns with your organization's needs and your team's familiarity with programming languages and infrastructure provisioning concepts.

Once you've made your choice, you can begin by setting up your development environment.

This involves installing the necessary tools, configuring your AWS credentials, and creating a project directory to organize your IaC code.

For AWS CloudFormation, you'll need to have the AWS Command Line Interface (CLI) installed, as it is often used in conjunction with CloudFormation to create and manage stacks.

AWS CDK requires the installation of the CDK CLI and the language-specific CDK libraries for your chosen programming language.

Terraform can be installed by downloading the binary for your platform and adding it to your system's PATH.

After setting up your development environment, you can start writing your first IaC code.

For AWS CloudFormation, this means creating a CloudFormation template in JSON or YAML format.

You'll define your AWS resources, their properties, and any dependencies between them within the template.

AWS CDK allows you to define your infrastructure using programming constructs in your chosen language.

You'll create a CDK app, define stacks, and use CDK constructs to define AWS resources and their relationships.

In Terraform, you'll create a Terraform configuration file with a ".tf" extension.

This file will contain resource blocks that define the AWS resources you want to create, their attributes, and any dependencies.

When writing IaC code, it's crucial to follow best practices and maintain a clear and organized structure.

Use meaningful names for your resources and avoid hardcoding sensitive information like credentials or secret keys.

Leverage parameterization and variables to make your code more reusable and configurable.

Modularize your IaC code by creating separate templates or modules for different components of your infrastructure, promoting reusability and maintainability.

Additionally, make use of version control systems like Git to track changes to your IaC code, enabling collaboration and providing a history of modifications.

Once you've written your IaC code, you can use the respective tool or service to deploy your infrastructure.

With AWS CloudFormation, you'll create a CloudFormation stack from your template, either using the AWS Management Console, AWS CLI, or SDKs.

The stack creation process will create the specified AWS resources according to your template.

AWS CDK requires you to synthesize your code into CloudFormation templates before deploying them using the AWS CLI or CDK CLI.

Terraform, on the other hand, uses the "terraform init" command to initialize your working directory and the "terraform apply" command to create or update resources as defined in your configuration.

As part of your IaC workflow, it's essential to test and validate your infrastructure code to catch any errors or misconfigurations before deployment.

AWS provides tools like AWS CloudFormation StackSets for deploying stacks across multiple AWS accounts and regions.

AWS CDK provides built-in testing features to validate your constructs, and Terraform offers a "terraform validate" command to check for configuration errors.

Once your infrastructure is deployed, you can monitor and manage it using AWS services like CloudWatch for logging and monitoring, CloudTrail for auditing, and AWS Config for tracking resource changes.

By adopting IaC practices, you gain several benefits, including repeatability, consistency, and version control of your infrastructure.

You can easily reproduce your environment in different AWS regions or accounts, ensuring consistency across your deployments.

IaC also enables you to roll back to previous infrastructure states in case of issues or changes.

Additionally, IaC encourages collaboration among development and operations teams, as infrastructure code becomes part of the application codebase.

As you become more proficient with AWS IaC, you can explore advanced topics like managing secrets and sensitive data, implementing CI/CD pipelines for automated deployments, and leveraging IaC tools and frameworks specific to AWS, such as AWS Serverless Application Model (SAM) for serverless applications.

In summary, getting started with AWS Infrastructure as Code is a valuable step towards achieving more efficient, reliable, and scalable infrastructure management in the AWS cloud.

Choose the IaC tool or service that suits your needs, set up your development environment, write clear and organized code, and deploy your infrastructure with confidence.

Embrace the benefits of IaC to enhance the agility and automation of your AWS deployments and streamline your development and operations workflows.

Writing your first AWS Infrastructure as Code (IaC) code is an exciting and pivotal moment in your journey to automate and manage your AWS resources efficiently.

It marks the beginning of your ability to define and provision infrastructure using code, enabling you to scale and manage your AWS environment with ease.

Before you start writing your IaC code, you should choose the tool or service that aligns best with your organization's requirements and your team's expertise.

AWS provides several options, including AWS CloudFormation, AWS CDK (Cloud Development Kit), and Terraform, each with its approach to defining and managing infrastructure.

AWS CloudFormation is a native IaC service that empowers you to create and provision AWS resources using templates written in JSON or YAML.

These templates describe the desired state of your infrastructure, including EC2 instances, S3 buckets, VPCs, and more, while CloudFormation handles the resource creation and management.

AWS CDK, on the other hand, offers a higher-level abstraction, allowing developers to define infrastructure using familiar programming languages such as TypeScript, Python, and Java.

CDK enables you to create reusable constructs and define complex infrastructure as code using object-oriented programming principles.

Terraform is an open-source IaC tool that supports multiple cloud providers, including AWS.

It uses HashiCorp Configuration Language (HCL) to define infrastructure as code and offers a wide range of providers and modules for managing AWS resources.

Once you've chosen your preferred IaC tool or service, it's time to set up your development environment.

This involves installing the necessary tools, configuring your AWS credentials, and creating a dedicated project directory to organize your IaC code.

For AWS CloudFormation, you'll need to have the AWS Command Line Interface (CLI) installed, as it is commonly used in conjunction with CloudFormation to create and manage stacks.

AWS CDK requires the installation of the CDK CLI and the language-specific CDK libraries for your chosen programming language.

Terraform can be installed by downloading the binary for your platform and adding it to your system's PATH.

After setting up your development environment, you can embark on the journey of writing your first IaC code.

For AWS CloudFormation, this means creating a CloudFormation template in either JSON or YAML format.

Within this template, you will define your AWS resources, their properties, and any dependencies between them.

AWS CDK takes a different approach. You'll create a CDK app and define stacks using programming constructs in your chosen language.

You'll use CDK constructs to define AWS resources and their relationships in a more programmatic manner.

In Terraform, you'll create a Terraform configuration file with a ".tf" extension.

This file will contain resource blocks that define the AWS resources you want to create, their attributes, and any dependencies.

While writing your IaC code, it's essential to adhere to best practices and maintain a clear and organized structure.

Use meaningful names for your resources, avoid hardcoding sensitive information like credentials or secret keys, and employ parameterization and variables to make your code more reusable and configurable.

To enhance code reusability and maintainability, modularize your IaC code by creating separate templates or modules for different components of your infrastructure.

This modularity promotes efficient collaboration among team members and simplifies the process of building and maintaining your infrastructure.

Furthermore, make use of version control systems like Git to track changes to your IaC code, ensuring collaboration, providing a history of modifications, and allowing you to roll back to previous states if needed.

Once you have written your IaC code and adhered to best practices, you can proceed to deploy your infrastructure.

With AWS CloudFormation, this involves creating a CloudFormation stack from your template using various deployment methods, including the AWS Management Console, AWS CLI, or SDKs.

During the stack creation process, CloudFormation will create the specified AWS resources according to the definitions in your template.

AWS CDK requires you to synthesize your code into CloudFormation templates before deploying them using the AWS CLI or CDK CLI.

Terraform, on the other hand, uses commands like "terraform init" to initialize your working directory and "terraform apply" to create or update resources according to your configuration.

As an essential part of your IaC workflow, you should test and validate your infrastructure code before deployment to identify and rectify errors or misconfigurations.

AWS offers tools like AWS CloudFormation StackSets to deploy stacks across multiple AWS accounts and regions, simplifying the process of managing and scaling infrastructure.

AWS CDK provides built-in testing features to validate your constructs, and Terraform offers a "terraform validate" command to check for configuration errors.

Upon successful deployment of your infrastructure, you can begin monitoring and managing it using AWS services such as Amazon CloudWatch for logging and monitoring, AWS CloudTrail for auditing, and AWS Config for tracking resource changes.

Embracing Infrastructure as Code (IaC) offers numerous benefits, including repeatability, consistency, and version control of your infrastructure.

It allows you to easily reproduce your environment in different AWS regions or accounts, ensuring consistency across your deployments.

IaC also enables you to roll back to previous infrastructure states in case of issues or changes.

Additionally, IaC encourages collaboration among development and operations teams, as infrastructure code becomes an integral part of the application codebase.

As you gain more experience with AWS IaC, you can explore advanced topics such as managing secrets and sensitive data, implementing continuous integration and continuous deployment (CI/CD) pipelines for automated deployments, and leveraging AWS-specific IaC tools and frameworks like AWS Serverless Application Model (SAM) for serverless applications.

In summary, writing your first AWS Infrastructure as Code (IaC) code is a significant step toward achieving more efficient, reliable, and scalable infrastructure management in the AWS cloud.

By choosing the right IaC tool or service, setting up your development environment, writing organized and best-practice-compliant code, and deploying your infrastructure, you can harness the power of automation and streamline your development and operations workflows.

Chapter 5: Advanced IaC Techniques for AWS

Leveraging AWS CloudFormation is a powerful approach to defining and managing infrastructure as code (IaC) in the Amazon Web Services (AWS) ecosystem.

CloudFormation allows you to create, update, and delete AWS resources in a declarative manner, ensuring your infrastructure remains consistent and reproducible.

With CloudFormation, you can describe your desired AWS resource configuration in a JSON or YAML template, specifying the resource types, properties, and relationships between resources.

Templates are at the heart of CloudFormation, serving as the blueprint for your infrastructure.

They enable you to codify your infrastructure requirements, making it easier to automate deployments and manage infrastructure at scale.

CloudFormation supports a wide range of AWS resource types, including compute resources like EC2 instances, networking resources like VPCs and subnets, and application resources like Lambda functions and RDS databases.

By defining your infrastructure in templates, you gain several benefits, including version control, rollback capabilities, and the ability to reproduce your environment in different AWS regions or accounts.

Templates also encourage collaboration among team members, as infrastructure code becomes an integral part of the application's codebase.

To get started with AWS CloudFormation, you need to understand the structure and components of CloudFormation templates.

Templates consist of sections, including the format version, description, parameters, mappings, resources, outputs, and optional conditions.

Parameters allow you to customize your template by accepting input values at deployment time.

Mappings provide a way to create reusable mappings between keys and corresponding values, making your templates more flexible.

Resources are the core building blocks of your infrastructure, representing AWS resources like EC2 instances, RDS databases, and S3 buckets.

Outputs allow you to expose information about your resources, such as their ARNs or DNS names, for use in other parts of your infrastructure or applications.

Conditions enable you to create conditional logic within your templates, allowing for resource creation or exclusion based on specific criteria.

Once you've defined your template, you can deploy it using various methods, including the AWS Management Console, AWS CLI, AWS SDKs, or AWS CloudFormation API.

During deployment, CloudFormation creates a stack, which is a set of AWS resources defined by your template.

Stacks can be created, updated, or deleted as a whole, ensuring that your infrastructure remains consistent and manageable.

CloudFormation provides mechanisms to handle dependencies and orchestrate the creation of resources, ensuring that resources are created in the correct order and that they can communicate with one another.

For example, if you have an EC2 instance that depends on a security group, CloudFormation will create the security group first and then the EC2 instance.

To facilitate resource management, CloudFormation offers features like stack updates and rollback capabilities.

When you update a stack, CloudFormation determines what changes are necessary to achieve the desired state defined in your template.

It then performs the necessary updates to your resources while minimizing disruptions to your infrastructure.

If a stack update fails, CloudFormation can automatically roll back to the previous stack state, ensuring that your infrastructure remains in a consistent state.

CloudFormation also supports drift detection, allowing you to identify and compare differences between your deployed stack's resources and their expected template definitions.

This feature helps you identify any manual changes made to your resources outside of CloudFormation.

To further enhance your CloudFormation templates, you can use intrinsic functions and built-in functions.

Intrinsic functions, such as Fn::Ref and Fn::GetAtt, allow you to reference resource attributes and parameters within your templates.

Built-in functions, like Fn::Sub and Fn::ImportValue, enable you to perform string manipulation and reference exported values from other stacks.

By using these functions, you can create dynamic and parameterized templates that adapt to various deployment scenarios.

CloudFormation also supports resource metadata, allowing you to add custom metadata to your resources, which can be useful for documentation or automation purposes.

To manage resource properties, you can use property types specific to each resource type.

Property types define the valid properties and values that can be associated with a resource, ensuring that your resource configurations are accurate and consistent.

To simplify the process of defining resources, CloudFormation provides resource specification files (also known as resource types reference) that detail the properties, attributes, and supported resource types for each AWS service.

These files can be valuable references when authoring your templates.

AWS CloudFormation Designer is a graphical tool that simplifies template authoring by providing a visual representation of your infrastructure.

It allows you to design templates by dragging and dropping resource icons onto a canvas, making it easier to understand and visualize your infrastructure.

CloudFormation Designer also generates the corresponding JSON or YAML template code, helping you get started with your templates.

As your infrastructure grows and evolves, you may need to manage multiple CloudFormation stacks that interoperate with one another.

To address this complexity, CloudFormation offers stack sets, a feature that enables you to deploy stacks across multiple AWS accounts and regions in a coordinated and automated fashion.

Stack sets can help you maintain consistency and enforce best practices across your organization's AWS environments.

To improve the reliability and performance of your CloudFormation deployments, you can use AWS CloudFormation Guard, an open-source tool that allows you to define and enforce policy rules on your templates.

These rules can help you ensure that your templates adhere to security, compliance, and naming conventions, reducing the risk of misconfigurations.

To manage CloudFormation stacks programmatically, you can use the AWS Cloud Development Kit (CDK), a higher-level abstraction for defining CloudFormation templates using familiar programming languages.

The CDK allows you to create reusable constructs and patterns for your infrastructure, making it easier to define complex architectures and share them across projects.

By leveraging the AWS CDK, you can take advantage of the flexibility and expressiveness of programming languages while benefiting from the automation and reliability of CloudFormation.

In summary, AWS CloudFormation is a robust and versatile tool for defining and managing infrastructure as code in AWS.

It enables you to create, update, and delete AWS resources in a declarative manner, ensuring your infrastructure remains consistent and reproducible.

With CloudFormation, you can codify your infrastructure requirements in templates, facilitating automation, version control, and collaboration among team members.

By understanding the structure and components of CloudFormation templates, utilizing intrinsic and built-in functions, and exploring advanced features like stack sets, CloudFormation Designer, and the AWS CDK, you can harness the full power of AWS CloudFormation to simplify and automate your infrastructure management.

Templating and modularization are essential concepts in AWS Infrastructure as Code (IaC) that enable you to create flexible, reusable, and maintainable infrastructure definitions.
Templates serve as the foundation of your IaC approach, allowing you to codify your infrastructure requirements in a structured and organized manner.
Templates define the desired state of your AWS resources, making it easier to automate deployments and manage infrastructure at scale.
Modularization, on the other hand, involves breaking down your IaC code into smaller, self-contained components or modules that can be easily reused across different projects and environments.
By combining templating and modularization, you can create IaC solutions that are not only more efficient but also adaptable to evolving infrastructure needs.
AWS CloudFormation, AWS CDK (Cloud Development Kit), and Terraform are popular tools and frameworks that support templating and modularization in AWS IaC.
CloudFormation templates, written in JSON or YAML, allow you to define the structure and properties of your AWS resources.
Templates are highly customizable, with support for parameters, mappings, conditions, and intrinsic functions.
Parameters enable you to accept input values at deployment time, making your templates adaptable to various scenarios without modification.
Mappings provide a way to create reusable mappings between keys and corresponding values, enhancing the flexibility of your templates.

Conditions allow you to introduce conditional logic within your templates, enabling resource creation or exclusion based on specific criteria.

Intrinsic functions, such as Fn::Ref and Fn::Sub, enable you to reference resource attributes and parameters within your templates, enhancing their dynamic capabilities.

AWS CDK takes a different approach to templating by allowing you to define infrastructure using programming constructs in languages like TypeScript, Python, and Java.

This higher-level abstraction makes it easier to express complex infrastructure concepts using familiar programming paradigms.

With CDK, you can create reusable constructs, which encapsulate the configuration of AWS resources and can be shared across projects.

Constructs enable you to define AWS resources and their relationships programmatically, providing a more expressive and dynamic way to model your infrastructure.

Terraform, an open-source IaC tool, uses HashiCorp Configuration Language (HCL) to define infrastructure as code.

In Terraform, you create templates using ".tf" configuration files that specify AWS resources, their attributes, and dependencies.

Terraform offers resource modules, which are pre-packaged templates for specific AWS resources or services.

Modules can be shared across projects and provide a level of reusability and abstraction similar to AWS CDK constructs.

To implement templating effectively, it's important to follow best practices.

Use meaningful names for your resources and parameters to make your templates more understandable and maintainable.

Leverage parameters and variables to make your templates flexible and adaptable to different environments.

Consider using conditionals and intrinsic functions to introduce dynamic behaviors and configurations into your templates.

Document your templates comprehensively to provide context and usage instructions for team members.

As your IaC solutions become more complex, modularization becomes crucial to maintain clarity and manageability.

Modularization involves dividing your IaC code into smaller, self-contained units, or modules, each responsible for specific aspects of your infrastructure.

Modules encapsulate AWS resources, their configurations, and any associated dependencies.

By creating modules, you can reuse common infrastructure patterns, promote consistency, and simplify the management of complex deployments.

AWS CloudFormation supports modularization through nested stacks and includes mechanisms for sharing templates and resources across stacks.

Nested stacks allow you to reference templates from within other templates, enabling you to break down complex infrastructure into manageable components.

Sharing templates and resources across stacks can help you standardize configurations and maintain consistency across multiple environments or projects.

AWS CDK natively supports modularization through constructs.

Constructs are reusable units of code that define AWS resources and their relationships.

You can package constructs into libraries or modules and share them across different CDK applications.

This approach enables you to create a library of commonly used infrastructure components that can be easily integrated into various projects.

Terraform offers module support as well, allowing you to create reusable templates for specific AWS resources or configurations.

Modules can be versioned and shared across different Terraform configurations, promoting code reuse and consistency.

To effectively modularize your IaC code, it's important to identify common patterns or components in your infrastructure and encapsulate them into separate modules.

Modules should have well-defined interfaces, making it clear how to use them and what inputs they require.

Documenting modules and providing examples of their usage can help team members understand their functionality and purpose.

When working with modularized IaC code, version control becomes even more critical.

Using a version control system like Git allows you to manage changes, track history, and collaborate effectively with team members on different modules and projects.

By combining templating and modularization, you can create powerful and flexible AWS IaC solutions that streamline infrastructure management.

Templating enables you to define your infrastructure in a structured and organized manner, while modularization promotes code reuse and maintainability.

Whether you choose AWS CloudFormation, AWS CDK, or Terraform, the principles of templating and modularization remain valuable in creating efficient and adaptable IaC solutions.

As your infrastructure evolves, these practices will help you maintain consistency, promote collaboration, and simplify the management of your AWS resources.

Chapter 6: AWS Security and Compliance in IaC

Implementing security best practices is paramount when managing infrastructure as code (IaC) in the cloud.

Security considerations should be integrated into every step of the IaC lifecycle to protect your AWS resources and data from potential threats.

One of the first security practices to implement is the principle of least privilege, which means granting only the minimum permissions necessary to perform a specific task.

In AWS, you can use Identity and Access Management (IAM) to create and manage user roles and policies, ensuring that users and services have only the permissions required for their respective functions.

IAM allows you to establish fine-grained access controls, minimizing the risk of unauthorized access to sensitive resources.

Another essential practice is to secure your AWS credentials and secrets.

Avoid hardcoding credentials or secrets directly into your IaC code, as this can expose them to potential attackers.

Instead, use AWS Secrets Manager or Parameter Store to securely store and manage sensitive data, and then reference these values in your templates or code.

Additionally, consider using AWS Identity and Access Management (IAM) roles and instance profiles for EC2 instances to avoid the need for explicit credential management.

Implementing encryption is crucial for protecting data at rest and in transit.

AWS offers services like AWS Key Management Service (KMS) for managing encryption keys and Amazon S3 to enable server-side encryption for your stored data.

When using Amazon RDS or EBS volumes, you can enable encryption to ensure that data is secure, even if physical storage media is compromised.

For securing data in transit, use encryption protocols like TLS/SSL when transferring data between AWS resources or communicating with external services.

It's essential to keep your software and infrastructure up to date with the latest security patches and updates.

Regularly patching your EC2 instances, using AWS Elastic Beanstalk's managed platform updates, or leveraging AWS Fargate for container deployments can help you stay protected against known vulnerabilities.

AWS also provides services like AWS Systems Manager for automating patch management and compliance checking.

Implementing network security is critical for protecting your AWS infrastructure.

Use Amazon Virtual Private Cloud (VPC) to isolate and segment your resources logically.

Define security groups and network access control lists (ACLs) to control inbound and outbound traffic to and from your instances.

Consider implementing AWS Web Application Firewall (WAF) and AWS Shield for protection against web application attacks and Distributed Denial of Service (DDoS) attacks, respectively.

To monitor and detect security incidents, leverage AWS CloudTrail for auditing and AWS Config for tracking resource configuration changes.

These services provide visibility into who accessed your resources and what changes were made.

Set up CloudWatch alarms to alert you to specific events or thresholds, helping you respond to security incidents in real time.

Implementing logging and monitoring is crucial for gaining insights into your AWS infrastructure's security.

Enable AWS CloudTrail to capture API calls and create logs that can be used for auditing and compliance purposes.

Use Amazon CloudWatch to collect and analyze logs from your resources, allowing you to identify suspicious activities or security breaches.

Implementing continuous security scanning and vulnerability assessments is essential to proactively identify and address security weaknesses in your infrastructure.

Leverage AWS Inspector to automatically assess the security of your EC2 instances and applications.

Additionally, use third-party security scanning tools or services to identify vulnerabilities in your IaC code and configurations.

Implementing secure DevOps practices is essential for integrating security into your development and deployment pipelines.

Adopting a DevSecOps approach means considering security throughout the entire development lifecycle.

Integrate security testing into your CI/CD pipelines to catch vulnerabilities early in the development process.

Use AWS CodePipeline, AWS CodeBuild, and AWS CodeDeploy to automate your application deployments securely.

Implement infrastructure as code (IaC) security scanning tools like AWS CloudFormation Guard or Terraform Static Analysis (TerraScan) to validate your IaC code for security best practices and compliance.

Additionally, enforce code reviews and security checks as part of your code review process to ensure that security concerns are addressed before deploying changes.

Implementing incident response and recovery procedures is crucial to minimizing the impact of security incidents.

Create an incident response plan that outlines roles and responsibilities, communication channels, and procedures for identifying, containing, and mitigating security breaches.

Regularly test your incident response plan through tabletop exercises or simulations to ensure your team is prepared to respond effectively.

Implement automated backups and disaster recovery plans to minimize downtime and data loss in case of a security incident.

AWS offers services like Amazon S3 versioning, Amazon RDS automated backups, and AWS Backup to help you protect your data and applications.

Implementing security automation is essential for maintaining a consistent and secure AWS environment.

Leverage AWS Config rules to automatically evaluate the compliance of your resources against predefined security policies.

Use AWS Lambda functions to automate security-related tasks, such as triggering alerts or remediation actions in response to security events.

Consider implementing Infrastructure as Code (IaC) security tools that can scan your templates for security vulnerabilities and compliance issues before deploying infrastructure changes.

AWS Config Rules can also help automate compliance checks and enforce security policies across your AWS resources.

Implementing identity and access management (IAM) best practices is essential to maintaining a secure AWS environment.

Regularly review and audit IAM roles, policies, and permissions to ensure that they align with your security requirements.

Leverage AWS IAM Access Analyzer to analyze resource policies for unintended access and vulnerabilities.

Use AWS Multi-Factor Authentication (MFA) to add an additional layer of security to your AWS accounts and ensure that only authorized users can access sensitive resources.

Finally, regularly review and rotate access keys and credentials to minimize the risk of unauthorized access.

In summary, implementing security best practices in AWS Infrastructure as Code (IaC) is crucial to safeguarding your resources, data, and applications in the cloud.

By following the principles of least privilege, securing credentials and secrets, implementing encryption, keeping your software and infrastructure up to date, and using network security controls, you can significantly reduce your security risks.

Monitoring and logging, continuous security scanning, and secure DevOps practices help you proactively identify and respond to security threats.

Incident response and recovery procedures, security automation, IAM best practices, and regular security audits round out a comprehensive security strategy for your AWS IaC deployments.

Remember that security is an ongoing process, and staying vigilant and proactive is essential to protecting your AWS environment effectively.

Compliance as code in AWS is a critical approach to ensuring that your infrastructure and applications meet regulatory requirements and security standards.

It involves codifying compliance rules and checks into your infrastructure as code (IaC) templates and workflows.

By doing so, you can automate compliance assessments, reduce manual efforts, and maintain a continuous and consistent state of compliance.

AWS provides a range of tools and services that enable you to implement compliance as code effectively.

One of the key foundations of compliance as code is the use of AWS Config, a service that provides configuration history, change tracking, and compliance checks for your AWS resources.

AWS Config allows you to define compliance rules using AWS Config Rules, which are essentially code-based policies that evaluate your AWS resources for compliance with specific security, operational, and regulatory requirements.

These rules can be predefined by AWS or custom-coded to match your organization's specific compliance needs.

When a rule is evaluated, AWS Config assesses the compliance state of your resources and provides detailed reports on any non-compliant configurations.

Using AWS Config Rules, you can automate checks for various compliance standards, including AWS Well-Architected Framework, CIS AWS Foundations Benchmark, and more.

Implementing compliance checks as code allows you to enforce policies consistently across your infrastructure and automatically remediate non-compliant resources.

For example, you can create a custom AWS Config Rule that checks whether all your Amazon S3 buckets are encrypted using server-side encryption.

If a bucket is found to be non-compliant, you can configure AWS Config to trigger an automated remediation action, such as enabling encryption on the bucket.

Another essential tool for compliance as code in AWS is AWS CloudFormation, which enables you to define and provision AWS resources and their configurations using code.

With CloudFormation, you can define your infrastructure as code, including the necessary security configurations, in a template.

This template becomes a version-controlled artifact, and you can use it to consistently deploy compliant infrastructure across your AWS accounts and regions.

By embedding compliance checks directly into your CloudFormation templates, you can ensure that your infrastructure is provisioned in a compliant state from the start.

For instance, you can define an Amazon RDS instance in your template and specify encryption options, ensuring that all RDS instances are encrypted by default.

Additionally, you can use AWS CloudFormation StackSets to deploy compliant stacks across multiple AWS accounts and regions, streamlining compliance management at scale.

AWS Organizations is another valuable resource for compliance as code, as it enables you to manage multiple AWS accounts within your organization.

By centralizing and managing AWS accounts using AWS Organizations, you can enforce compliance policies and service control policies (SCPs) across your entire organization.

SCPs allow you to set guardrails that restrict what actions can be performed within your accounts, helping you maintain a secure and compliant AWS environment.

You can use SCPs to limit access to specific AWS services, control resource creation, and enforce compliance standards across all member accounts.

AWS Identity and Access Management (IAM) is instrumental in enforcing compliance as code by controlling who can perform actions within your AWS accounts.

IAM policies can be defined and managed as code, specifying fine-grained permissions for users, groups, and roles.

You can create custom IAM policies that align with your organization's compliance requirements and attach them to users and resources accordingly.

For example, you can create an IAM policy that restricts access to certain AWS resources or actions, ensuring that only authorized users can perform compliance-sensitive operations.

AWS also provides a set of managed IAM policies that align with best practices and compliance standards, such as the AWS managed policy for Amazon S3 bucket encryption, which enforces encryption requirements.

To further automate compliance checks, you can use AWS Lambda functions to trigger actions based on AWS Config Rule evaluations.

For instance, when AWS Config detects non-compliance, a Lambda function can be automatically invoked to initiate remediation actions.

Lambda functions can be written as code and deployed using AWS SAM (Serverless Application Model) or the AWS Management Console.

This enables you to create custom automation scripts that align with your compliance as code requirements.

Additionally, you can use AWS Step Functions to orchestrate complex compliance workflows involving multiple AWS services and Lambda functions.

Step Functions allow you to build serverless workflows that automate compliance checks, remediation, and reporting processes.

By defining these workflows as code, you can ensure that compliance processes are consistently executed and auditable.

AWS Security Hub is a centralized security and compliance service that provides a comprehensive view of your security posture across AWS accounts.

Security Hub aggregates findings from AWS Config, AWS GuardDuty, and other AWS security services, allowing you to prioritize and respond to security and compliance issues effectively.

You can enable automated security standards checks in Security Hub, which align with common compliance frameworks like CIS AWS Foundations Benchmark and AWS Foundational Security Best Practices.

Security Hub findings can be used to trigger automated actions or integrate with third-party security tools for further analysis and response.

In summary, compliance as code in AWS is a powerful approach to ensuring that your infrastructure and applications adhere to regulatory requirements and security standards.

By codifying compliance checks, policies, and remediation actions, you can automate the assessment and enforcement of compliance across your AWS environment.

Key tools and services like AWS Config, AWS CloudFormation, AWS Organizations, IAM, Lambda, Step Functions, and Security Hub enable you to implement compliance as code effectively.

With this approach, you can maintain a secure and compliant AWS environment while streamlining operations and reducing manual effort.

Chapter 7: Infrastructure Testing and Validation

Testing your AWS Infrastructure as Code (IaC) code is a critical step in ensuring the reliability, security, and correctness of your infrastructure deployments.

IaC testing involves systematically evaluating your code to identify and address issues before deploying resources to your AWS environment.

One of the primary reasons to test your IaC code is to catch errors and misconfigurations early in the development process.

Testing helps you avoid costly and time-consuming issues that can arise when deploying infrastructure without validation.

Several types of tests can be performed on your AWS IaC code, including unit tests, integration tests, and end-to-end tests.

Unit tests focus on individual components or modules of your IaC code, verifying that they function correctly in isolation.

These tests are particularly useful for checking the behavior of specific resources or configurations.

For example, you can write unit tests to ensure that an Amazon S3 bucket is created with the correct permissions and settings.

Integration tests, on the other hand, evaluate how different components of your IaC code work together.

They examine how resources interact with each other and whether dependencies are properly configured.

Integration tests can uncover issues that may not be apparent when testing individual components.

For example, you can write an integration test to confirm that an Amazon RDS database can communicate with an Amazon EC2 instance as expected.

End-to-end tests validate the entire deployment process, from provisioning resources to verifying their functionality.

These tests mimic real-world scenarios and can help ensure that your IaC code not only deploys infrastructure correctly but also achieves the desired business outcomes.

For example, an end-to-end test can validate that a web application deployed on AWS serves web pages without errors.

To perform these tests effectively, you need testing frameworks and tools that support your chosen IaC language or framework.

For example, if you're using AWS CloudFormation, you can use tools like AWS CloudFormation Testing Framework (Cfn-Test) or open-source libraries to write and run tests for your templates.

When conducting unit tests, you can use mock AWS services to simulate AWS resource behavior without actually creating resources in your AWS account.

This approach allows you to test your code quickly and without incurring AWS usage costs.

For integration and end-to-end tests, you may need to use live AWS services to validate your code's behavior in a real AWS environment.

It's essential to set up dedicated testing environments that closely resemble your production environment to ensure accurate test results.

Automating your IaC tests is a best practice for maintaining consistent and repeatable testing processes.

Continuous Integration/Continuous Deployment (CI/CD) pipelines can be configured to automatically run tests whenever changes are made to your IaC code.

This automation ensures that tests are consistently executed, reducing the risk of human error and speeding up the development cycle.

AWS CodePipeline, GitHub Actions, Jenkins, and Travis CI are popular CI/CD platforms that can integrate with your IaC testing framework.

When writing tests for your AWS IaC code, consider the following best practices:

Test early and often: Start writing tests as soon as you begin developing your IaC code. Frequent testing helps catch issues early in the development process.

Use meaningful test names: Create descriptive test names that clearly indicate the purpose and expected outcome of each test.

Isolate tests: Ensure that tests do not depend on external factors or shared state to maintain test independence and reproducibility.

Include edge cases: Test scenarios that cover both typical use cases and exceptional conditions to uncover potential vulnerabilities.

Validate security configurations: Implement tests that confirm your IaC code follows security best practices and adheres to your organization's security policies.

Automate cleanup: When running tests that create AWS resources, include code to clean up or delete those resources after the tests complete.

Monitor test results: Establish a process for reviewing and acting upon test results to address issues promptly.

Use test reporting and logging: Implement robust reporting and logging mechanisms to capture test results and diagnose failures effectively.

Version control tests: Store your tests alongside your IaC code in version control repositories, ensuring that tests remain consistent with code changes.

Test across environments: Conduct tests in development, staging, and production environments to validate that code behaves consistently.

It's important to note that testing IaC code goes beyond validating AWS resource creation.

It includes testing for compliance, security, performance, and scalability, depending on your specific requirements and use cases.

Compliance tests can verify that your infrastructure adheres to regulatory standards, while security tests can uncover vulnerabilities and misconfigurations.

Performance and scalability tests assess your infrastructure's ability to handle increased workloads and traffic.

When implementing IaC testing, consider using test-driven development (TDD) practices, where you write tests before writing the code.

This approach helps ensure that your code meets specific requirements and behaves as expected.

In summary, testing your AWS Infrastructure as Code (IaC) is a fundamental practice for ensuring the reliability, security, and correctness of your infrastructure deployments.

By incorporating unit tests, integration tests, and end-to-end tests into your development process, you can catch errors early, validate compliance and security, and automate testing to streamline development.

Follow best practices for test naming, isolation, coverage, and automation, and consider test-driven development to enhance the quality of your IaC code and infrastructure.

Validation and error handling are essential aspects of any robust Infrastructure as Code (IaC) implementation on AWS.

Proper validation ensures that your IaC templates and configurations meet your requirements, while effective error handling helps you respond gracefully to unexpected issues.

Validation begins with defining clear and well-documented requirements for your infrastructure.

Before writing any IaC code, you should have a thorough understanding of what you want to achieve and how your infrastructure should be configured.

These requirements serve as the foundation for your validation process.

As you write your IaC code, you should validate it against these requirements at each stage of development.

For example, if your requirement is to create an Amazon RDS database instance with specific parameters, your IaC code should ensure that those parameters are correctly defined in the template.

This early validation helps catch errors and deviations from your requirements as soon as they occur.

AWS provides various tools and services that can assist in the validation process.

AWS CloudFormation, for instance, allows you to define constraints and validation rules within your templates.

You can use AWS CloudFormation intrinsic functions and AWS CloudFormation macros to implement custom validation checks.

For example, you can create a custom macro that verifies whether the specified Amazon EC2 instance type is within the approved list for your organization.

These validation checks can prevent the deployment of resources that do not comply with your requirements.

Additionally, AWS CloudFormation provides Rollback Triggers, which allow you to specify conditions that trigger a rollback of the stack if validation checks fail during the update process.

This ensures that your infrastructure remains in a consistent state even in the presence of errors.

When working with AWS CloudFormation, you can also enable termination protection for critical resources, preventing accidental deletions that could lead to data loss or service disruptions.

Validation is not limited to AWS CloudFormation; it applies to all IaC tools and frameworks.

For example, if you use AWS CDK (Cloud Development Kit) to define your infrastructure, you can incorporate custom validation checks using programming constructs.

In the case of Terraform, the **terraform validate** command can be used to check the validity of your configuration files against the provider's schema.

This command helps ensure that your Terraform code adheres to the correct resource types and attributes.

In addition to validating your IaC code, it's crucial to handle errors effectively during the deployment process.

Errors can occur at various stages, from template validation to resource provisioning.

Your error-handling strategy should include both preventive measures and responses to unforeseen errors.

Preventive measures involve rigorous code review processes and thorough testing.

Code reviews should involve multiple team members to identify issues that may have been overlooked.

Testing should encompass unit tests, integration tests, and end-to-end tests, as discussed in previous chapters.

By addressing issues early in the development cycle, you can reduce the likelihood of errors making their way into your production environment.

However, despite your best efforts, errors can still occur during deployment.

For example, a resource creation might fail due to a capacity issue in a specific AWS Availability Zone.

To handle such errors gracefully, you can implement retry mechanisms in your IaC code.

AWS CloudFormation allows you to specify a **DependsOn** attribute for resources, indicating dependencies between resources.

By configuring dependencies correctly, you can ensure that resources are created or updated in the correct order.

If a resource creation fails, AWS CloudFormation can automatically retry the operation after resolving the issue.

In the case of AWS Lambda functions, you can implement custom error handling and retry logic using Lambda's event-driven architecture.

For example, you can configure an AWS Lambda function to respond to AWS CloudWatch Events that signal errors in your infrastructure.

Upon receiving such an event, the Lambda function can trigger a retry or initiate corrective actions.

AWS Step Functions can be used to create complex workflows that handle errors gracefully.

You can define state machines that include retry, catch, and rollback states to manage error scenarios effectively.

In the event of an error, Step Functions can transition to a specific error-handling state, allowing you to trigger remediation actions or notifications.

When implementing error handling, it's crucial to log errors and diagnostic information comprehensively.

Logging provides visibility into the deployment process, making it easier to diagnose issues and troubleshoot errors.

AWS services like AWS CloudTrail, AWS Config, and Amazon CloudWatch Logs capture essential information about API calls, resource changes, and application logs.

By analyzing these logs, you can gain insights into the root causes of errors and take corrective actions.

Alerting mechanisms, such as AWS CloudWatch Alarms, can be configured to notify you when specific error conditions are detected.

These alarms can trigger automated responses or notify your operations team for manual intervention.

In addition to technical error handling, it's important to have a well-defined incident response plan in place.

Your incident response plan should outline roles and responsibilities, communication channels, and procedures for addressing and resolving errors.

Regularly test your incident response plan through tabletop exercises or simulations to ensure that your team is prepared to respond effectively to unexpected issues.

In summary, validation and error handling are integral components of successful IaC implementations on AWS.

Validation ensures that your infrastructure adheres to requirements, while error handling mechanisms help you respond to unforeseen issues.

AWS provides a range of tools and services that facilitate validation and error handling, including AWS CloudFormation, AWS CDK, Terraform, AWS Lambda, AWS Step Functions, and logging services.

By incorporating robust validation and error handling practices into your IaC processes, you can enhance the reliability, security, and stability of your AWS infrastructure deployments.

Chapter 8: Scaling and Optimization Strategies

Scalability is a fundamental concept in cloud computing, and AWS offers a wide range of patterns and services to help you design and implement scalable solutions.

Scalability is the ability of a system to handle increasing workloads by adapting and expanding its resources dynamically.

In AWS, scalability can be achieved through various patterns and practices that allow your applications and infrastructure to grow seamlessly as demand increases.

One common scalability pattern in AWS is horizontal scaling, also known as scaling out.

Horizontal scaling involves adding more identical instances or resources to distribute the load and accommodate increased traffic.

For example, if you're running a web application on Amazon EC2 instances and you expect higher user traffic during peak hours, you can set up an Auto Scaling group.

The Auto Scaling group automatically launches additional EC2 instances based on defined triggers, such as CPU utilization or network traffic.

This ensures that your application can handle increased user requests by scaling out horizontally.

Vertical scaling, on the other hand, involves increasing the size or capacity of individual resources.

In AWS, vertical scaling can be achieved by resizing instances or changing the instance type to one with more resources, such as CPU, memory, or storage.

For example, if your database server is experiencing increased query loads, you can vertically scale by upgrading the instance type to a larger one with more processing power and memory.

AWS provides services like Amazon RDS (Relational Database Service) that allow you to perform vertical scaling with ease.

Another important scalability pattern is the use of serverless computing, which allows you to build and deploy applications without managing the underlying infrastructure.

AWS Lambda is a prime example of serverless computing, where you write code in response to events, and AWS automatically manages the execution environment.

Lambda functions can be triggered by various AWS services, such as Amazon S3, Amazon DynamoDB, or AWS API Gateway.

This serverless approach enables automatic scaling without the need to provision or manage servers.

In addition to serverless computing, AWS offers container orchestration services like Amazon ECS (Elastic Container Service) and Amazon EKS (Elastic Kubernetes Service).

Containers allow you to package your application and its dependencies into a portable unit, making it easier to scale and manage.

With container orchestration, you can deploy and manage containers at scale, allowing your application to adapt to changing workloads.

Auto Scaling is a fundamental AWS service for achieving scalability.

Auto Scaling groups can be configured to automatically add or remove instances based on metrics and policies.

For example, if you have a fleet of EC2 instances running a web application, you can create an Auto Scaling group that adjusts the number of instances based on CPU utilization.

When CPU utilization exceeds a specified threshold, new instances are launched; when it decreases, instances are terminated.

This dynamic scaling ensures that your application always has the right number of instances to handle the workload efficiently.

In addition to Auto Scaling, AWS offers Application Load Balancers and Network Load Balancers, which distribute incoming traffic across multiple instances to ensure high availability and improved scalability.

Load balancers can automatically route traffic to healthy instances and distribute it evenly, preventing overloading of individual resources.

AWS Global Accelerator is another service that enhances scalability by routing traffic over AWS's global network infrastructure to the nearest healthy application endpoint.

It provides advanced traffic management and availability features to improve the performance and availability of your applications.

Caching is a valuable technique for improving the scalability and performance of applications.

AWS offers Amazon ElastiCache, a managed caching service that supports popular in-memory data stores like Redis and Memcached.

By caching frequently accessed data, ElastiCache reduces the load on your backend databases and accelerates response times, making your applications more scalable and responsive.

Distributed caching with ElastiCache can also be combined with horizontal scaling to further enhance your application's performance.

To achieve scalability in data processing, AWS provides managed services like Amazon EMR (Elastic MapReduce) for big data processing and Amazon Kinesis for real-time data streaming and analytics.

These services allow you to process large volumes of data efficiently and elastically scale resources based on demand.

When it comes to storage scalability, Amazon S3 (Simple Storage Service) is a highly scalable and durable object storage service that can handle virtually unlimited data.

You can store and retrieve objects in S3 with low latency and high throughput, making it suitable for a wide range of applications, from static website hosting to data lakes.

Elastic File System (EFS) is another AWS service that offers scalable and shared file storage for applications and workloads that require file-based access.

EFS grows and shrinks automatically as you add or remove files, making it a convenient choice for scalable file storage.

Database scalability is a crucial consideration for applications with changing data demands.

AWS offers managed database services like Amazon RDS, Amazon Aurora, and Amazon DynamoDB, which provide automated scaling capabilities.

Amazon RDS, for instance, allows you to scale your relational database vertically by changing the instance type or horizontally by using Read Replicas for read-heavy workloads.

Amazon DynamoDB, a NoSQL database service, automatically scales to handle varying read and write requests, making it suitable for high-traffic applications.

AWS also provides services for managing containers and serverless applications at scale.

Amazon ECS and Amazon EKS allow you to deploy and manage containers with ease, while AWS Lambda takes care of serverless application scaling automatically.

Implementing scalable solutions in AWS requires careful planning and monitoring.

You should continuously monitor your application's performance and use AWS services like Amazon CloudWatch to set up alarms and scaling policies based on key performance metrics.

By leveraging AWS's diverse set of services and scalability patterns, you can build resilient and responsive applications that can adapt to changing workloads and user demands effectively.

Optimization of AWS resources is a continuous process that aims to maximize the efficiency, performance, and cost-effectiveness of your cloud infrastructure.

To achieve optimal resource utilization, it's essential to follow a set of best practices and employ various optimization techniques available in AWS.

One key aspect of resource optimization is cost management, as AWS bills are based on actual resource consumption.

A fundamental practice is to monitor and analyze your AWS usage regularly using AWS Cost Explorer, AWS Trusted Advisor, and AWS Cost and Usage Reports.

By understanding your resource costs and usage patterns, you can identify opportunities for optimization.

Right-sizing your AWS resources is a crucial optimization technique.

Right-sizing involves selecting the appropriate instance types and sizes based on your application's actual resource requirements.

Many AWS customers initially overprovision resources to ensure performance, but this can lead to unnecessary costs.

By using AWS tools like AWS Compute Optimizer, which recommends optimal instance types based on historical usage data, you can resize instances to match your workload more precisely.

Implementing Auto Scaling is another effective cost optimization technique.

Auto Scaling allows your infrastructure to automatically adjust the number of instances based on traffic or resource utilization.

This ensures that you have the right number of resources to handle varying workloads, reducing the risk of overprovisioning.

Elastic Load Balancers (ELBs) can be used in conjunction with Auto Scaling to distribute traffic evenly among instances, improving availability and fault tolerance.

Reserved Instances (RIs) and Savings Plans are cost-saving options provided by AWS.

RIs offer significant discounts compared to On-Demand pricing in exchange for a one- or three-year commitment.

AWS Savings Plans provide similar savings but offer more flexibility in terms of instance types and regions.

By strategically purchasing RIs or Savings Plans, you can achieve substantial cost reductions for your long-term workloads.

AWS provides recommendations for RIs and Savings Plans through tools like AWS Cost Explorer and AWS Compute Optimizer.

Storage optimization is a critical aspect of AWS resource optimization.

Unused or obsolete data should be identified and removed to free up storage space and reduce costs.

Amazon S3 provides lifecycle policies that can automatically transition objects to lower-cost storage classes or delete them when they are no longer needed.

Elastic Block Store (EBS) volumes can be resized or snapshots can be managed efficiently to optimize storage costs.

Amazon EFS can be used to share and manage file storage resources more cost-effectively.

Data transfer costs can also be reduced by selecting the right AWS region and using services like Amazon CloudFront for content delivery.

Optimizing database resources is essential for cost and performance efficiency.

Amazon RDS offers options to scale your databases vertically by resizing instances or horizontally by using Read Replicas.

You can use Amazon DynamoDB's on-demand capacity mode to automatically scale read and write capacity based on your application's needs, eliminating overprovisioning.

Database caching with Amazon ElastiCache can improve query performance and reduce database load.

Using Amazon Aurora's serverless mode allows databases to automatically pause during inactivity, saving costs.

To optimize network resources, AWS offers services like Amazon VPC (Virtual Private Cloud) that allow you to design and manage your network architecture efficiently.

You can use VPC peering to connect VPCs privately, use VPN or Direct Connect for secure connectivity to on-premises networks, and utilize AWS Global Accelerator for enhanced availability and performance.

Security and compliance are integral aspects of resource optimization.

Implementing security best practices and utilizing AWS Identity and Access Management (IAM) effectively can help protect your resources from unauthorized access and potential threats.

AWS Config can be used to monitor and enforce compliance with security policies and configurations.

By following the principle of least privilege and regularly reviewing IAM permissions, you can reduce security risks and optimize resource security.

Another optimization technique is taking advantage of AWS Trusted Advisor, which provides real-time recommendations across various categories, including cost, performance, security, and fault tolerance.

Trusted Advisor can identify opportunities for cost savings, security improvements, and resource optimization.

For example, it may recommend removing unused Elastic IP addresses, adjusting instance size, or improving security group configurations.

When optimizing AWS resources, it's important to consider performance alongside cost.

Resource optimization should not compromise the performance and reliability of your applications.

AWS offers Performance Insights for Amazon RDS, which provides visibility into database performance metrics and helps you identify and resolve performance bottlenecks.

Amazon CloudWatch can be used to monitor performance metrics for various AWS resources, allowing you to make data-driven optimization decisions.

AWS also provides tools like AWS Trusted Advisor and AWS Well-Architected Review, which assess your workload's performance, security, reliability, and cost-efficiency.

These assessments can guide you in making optimization improvements based on best practices.

Continuous monitoring and optimization are key to maintaining an efficient AWS environment.

As your workloads evolve and usage patterns change, you should regularly revisit your optimization strategies and adjust resource configurations accordingly.

By continuously optimizing your AWS resources, you can achieve cost savings, improve performance, enhance security, and ensure the overall efficiency of your cloud infrastructure.

AWS offers a rich set of tools and services to help you in this ongoing process, making resource optimization a manageable and rewarding effort in the cloud.

Chapter 9: Continuous Integration and Deployment (CI/CD) with AWS

Implementing Continuous Integration and Continuous Deployment (CI/CD) pipelines is a crucial step in the journey of managing Infrastructure as Code (IaC) on AWS.

CI/CD pipelines streamline the process of deploying and managing infrastructure changes, ensuring efficiency, reliability, and rapid development cycles.

CI/CD is a software development practice that involves integrating code changes into a shared repository continuously and automating the deployment of those changes to production or testing environments.

In the context of IaC, CI/CD extends this concept to the automation of infrastructure provisioning and configuration.

The primary goals of implementing CI/CD pipelines for AWS IaC are to eliminate manual processes, reduce human error, accelerate deployment cycles, and enhance the consistency and reliability of infrastructure changes.

To begin implementing CI/CD for AWS IaC, you should first choose a version control system (VCS) to manage your IaC codebase.

Popular VCS options include Git and AWS CodeCommit, a fully managed Git service provided by AWS.

Using a VCS allows you to track changes to your IaC code, collaborate with team members, and roll back to previous versions if issues arise.

Once you have a VCS in place, the next step is to set up a CI/CD pipeline.

AWS offers various tools and services to help you create CI/CD pipelines tailored to your IaC needs.

AWS CodePipeline is a fully managed CI/CD service that orchestrates the entire pipeline, from source code changes to deployment.

You can define a series of stages in your pipeline, such as source, build, test, and deploy, and specify the actions to be taken at each stage.

For AWS IaC, the source stage typically connects to your VCS repository, where you store your Terraform or CloudFormation code.

CodePipeline can automatically trigger pipeline executions whenever changes are pushed to the repository.

In the build and test stages, you can use AWS CodeBuild, a managed build service, to compile and validate your IaC code.

CodeBuild can run custom scripts or commands, execute unit tests, and perform syntax checks to ensure the code is error-free.

It also integrates with popular build tools like Terraform and AWS CDK, making it suitable for building IaC projects.

During the deploy stage, you can use AWS CodeDeploy to automate the deployment of your IaC changes.

CodeDeploy can deploy your Terraform or CloudFormation templates to AWS environments, such as development, testing, or production.

You can define deployment strategies and rollbacks to ensure safe and controlled updates.

Additionally, CodeDeploy can integrate with AWS CloudFormation to manage stack updates, allowing you to follow infrastructure-as-code best practices.

To configure your CI/CD pipeline for IaC, you'll need to create a pipeline definition in AWS CodePipeline.

This definition specifies the source, build, and deployment actions, as well as any required input parameters or environment variables.

For Terraform-based IaC, you can pass variables like AWS region, AWS access keys, or environment-specific configuration files as parameters to your pipeline.

Using parameterization ensures that your infrastructure deployments are adaptable and can target different AWS environments without code duplication.

Security is a critical consideration when implementing CI/CD pipelines for AWS IaC.

You should follow AWS security best practices to protect your pipeline and associated resources.

Access control policies should be applied to AWS IAM roles and permissions, ensuring that only authorized users or systems can trigger pipeline executions or make changes to infrastructure.

AWS Key Management Service (KMS) can be used to encrypt sensitive configuration data or secrets required during pipeline execution.

Regularly review and audit your CI/CD pipeline configurations to identify and remediate security vulnerabilities or misconfigurations.

Monitoring and logging are essential components of a robust CI/CD pipeline for AWS IaC.

AWS CloudWatch can be used to capture and analyze logs, metrics, and events generated by pipeline executions.

CloudWatch Alarms can notify you of pipeline failures or anomalies in real-time.

Integrating AWS CloudTrail with your pipeline allows you to track API calls and actions performed by the pipeline, enhancing visibility into pipeline activity and potential security threats.

Testing plays a crucial role in the CI/CD pipeline for AWS IaC.

Automated testing should be an integral part of your pipeline to validate changes to infrastructure code.

For Terraform, tools like Terratest can be used to write automated tests that provision infrastructure, verify resource properties, and clean up resources after testing.

For CloudFormation, AWS offers the AWS Cloud Development Kit (CDK) for creating infrastructure as code using programming languages like TypeScript or Python.

The CDK allows you to write unit tests and integration tests using familiar programming frameworks.

Integration tests can be performed on AWS environments that replicate the production environment, ensuring that changes behave as expected before being deployed to production.

Continuous monitoring and feedback loops are essential for the success of your CI/CD pipeline.

Collect feedback from developers, operations teams, and other stakeholders to identify areas for improvement in your IaC code and pipeline configuration.

Use this feedback to refine your pipeline and enhance the automation and reliability of your infrastructure changes.

In summary, implementing CI/CD pipelines for AWS IaC is a best practice that can significantly enhance the efficiency, consistency, and security of your infrastructure management processes.

By using AWS services like CodePipeline, CodeBuild, and CodeDeploy, you can automate the provisioning and deployment of infrastructure changes, while also ensuring the adherence to security and testing standards.

Regular monitoring and continuous improvement are key to maintaining a reliable and effective CI/CD pipeline for AWS IaC, enabling you to respond quickly to changing requirements and deliver value to your organization.

Automated testing and deployment are essential practices in modern software development and infrastructure management.

These practices are critical for ensuring the reliability, stability, and security of your applications and infrastructure.

Next, we will explore the concepts and benefits of automated testing and deployment, as well as best practices for implementing them in your development and operations workflows.

Automated testing involves the use of automated tools and scripts to assess the correctness and quality of your code, infrastructure, and applications.

Automated tests can encompass a wide range of activities, from unit tests that evaluate individual code components to integration tests that verify the interaction between multiple components.

The primary goal of automated testing is to catch and fix defects early in the development process, reducing the likelihood of bugs and issues in production.

Automated testing provides several key advantages over manual testing.

First, it saves time and effort by automating repetitive and time-consuming testing tasks, allowing developers and testers to focus on more complex and creative aspects of testing.

Second, it ensures consistency in testing, as automated tests follow predefined test cases and procedures consistently.

Third, automated tests can be executed quickly and frequently, enabling rapid feedback on code changes and reducing the time between development and testing cycles.

Fourth, automated tests are highly reproducible, which means that you can easily rerun the same tests to verify the correctness of your code and infrastructure across different environments.

Fifth, automated tests can be incorporated into your continuous integration (CI) and continuous deployment (CD) pipelines, enabling automated validation of code changes before deployment.

There are various types of automated tests that you can use to validate different aspects of your code and infrastructure.

Unit tests focus on evaluating individual functions, methods, or code components in isolation.

These tests are designed to catch small-scale defects and ensure that each piece of code behaves as expected.

Integration tests, on the other hand, assess the interaction between multiple components or services.

Integration tests verify that different parts of your application or infrastructure work together correctly.

End-to-end (E2E) tests simulate user interactions with your application, checking whether the entire system functions as intended from start to finish.

Load tests assess the performance and scalability of your infrastructure by subjecting it to various levels of simulated traffic.

Security tests examine your code and infrastructure for vulnerabilities and security weaknesses.

These tests can help you identify and address security risks before they become serious issues.

Automated tests should be an integral part of your development process, starting from the early stages of code development.

In a CI/CD workflow, automated tests are typically executed in a CI environment whenever code changes are pushed to a version control system like Git.

This process is known as continuous integration, and it ensures that code changes are automatically validated before they are merged into the main codebase.

Continuous deployment extends the concept of CI by automating the deployment of code changes to production or staging environments after passing automated tests.

CI/CD pipelines are a key component of an automated testing and deployment strategy.

A CI/CD pipeline is a series of automated steps that take code changes from development through testing and ultimately to production.

The pipeline includes stages for building, testing, and deploying code changes.

In a typical CI/CD pipeline, code changes are first built and tested in a controlled environment to catch defects early.

Once the code changes pass all automated tests, they are automatically deployed to a staging environment for further testing and validation.

If the changes are successful in the staging environment, they can be promoted to production with minimal manual intervention.

One of the most popular CI/CD tools for automating testing and deployment is Jenkins.

Jenkins is an open-source automation server that supports the entire CI/CD process.

Other cloud-based CI/CD services like AWS CodePipeline, Travis CI, CircleCI, and GitLab CI/CD also offer robust automation capabilities for testing and deployment.

These services integrate with popular version control systems and provide preconfigured templates for building and deploying code to various cloud platforms.

When implementing automated testing and deployment for infrastructure as code (IaC), tools like Terraform, AWS CloudFormation, and Ansible play a crucial role.

These tools allow you to define infrastructure in code and use version control to manage changes.

By incorporating automated testing into your IaC workflows, you can validate the correctness of your infrastructure code before provisioning resources.

For example, you can use Terraform's built-in testing framework, Terratest, to write automated tests that create, modify, and destroy infrastructure resources in a test environment.

These tests can ensure that your infrastructure code correctly provisions and configures resources, as well as validate that the desired state matches the actual state of the resources.

In addition to functional testing, you can perform security assessments on your IaC templates to identify potential vulnerabilities and compliance issues.

Tools like Checkov, AWS Config Rules, and AWS Trusted Advisor can help automate security and compliance checks for your IaC code.

By integrating these tools into your CI/CD pipeline, you can automatically validate the security and compliance of your infrastructure before deploying it to production.

Another important aspect of automated testing and deployment is the ability to roll back changes in case of issues or failures.

A well-designed CI/CD pipeline should include mechanisms for safely rolling back to a previous version of your code or infrastructure in case of unexpected problems.

By automating the rollback process, you can minimize downtime and impact on your users.

In summary, automated testing and deployment are essential practices for ensuring the reliability, stability, and security of your code and infrastructure.

These practices help catch defects early, reduce manual effort, and accelerate development and deployment cycles.

By incorporating automated testing into your CI/CD pipeline and leveraging tools designed for IaC, you can ensure that your infrastructure is as reliable as your code, allowing you to deliver high-quality applications and services to your users.

In this case study, we will explore the design and implementation of a high-availability web application using cloud services and Infrastructure as Code (IaC) principles.

The goal of this case study is to illustrate how IaC can be applied to build a resilient and scalable web application that can withstand traffic spikes and hardware failures.

Our fictitious company, "CloudTech Solutions," is launching a new web application called "CloudConnect" that allows users to securely store and share files in the cloud.

To ensure high availability and fault tolerance, CloudTech Solutions has chosen to host CloudConnect on Amazon Web Services (AWS).

The first step in building a high-availability web application is to design the architecture.

For CloudConnect, we'll use a multi-tier architecture with redundancy at each layer.

At the front end, we'll deploy a load balancer to distribute incoming traffic across multiple web servers.

This load balancer will ensure that even if one server fails, the application remains accessible.

The web servers will run the application code and serve user requests.

To achieve redundancy, we'll create an Auto Scaling group that automatically adds or removes web server instances based on traffic demand.

This dynamic scaling ensures that the application can handle increased load during peak times and scale down during periods of lower demand, optimizing costs.

Behind the web servers, we'll deploy a database cluster using Amazon RDS (Relational Database Service).

RDS provides automated backups, failover, and replication, ensuring data durability and availability.

By using a multi-Availability Zone (AZ) deployment, we can withstand AZ failures without impacting the application's availability.

Next, we'll implement Infrastructure as Code (IaC) to define and provision the architecture.

For this case study, we'll use AWS CloudFormation, a service that allows us to define infrastructure resources as code templates.

These templates can be version-controlled, reviewed, and automatically deployed, providing consistency and reproducibility.

With IaC, CloudTech Solutions can easily recreate the entire infrastructure in case of disaster recovery or when scaling up for additional capacity.

To enhance security, we'll follow AWS best practices, such as limiting access to resources using IAM (Identity and Access Management) roles and policies.

CloudConnect's infrastructure will also leverage AWS WAF (Web Application Firewall) to protect against common web application attacks.

Additionally, CloudTech Solutions will set up continuous monitoring and logging using Amazon CloudWatch and AWS Config.

These services provide real time insights into the health and performance of the application and infrastructure, allowing proactive issue resolution.

To further optimize the application's performance, we'll use Amazon CloudFront, AWS's content delivery network (CDN).

CloudFront caches and serves static content from edge locations worldwide, reducing latency for users and improving the application's responsiveness.

With AWS's global network of edge locations, CloudConnect can provide low-latency access to users around the world.

Another key aspect of high availability is disaster recovery planning.

CloudTech Solutions will implement automated backups and snapshots of the database, allowing for point-in-time recovery.

Additionally, a well-defined disaster recovery plan will outline procedures to follow in case of catastrophic events, ensuring minimal downtime and data loss.

CloudConnect's architecture will also be designed to support blue-green deployments.

This deployment strategy involves running two identical environments: one (the blue environment) is currently in production, while the other (the green environment) is a clone of the blue environment with updated code.

By switching traffic from the blue to the green environment, CloudTech Solutions can perform updates or rollbacks without impacting users.

Continuous integration and continuous deployment (CI/CD) pipelines will be established to automate the testing and deployment of new code changes.

Using AWS CodePipeline and AWS CodeDeploy, CloudTech Solutions can ensure that code updates are thoroughly tested in a staging environment before being promoted to production.

In case of issues, the pipeline can be configured to automatically roll back to the previous version.

In summary, this case study illustrates how Infrastructure as Code (IaC), cloud services, and best practices can be leveraged to build a high-availability web application.

CloudTech Solutions' CloudConnect application benefits from a multi-tier architecture, redundancy, scalability, security, monitoring, and disaster recovery measures.

By adopting these principles and tools, organizations can ensure that their web applications are not only available but also resilient and adaptable to changing demands and challenges in the cloud computing landscape.

Book 3
Azure IaC Mastery
Advanced Techniques and Best Practices

ROB BOTWRIGHT

Chapter 1: Azure Infrastructure as Code (IaC) Fundamentals

Understanding the core concepts of Infrastructure as Code (IaC) in the context of Microsoft Azure is crucial for efficiently managing and automating your cloud infrastructure.

Azure IaC enables you to define, provision, and manage infrastructure using code and templates, bringing consistency, scalability, and agility to your cloud deployments.

At its core, Azure IaC revolves around the idea of treating infrastructure as code, which means that infrastructure definitions are expressed in a structured and human-readable format.

Azure Resource Manager (ARM) templates are the foundation of Azure IaC.

These templates are JSON files that describe the desired state of your Azure resources and their configurations.

ARM templates allow you to define resources, their properties, dependencies, and even complex configurations in a declarative manner.

One of the key advantages of Azure IaC is the ability to define infrastructure in a repeatable and automated way.

By using templates, you can recreate and provision identical environments for various purposes, such as development, testing, and production.

This repeatability eliminates the manual configuration of resources, reducing the risk of human errors and ensuring consistency.

Azure IaC also enhances collaboration among teams, as templates can be version-controlled and shared, enabling multiple stakeholders to contribute to infrastructure definitions.

Infrastructure as Code principles in Azure emphasize the importance of automation.

You can leverage Azure DevOps, PowerShell, or other automation tools to orchestrate the deployment of your ARM templates.

This automation streamlines the process of provisioning and managing Azure resources, saving time and effort.

With Azure IaC, you can employ version control systems like Git to track changes made to your infrastructure code over time.

This enables you to maintain a historical record of infrastructure changes, collaborate effectively with team members, and roll back to previous versions if issues arise.

Azure IaC also promotes the use of modules and parameterization to create reusable and flexible templates.

Modules allow you to encapsulate a set of resources and configurations into a single template, making it easier to manage and maintain.

Parameters enable you to customize the behavior of templates by providing inputs that can be adjusted for different environments or scenarios.

Azure IaC encourages the use of best practices for infrastructure security.

You can incorporate Azure Policy and Azure Blueprints into your templates to enforce compliance, security, and governance standards.

Azure Policy allows you to define rules that check the compliance of resources with specific policies, while Azure Blueprints provide a way to define a repeatable set of policies, role assignments, and resource templates that align with your organization's standards.

By implementing these practices, you can ensure that your Azure resources are deployed and configured securely and in alignment with your organization's requirements.

Another crucial aspect of Azure IaC is the concept of idempotence, which means that applying the same template multiple times has the same outcome as applying it once.

Idempotent templates ensure that changes are only applied when necessary and that they don't cause unintended side effects.

Azure Resource Manager evaluates the current state of resources and updates them only if there is a divergence from the desired state defined in the template.

This behavior minimizes disruptions to existing resources and reduces the risk of misconfigurations.

Azure IaC promotes the use of testing and validation as integral parts of the deployment process.

You can implement automated testing and validation checks to ensure that your templates are correct and that they meet your requirements.

Testing frameworks like Pester for PowerShell enable you to validate templates and configurations, helping you catch issues early in the development process.

Azure DevTest Labs can also be used to create isolated environments for testing and validation purposes.

Azure IaC empowers organizations to adopt a DevOps culture by fostering collaboration between development and operations teams.

The use of automation, version control, and repeatable processes facilitates the integration of infrastructure changes into the software delivery pipeline.

This integration ensures that infrastructure is treated as code, allowing it to evolve and adapt alongside application code.

Azure IaC templates are designed to be infrastructure-agnostic, meaning that they can define resources not only in Azure but also in other cloud providers or on-premises environments.

This flexibility enables organizations to adopt a multi-cloud or hybrid cloud strategy while maintaining a consistent IaC approach.

Azure IaC templates can be deployed using various tools and methods, including Azure Portal, Azure PowerShell, Azure CLI, Azure DevOps pipelines, and third-party tools like Terraform.

These deployment options cater to different preferences and scenarios, ensuring that you can use Azure IaC in a way that best fits your organization's needs.

Azure IaC templates can be authored manually, generated using visual tools like the Azure Resource Manager template designer, or created from existing resources using Azure Resource Mover.

The choice of method depends on your familiarity with JSON, your specific use case, and your preferred workflow.

To effectively manage your templates and deployments, Azure provides services like Azure Resource Manager, which acts as the orchestration layer for deploying and managing resources.

Resource groups help organize and manage related resources, and Azure Resource Explorer provides a graphical interface to explore and interact with resources defined in templates.

In summary, understanding the core concepts of Azure IaC is essential for harnessing the power of automation, repeatability, and collaboration in your cloud infrastructure management.

By adopting IaC principles and leveraging ARM templates, organizations can achieve consistency, security, and efficiency in their Azure deployments while seamlessly integrating infrastructure management into their DevOps workflows.

Adopting Infrastructure as Code (IaC) in Azure environments offers a wide array of benefits that can transform the way organizations manage and deploy their infrastructure.

One of the primary advantages of IaC in Azure is increased agility.

With IaC, organizations can define and provision infrastructure using code templates, enabling rapid and automated resource provisioning.

This agility is especially valuable in dynamic and fast-paced environments where the ability to respond quickly to changing requirements is essential.

IaC also enhances scalability by allowing organizations to easily replicate and scale resources up or down as needed.

By defining infrastructure as code, it becomes straightforward to adjust the number of instances or resources based on demand, optimizing costs and performance.

Consistency is another significant benefit of IaC in Azure environments.

IaC templates ensure that infrastructure configurations are standardized and reproducible.

This consistency reduces the risk of configuration drift and minimizes the potential for misconfigurations that can lead to security vulnerabilities or operational issues.

Azure IaC templates are version-controlled, making it possible to track changes and maintain a historical record of infrastructure modifications.

This version control facilitates collaboration among team members and enables rollbacks to previous configurations if issues arise.

Additionally, IaC promotes automation, reducing manual intervention and human errors in infrastructure management.

Automation tools and scripts can be used to orchestrate the deployment and configuration of Azure resources, saving time and effort.

Furthermore, Azure IaC templates can be reused across different environments, such as development, testing, and production.

This reusability streamlines the deployment process and ensures that resources are provisioned consistently across various stages of the development lifecycle.

Security and compliance are paramount in Azure environments, and IaC can significantly contribute to achieving these goals.

Azure Policy and Azure Blueprints can be integrated with IaC templates to enforce security and governance standards.

These policies and blueprints ensure that resources are deployed and configured in alignment with organizational requirements and industry best practices.

By adhering to these standards, organizations can enhance the security and compliance posture of their Azure environments.

Idempotence is a key concept in IaC that ensures applying the same configuration multiple times has the same outcome as applying it once.

Azure Resource Manager evaluates the current state of resources and updates them only if there is a deviation from the desired state defined in the template.

This idempotent behavior minimizes disruptions to existing resources and mitigates the risk of unintentional changes.

Testing and validation are integral components of IaC in Azure.

Automated testing frameworks like Pester for PowerShell can be employed to validate templates and configurations, ensuring that they are correct and meet requirements.

This testing approach helps identify issues early in the development process, reducing the likelihood of errors in production deployments.

Azure DevTest Labs can also be used to create isolated environments for testing and validation purposes. IaC promotes collaboration between development and operations teams, fostering a DevOps culture within organizations. By treating infrastructure as code, development and operations teams can work together seamlessly to automate the deployment and management of resources. This collaboration streamlines the delivery pipeline, enabling both infrastructure and application code to evolve and adapt in tandem.

Furthermore, Azure IaC templates are designed to be infrastructure-agnostic, meaning they can define resources not only in Azure but also in other cloud providers or on-premises environments. This flexibility empowers organizations to adopt a multi-cloud or hybrid cloud strategy while maintaining a consistent IaC approach. Azure IaC templates can be deployed using various methods, including Azure Portal, Azure PowerShell, Azure CLI, Azure DevOps pipelines, and third-party tools like Terraform. These deployment options cater to different preferences and scenarios, ensuring that organizations can choose the method that best suits their needs.

To effectively manage IaC templates and deployments, Azure provides services like Azure Resource Manager, which acts as the orchestration layer for deploying and managing resources.

Resource groups help organize and manage related resources, and Azure Resource Explorer provides a graphical interface to explore and interact with resources defined in templates.

In summary, the benefits of adopting Infrastructure as Code in Azure environments are numerous and impactful.

Agility, scalability, consistency, security, automation, version control, idempotence, testing, collaboration, and flexibility are all advantages that organizations can leverage to optimize their Azure infrastructure management.

By embracing IaC principles and incorporating them into their Azure deployments, organizations can realize the full potential of cloud infrastructure while ensuring efficiency, reliability, and compliance.

Chapter 2: Setting Up Your Azure Environment for IaC

Preparing your Azure environment for Infrastructure as Code (IaC) is a critical step in streamlining the deployment and management of your cloud infrastructure.

Before diving into IaC, it's essential to ensure that your Azure environment is well-organized and properly configured.

A well-prepared environment will set the stage for successful IaC implementation and help you avoid common pitfalls.

The first aspect of preparation involves understanding your organization's Azure subscription model.

Azure offers various subscription types, such as Pay-As-You-Go, Enterprise Agreement, and others, each with its own billing and governance characteristics.

Choosing the right subscription type and properly managing subscriptions is fundamental for cost control and resource governance.

Additionally, it's important to determine who will have access to the Azure portal and resources.

Azure Identity and Access Management (IAM) allows you to assign roles and permissions to users and groups, ensuring that only authorized individuals can make changes to your resources.

Implementing least privilege access is a best practice to minimize security risks.

Resource groups are a fundamental concept in Azure and play a crucial role in organizing and managing resources.

Before adopting IaC, consider how you want to structure your resource groups to align with your organization's projects, applications, or environments.

A well-thought-out resource group strategy can simplify resource management and isolation.

Another important aspect of preparing your Azure environment for IaC is defining naming conventions for resources.

Consistent and meaningful naming conventions make it easier to identify resources, track costs, and manage resources programmatically using IaC templates.

Resource tagging is also a valuable practice for categorizing resources based on attributes like cost center, environment, or owner.

Once your Azure environment is structured, it's time to think about network architecture.

Consider how you want to design your virtual networks (VNets), subnets, and network security groups (NSGs) to meet your application's connectivity and security requirements.

Planning your network architecture in advance ensures that your IaC templates can provision the necessary networking resources accurately.

Azure provides a wide range of services for data storage, including Azure Storage, Azure SQL Database, and Azure Cosmos DB.

Determine which data storage services your applications will rely on, and plan the configurations and access controls accordingly.

Azure Key Vault is a critical service for securely storing and managing sensitive information such as secrets, keys, and certificates.

Integrate Azure Key Vault into your environment to ensure secure storage and retrieval of secrets used by your IaC templates.

As part of your preparation, consider the Azure regions where you want to deploy resources.

Azure offers a global network of data centers, allowing you to choose regions that are geographically close to your users or that comply with data sovereignty requirements.

Understanding your data residency and compliance needs is crucial when selecting Azure regions.

Azure provides various monitoring and logging services, including Azure Monitor and Azure Security Center.

Configuring monitoring and alerting rules early in your preparation phase enables you to proactively identify and address issues in your Azure environment.

In addition to monitoring, implementing backup and disaster recovery solutions is essential to protect your data and applications.

Azure Backup and Azure Site Recovery are Azure services that can be integrated into your IaC templates to ensure data resilience.

When it comes to cost management, Azure Cost Management and Billing provide tools to monitor and control spending.

Set up cost alerts and budgets to avoid unexpected charges and optimize your Azure resources.

Security should be a top priority in your Azure environment.

Azure Security Center helps you identify and mitigate security threats by providing recommendations and threat detection capabilities.

Integrate Azure Security Center into your environment to enhance the security posture of your IaC deployments.

Azure Policy is a powerful service that allows you to define and enforce organizational standards and compliance requirements.

Implement Azure Policy definitions to ensure that resources deployed through IaC adhere to your organization's policies.

Now that you've prepared your Azure environment by structuring it, defining access controls, planning network architecture, and configuring monitoring and security, you're ready to start working with IaC.

Azure provides several tools and services for implementing IaC, including Azure Resource Manager (ARM) templates, Azure CLI, and Azure PowerShell.

Choose the tool that best aligns with your skills and requirements.

ARM templates are JSON files that define the desired state of your Azure resources.

They are the foundation of Azure IaC and enable you to declaratively specify resources, properties, and dependencies.

Azure CLI and Azure PowerShell are command-line interfaces that allow you to interact with Azure resources programmatically.

These tools are useful for deploying and managing resources using scripts and automation.

Before writing your IaC templates, it's essential to have a clear understanding of the resources you want to deploy.

Refer to your previously prepared resource group structure, naming conventions, and network architecture plans when designing your templates.

Azure Quickstart Templates provide a repository of pre-built ARM templates for common scenarios, which can serve as valuable references and starting points for your IaC projects.

When writing your IaC templates, focus on defining resources, their properties, dependencies, and configurations in a structured and modular manner.

Leverage Azure Policy to enforce governance standards and security requirements in your templates.

Parameterization is a key aspect of IaC templates.

Use parameters to make your templates flexible and reusable across different environments or projects.

Parameters enable you to customize resource configurations without modifying the template code.

To ensure the quality of your IaC templates, implement testing and validation practices.

Automated testing frameworks like Pester for PowerShell can help validate your templates to ensure they are correct and meet your requirements.

Azure DevTest Labs can be utilized to create isolated environments for testing and validation purposes.

Continuous integration and continuous deployment (CI/CD) pipelines are integral to the IaC development workflow.

Use Azure DevOps or other CI/CD tools to automate the testing and deployment of your IaC templates.

These pipelines ensure that changes to your templates are thoroughly tested and deployed in a controlled and reproducible manner.

Monitoring and logging should not be overlooked in your IaC implementation.

Configure Azure Monitor and Azure Application Insights to gain real-time insights into the health and performance of your resources and applications.

Implement logging to capture relevant information for troubleshooting and auditing purposes.

Incorporate Azure Policy into your IaC development process to enforce organizational standards and compliance requirements.

By defining policy definitions and assignments in your templates, you can ensure that deployed resources adhere to your policies from the outset.

Finally, document your IaC templates and deployment processes.

Clear documentation helps your team understand how to use and modify the templates effectively.

Include information on parameters, resource dependencies, deployment steps, and any specific considerations.

In summary, preparing your Azure environment for Infrastructure as Code involves structuring, configuring, securing, and optimizing your resources and services.

This preparation lays the foundation for successful IaC implementation, enabling you to deploy and manage Azure resources efficiently and consistently.

With a well-prepared Azure environment, you can leverage IaC to automate, scale, and govern your cloud infrastructure effectively.

Azure credentials and configuration are essential components of working with Microsoft Azure, especially when implementing Infrastructure as Code (IaC) solutions.

To interact with Azure programmatically, you need appropriate credentials and a well-defined configuration.

Azure supports various authentication methods, including Azure Active Directory (Azure AD) service principals, managed identities, and shared access signatures.

Azure AD service principals are commonly used for IaC scenarios.

A service principal is essentially a non-human identity that can be used to authenticate and authorize applications and automation tools.

When creating a service principal, you receive a client ID and client secret or a certificate, which are used as credentials to access Azure resources.

These credentials must be stored securely, and best practices should be followed to protect them.

Azure Managed Identities are a more secure way to authenticate applications running on Azure services.

With managed identities, you don't need to manage credentials directly, as Azure automatically handles the authentication process.

Managed identities are assigned to Azure resources, such as virtual machines or Azure Functions, and can be used to access other Azure resources.

When using IaC, it's important to provision and configure managed identities where applicable to enhance security.

In addition to service principals and managed identities, you can also use shared access signatures (SAS) for temporary and limited access to Azure resources.

SAS tokens can be generated for specific resources and actions and are often used for scenarios like temporary data sharing.

Once you have chosen an authentication method, you need to configure your development environment with the necessary credentials.

This involves setting up the authentication details in the tools and scripts you use for IaC.

For Azure CLI and Azure PowerShell, you can log in using the **az login** and **Connect-AzAccount** commands, respectively.

These commands will prompt you to provide your Azure AD credentials or use a service principal's credentials.

When working with Azure DevOps pipelines, you can securely store credentials as secrets in the pipeline's variables, ensuring that they are protected and not exposed.

Azure Resource Manager (ARM) templates, which are at the core of Azure IaC, also require authentication.

You can use the **az login** command in your deployment scripts to authenticate and access Azure resources during template deployment.

It's important to note that Azure AD service principals should have the appropriate permissions (Azure role assignments) to access the necessary resources in your subscription.

These permissions are defined in Azure role-based access control (RBAC) roles, such as "Contributor" or custom roles that you create.

Managing permissions effectively is crucial for ensuring that IaC deployments can perform the required operations without unnecessary access rights.

Furthermore, you should follow the principle of least privilege when assigning permissions to service principals, ensuring that they have only the permissions necessary to perform their tasks.

In addition to credentials, configuration settings play a vital role in Azure IaC.

Configuration settings include details such as the Azure subscription ID, resource group names, and Azure region settings.

These settings should be defined and stored in a structured manner to ensure consistency across deployments.

One common approach is to use parameter files in ARM templates or configuration files in your IaC scripts.

By using parameter files, you can customize deployments for different environments or scenarios while maintaining a consistent template.

Configuration settings should be version-controlled along with your IaC code to ensure that changes to settings are tracked and documented.

Secrets, such as connection strings or encryption keys, should never be hard-coded in your IaC scripts or templates.

Instead, use Azure Key Vault to securely store and manage secrets.

Key Vault allows you to create secrets and access them programmatically using managed identities or service principals.

Integrating Key Vault into your IaC deployments ensures that sensitive information remains protected and can be easily rotated when needed.

Another crucial aspect of Azure credentials and configuration is the management of multiple environments.

Typically, organizations have multiple Azure environments, such as development, testing, and production.

To work effectively with these environments, you can use environment-specific configuration files or parameter files.

These files specify settings unique to each environment while using the same IaC codebase.

This approach promotes consistency and ensures that the IaC code can be reused across different stages of the development lifecycle.

Additionally, consider the use of deployment scripts or automation pipelines that handle environment-specific settings and credentials.

These scripts can streamline the deployment process and minimize the risk of configuration errors.

When transitioning from development to production environments, it's crucial to update configuration settings and credentials appropriately.

Azure DevOps Release Pipelines, for example, allow you to automate the deployment process while injecting environment-specific configuration values.

This ensures a smooth and controlled transition from one environment to another.

In summary, Azure credentials and configuration are integral to successful IaC implementations.

Selecting the appropriate authentication method, managing credentials securely, and defining configuration settings systematically are essential steps in the IaC workflow.

Using service principals, managed identities, or shared access signatures, along with Azure Key Vault for secret management, helps protect sensitive information.

Ensuring proper permissions and adhering to the principle of least privilege guarantees that IaC deployments have the necessary access without unnecessary exposure. By structuring configuration settings and parameterizing templates, you can maintain consistency across multiple environments and stages of the development lifecycle. Managing credentials and configuration effectively contributes to the reliability, security, and maintainability of your Azure IaC solutions.

Exploring Azure resource types is a fundamental step in understanding how to manage and deploy infrastructure using Infrastructure as Code (IaC) in the Microsoft Azure cloud.

Azure offers a vast array of resource types, each representing a specific type of infrastructure component or service that you can provision and manage programmatically.

These resource types cover various aspects of cloud computing, from compute and storage to networking and databases.

Azure resources are organized into resource groups, which act as containers for resources related to a specific project, application, or environment.

Resource groups enable you to manage and organize resources effectively, making it easier to apply policies, control access, and track costs.

One of the most common and foundational resource types in Azure is the virtual machine (VM).

Azure VMs provide scalable and flexible compute resources, allowing you to run virtualized Windows or Linux operating systems in the cloud.

You can define the size, configuration, and operating system of a VM using IaC templates, making it possible to create and manage VMs consistently and efficiently.

Azure also offers various storage-related resource types, such as Azure Storage Accounts and Azure Blob Storage.

Azure Storage Accounts provide a scalable and secure way to store data, and you can use them to create containers for storing blobs, tables, queues, and files.

Blob Storage, in particular, is commonly used for storing unstructured data, such as images, videos, and backups.

Azure Networking plays a crucial role in building and connecting resources in the cloud.

Resource types like Virtual Networks (VNets), Network Security Groups (NSGs), and Application Gateways are essential for creating secure and isolated network architectures.

VNets allow you to define the network topology, subnets, and IP address ranges for your Azure resources.

NSGs, on the other hand, control inbound and outbound traffic to network interfaces, VMs, or subnets.

Application Gateways provide advanced load balancing and web application firewall (WAF) capabilities for web applications.

Another resource type critical for cloud-based applications is Azure App Service.

Azure App Service allows you to build, host, and scale web applications and APIs, and it supports various programming languages and platforms.

You can define the configuration and settings of App Service plans, web apps, and deployment slots using IaC templates.

Azure also offers managed database services, including Azure SQL Database and Azure Cosmos DB.

Azure SQL Database is a fully managed relational database service, while Azure Cosmos DB is a globally distributed, multi-model database service.

Both of these services can be provisioned and configured using IaC, enabling you to automate database deployments and management.

Azure Kubernetes Service (AKS) is another essential resource type for container orchestration and management.

AKS simplifies the deployment, scaling, and management of containerized applications using Kubernetes.

You can create and manage AKS clusters and deploy containerized workloads using IaC templates.

Azure also provides resource types for identity and access management.

Azure Active Directory (Azure AD) is a comprehensive identity and access management solution that allows you to manage user identities, secure access to resources, and enable single sign-on (SSO) for applications.

You can use IaC to define Azure AD configurations, including users, groups, roles, and authentication settings.

Azure Key Vault is a resource type that provides secure and centralized management of keys, secrets, and certificates.

You can use Azure Key Vault to store and retrieve secrets, encryption keys, and certificates securely in your IaC templates and applications.

Azure Monitor and Azure Log Analytics are resource types for monitoring and managing the performance and health of Azure resources.

You can use these services to collect and analyze telemetry data, set up alerts, and gain insights into the behavior of your applications and infrastructure.

Azure Functions is a serverless compute service that allows you to run code in response to events.

You can use IaC to define Azure Functions and configure triggers, bindings, and function code.

Azure Logic Apps is a workflow automation service that enables you to create and run workflows that integrate with various services and applications.

You can define Logic App workflows using IaC templates to automate business processes and data flows.

Azure Cognitive Services is a family of AI and machine learning services that provide capabilities such as computer vision, speech recognition, and natural language processing.

You can use IaC to provision and configure Cognitive Services resources for your applications.

Azure DevOps Services is a resource type that supports continuous integration and continuous delivery (CI/CD) pipelines.

You can define build and release pipelines using IaC to automate the building, testing, and deployment of your applications.

Azure Resource Manager (ARM) templates are at the heart of Azure IaC and are used to define the desired state of your Azure resources.

ARM templates are JSON files that describe the resources, their properties, dependencies, and configurations.

By authoring ARM templates, you can specify the infrastructure and services required for your applications in a declarative manner.

Azure Resource Manager evaluates the templates and deploys the resources accordingly, ensuring that the desired state is achieved.

Resource dependencies are managed automatically by Azure Resource Manager, making it possible to create complex architectures and applications with ease.

In summary, exploring Azure resource types is a crucial step in leveraging IaC for managing and deploying infrastructure in the Microsoft Azure cloud.

Azure offers a wide range of resource types that cover compute, storage, networking, databases, identity, monitoring, and more.

These resources can be provisioned, configured, and managed programmatically using IaC templates and scripts, allowing you to automate and streamline your cloud operations.

Understanding the capabilities and use cases of these resource types is essential for building robust and scalable Azure solutions using IaC.

Resource groups and resource management are foundational concepts in Microsoft Azure that play a critical role in organizing, governing, and deploying cloud resources efficiently and effectively.

In Azure, a resource group is a logical container for resources that share a common lifecycle, management policies, or access control requirements.

Resource groups serve as a means of grouping related resources together, making it easier to manage and govern those resources as a unit.

When you create a resource group, you give it a unique name and choose a region where the resource group's metadata is stored.

It's important to note that the region of the resource group's metadata does not restrict the location of the resources within the group.

Resource groups are not bound to a specific region, and you can place resources in different Azure regions while still associating them with the same resource group.

Resource groups are designed to simplify resource management tasks, such as deploying, updating, and deleting resources.

By grouping resources together, you can perform these operations on all the resources in the group collectively, rather than managing each resource individually.

This approach streamlines administrative tasks and reduces the risk of configuration errors.

Resource groups also provide a means of managing access control to resources.

Azure role-based access control (RBAC) allows you to define who can perform actions on resources within a resource group.

By assigning roles to users or security groups at the resource group level, you grant permissions to manage all resources within that group.

This simplifies access management and ensures that users have the appropriate level of access to resources based on their roles and responsibilities.

Resource groups can be created using various methods, including the Azure portal, Azure CLI, Azure PowerShell, Azure SDKs, and Infrastructure as Code (IaC) templates.

IaC templates, such as Azure Resource Manager (ARM) templates, allow you to define resource groups and their associated resources declaratively.

With ARM templates, you specify the resources you need, their configurations, and dependencies, and then Azure Resource Manager deploys those resources into the specified resource group.

Resource groups can also be used to define policies and governance standards.

Azure Policy, a service within Azure, enables you to define and enforce organizational standards and compliance requirements at the resource group level.

You can create policy definitions that specify rules and constraints for resources within a resource group, ensuring that they adhere to your organization's policies.

Azure Policy can help prevent non-compliant resource deployments and ensure that resources stay in compliance throughout their lifecycle.

Additionally, resource groups play a key role in cost management.

Azure Cost Management and Billing allows you to view and manage costs at the resource group level, making it easier to track spending and allocate costs to specific projects or departments.

Resource group tagging can further enhance cost allocation by categorizing resources based on attributes like cost center or project.

Resource management in Azure involves the process of creating, configuring, updating, and deleting resources within resource groups.

Azure offers a wide range of resource types, including virtual machines, databases, storage accounts, networking components, and more.

When creating resources, you specify their configurations, such as size, location, and settings, based on your application's requirements.

Resource management can be done interactively through the Azure portal, command-line interfaces (CLI and PowerShell), Azure SDKs, or programmatically through APIs.

Many organizations choose to automate resource management using Infrastructure as Code (IaC) principles and tools.

IaC allows you to define and provision resources and their configurations using code-based templates.

One of the primary advantages of IaC is repeatability.

You can create, update, and delete resources consistently and predictably by applying the same template to different environments or resource groups.

This approach ensures that your infrastructure remains consistent across development, testing, and production environments.

Azure Resource Manager (ARM) templates are a common choice for implementing IaC in Azure.

ARM templates are JSON files that define the desired state of Azure resources, including their properties, dependencies, and configurations.

Templates can be version-controlled and shared among teams, promoting collaboration and code reuse.

Azure Resource Manager evaluates the templates and deploys the resources into the specified resource group, ensuring that the desired configuration is achieved.

Resource management also encompasses resource updates and modifications.

As application requirements evolve, you may need to scale resources, apply configuration changes, or update resource settings.

IaC templates provide a structured and controlled way to make these modifications while maintaining consistency and minimizing the risk of configuration drift.

Resource deletion is another aspect of resource management.

When resources are no longer needed or have reached the end of their lifecycle, they should be decommissioned to avoid unnecessary costs and resource clutter.

Azure Resource Manager allows you to delete entire resource groups, which in turn deletes all the resources contained within them.

This makes resource cleanup a straightforward and efficient process. Resource management best practices include proper resource naming conventions, consistent tagging, and documentation.

Naming conventions help you identify resources and their purposes easily, especially in large-scale deployments. Tags allow you to categorize and label resources for cost allocation, tracking, and reporting.

Documentation ensures that your team understands the purpose and configurations of resources, making it easier to manage and troubleshoot issues.

Resource management in Azure is a critical component of cloud operations.

By leveraging resource groups and following best practices for resource management, organizations can effectively organize, govern, and automate the deployment and maintenance of their Azure resources.

Whether through manual interactions or the use of IaC, resource management helps ensure that Azure resources are provisioned, configured, updated, and deleted in a controlled and efficient manner, contributing to the overall success of cloud-based applications and services.

Advanced Azure Infrastructure as Code (IaC) patterns encompass a set of best practices and strategies that go beyond the basics of resource provisioning and configuration.

These patterns are designed to help organizations achieve greater efficiency, scalability, and maintainability in their Azure deployments.

One advanced pattern is the use of parameterized templates, which allows you to create reusable and customizable IaC solutions.

Parameterized templates enable you to define parameters for your templates, allowing users to provide input values when deploying resources.

This flexibility allows you to reuse the same template for different scenarios by adjusting the input parameters, reducing the need for template duplication.

Another advanced pattern is the use of nested templates, which enables the decomposition of complex infrastructure into smaller, more manageable units.

Nested templates can be linked together to form a hierarchy, where parent templates reference and deploy child templates.

This approach promotes modularity and simplifies template maintenance, as changes can be made to individual templates without affecting the entire infrastructure.

Azure Resource Manager (ARM) template functions are a powerful feature that can be leveraged to create dynamic and data-driven templates.

These functions allow you to generate values, perform calculations, and manipulate data within your templates.

For example, you can use functions to generate unique resource names, compute resource properties, or retrieve information from Azure resources.

Another advanced pattern is the use of template conditionals and loops to handle dynamic scenarios.

Conditionals allow you to define logic that determines whether a resource should be deployed or configured based on specific conditions.

Loops, on the other hand, enable you to iterate over a list of items and apply the same configuration to multiple resources.

These patterns are particularly valuable when dealing with variable workloads or environments.

Resource tagging is an advanced practice that involves assigning metadata to Azure resources using key-value pairs.

Tags provide additional context and categorization for resources, making it easier to track, manage, and report on resources in a structured manner.

Advanced tagging strategies may involve the enforcement of tagging policies and automated tagging through IaC templates.

Azure Blueprints is an advanced IaC pattern that allows organizations to define and enforce standards and compliance requirements across their Azure environments.

Blueprints provide a way to package together resource templates, policies, and role assignments into a single reusable blueprint definition.

This ensures that every deployment adheres to predefined standards and configurations.

Incorporating infrastructure as code testing and validation into your Azure IaC pipeline is crucial for maintaining the quality and reliability of your deployments.

Advanced patterns include the use of automated testing frameworks and tools to verify that templates and configurations meet desired outcomes.

Continuous integration (CI) and continuous deployment (CD) pipelines can be extended with IaC testing, allowing you to catch errors and issues early in the development process.

Security is a paramount concern in cloud environments, and advanced Azure IaC patterns include implementing robust security practices.

This may involve leveraging Azure Policy to enforce security controls, using Azure Key Vault for secure secret management, and implementing identity and access management (IAM) strategies.

Additionally, Azure Security Center can be integrated into your IaC pipeline to continuously assess and monitor the security posture of your Azure resources.

Scalability patterns in Azure IaC are essential for handling changing workloads and resource demands.

Advanced patterns include the use of auto-scaling templates and configurations that dynamically adjust resource capacity based on load or performance metrics.

These patterns ensure that your Azure resources can scale up or down as needed, optimizing cost and performance.

Another advanced pattern is the use of Azure DevTest Labs for provisioning and managing development and testing environments in a cost-effective manner.

DevTest Labs allows you to automate the creation of lab environments, including virtual machines, databases, and other resources, for development and testing purposes.

This pattern promotes resource efficiency and agility in software development and testing workflows.

Cost optimization is a key consideration in advanced Azure IaC patterns.

This involves regularly monitoring and optimizing your Azure resource usage to minimize unnecessary costs.

Advanced patterns may include implementing budget alerts, resource tagging for cost allocation, and using reserved instances for predictable workloads.

Advanced Azure IaC patterns also address cross-resource and cross-environment orchestration.

For complex scenarios that involve multiple resource groups, regions, or subscriptions, you can use Azure Automation or Azure Logic Apps to create workflows that coordinate actions across resources and environments.

This advanced pattern enables you to automate intricate processes and maintain consistency in complex architectures.

Lastly, advanced Azure IaC patterns involve disaster recovery and high availability strategies.

This includes the use of Azure Site Recovery for replicating and recovering critical workloads in case of outages or disasters.

High availability designs may incorporate Azure Load Balancer, Availability Sets, and Azure Functions to ensure that applications and services remain accessible and resilient.

In summary, advanced Azure Infrastructure as Code patterns are essential for organizations seeking to optimize, secure, and automate their cloud deployments effectively.

These patterns encompass a range of strategies and best practices, from parameterized templates to security enforcement, scalability, and disaster recovery planning.

By leveraging advanced IaC patterns, organizations can achieve greater flexibility, efficiency, and reliability in their Azure environments, ultimately supporting their business goals and objectives in the cloud.

Managing dependencies and complex scenarios is a critical aspect of Infrastructure as Code (IaC) in cloud environments like Azure, where resources often rely on one another and intricate architectures are common.

One of the primary challenges in managing dependencies is ensuring that resources are created and configured in the correct order.

This is vital because certain resources may depend on the existence or configuration of other resources to function properly.

For example, a virtual machine (VM) might require a virtual network (VNet) and a storage account to be created before it can be provisioned.

To address this challenge, you can use resource dependencies in your IaC templates.

Azure Resource Manager (ARM) templates allow you to define explicit dependencies between resources so that Azure deploys them in the correct order.

By specifying dependencies, you ensure that resources are created or updated in a coordinated manner, avoiding potential issues caused by missing dependencies.

Another common complexity in cloud scenarios is the need to parameterize IaC templates to accommodate different configurations for various environments or use cases.

Parameterization allows you to make templates more flexible and reusable by externalizing values that can vary between deployments.

For instance, you can parameterize the VM size, storage account name, or the number of virtual machines to deploy, allowing users to provide these values when deploying the template.

This flexibility enables you to reuse the same template across different scenarios, reducing the need for template duplication and maintenance.

Handling secrets and sensitive information is another critical aspect of managing dependencies and complex scenarios.

In many cases, IaC templates require sensitive data, such as passwords or API keys, to be used during resource provisioning.

Storing and managing secrets securely is essential to maintaining the integrity and security of your infrastructure.

Azure Key Vault is a service that can be leveraged to store and manage secrets, keys, and certificates securely.

You can reference secrets stored in Azure Key Vault directly in your IaC templates, ensuring that sensitive information is not exposed in the templates themselves.

Managing dependencies also involves dealing with resources that are shared across multiple deployments or environments.

For example, you may have a central database server that multiple applications need to connect to.

In such cases, it's important to manage the configuration and access to shared resources consistently.

One approach is to create a dedicated resource group for shared resources and define strict access control policies to ensure that only authorized deployments can access them.

Additionally, you can use Azure policies to enforce naming conventions and tagging standards for shared resources, making them easily identifiable and traceable.

Complex scenarios often involve the need to coordinate actions across multiple Azure regions or subscriptions.

This could be for disaster recovery, load balancing, or other cross-environment requirements.

Azure provides tools and services to help manage these complex scenarios.

Azure Traffic Manager, for instance, allows you to distribute traffic across multiple Azure regions for high availability and load balancing.

Azure Site Recovery is a service that facilitates disaster recovery planning and replication of workloads across regions or subscriptions.

Resource groups can also be used to organize resources by region or environment, simplifying management and deployment across complex scenarios.

In some cases, complex scenarios require the use of advanced networking configurations.

Azure Virtual WAN, for example, allows you to connect multiple Azure regions, on-premises locations, and remote users through a unified and scalable network infrastructure.

Virtual WAN simplifies complex networking tasks, such as routing, and ensures secure connectivity across distributed environments.

Testing and validation play a crucial role in managing dependencies and complex scenarios.

Before deploying IaC templates in a production environment, it's essential to thoroughly test and validate them in a controlled and isolated environment.

Azure DevTest Labs provides a cost-effective way to create and manage test environments for IaC templates.

You can automate the provisioning of lab environments, deploy templates, and run tests to ensure that dependencies are correctly managed, configurations are accurate, and resource interactions are as expected.

Furthermore, implementing continuous integration and continuous deployment (CI/CD) pipelines for IaC templates is recommended for managing dependencies effectively.

CI/CD pipelines allow you to automate the building, testing, and deployment of templates, ensuring that changes and updates are applied consistently and reliably across environments.

Azure DevOps Services and Azure Pipelines provide tools and capabilities for setting up CI/CD pipelines tailored to your IaC workflows.

In summary, managing dependencies and complex scenarios in Azure IaC requires careful planning, parameterization, secure handling of secrets, and the use of tools and services that facilitate coordination across regions, subscriptions, and environments.

By addressing these challenges and implementing best practices, organizations can effectively manage dependencies and ensure the reliable deployment of complex infrastructure in Azure.

Chapter 5: Azure IaC Security and Compliance

Implementing security controls with Azure Infrastructure as Code (IaC) is paramount in ensuring the integrity and protection of your cloud resources.

Security should be a top priority in any Azure deployment, and IaC provides a structured and consistent way to enforce security policies and configurations.

One of the foundational aspects of security in Azure IaC is the use of Azure Role-Based Access Control (RBAC).

RBAC allows you to define who can perform actions on resources within your Azure subscription.

By assigning roles to users or security groups, you can control access to resources and ensure that only authorized personnel have the permissions required to manage or modify them.

To enforce RBAC through IaC, you can include role assignments in your templates, specifying which users or groups should have specific roles on resources.

Azure Policy is another critical tool for enforcing security controls through IaC.

Azure Policy allows you to define and enforce organizational standards and compliance requirements across your Azure environment.

You can create policy definitions that specify rules and constraints for resources, ensuring that they adhere to your organization's security policies.

For example, you can define policies that require the use of encryption for storage accounts or prohibit the exposure of certain ports in network security groups.

Azure Policy can be applied to resource groups, subscriptions, or management groups, making it a powerful tool for maintaining consistent security configurations.

To implement Azure Policy through IaC, you can include policy definitions and assignments in your templates, ensuring that all deployments adhere to your security policies.

Secret management is a critical aspect of security in Azure IaC.

Secrets, such as passwords, API keys, and connection strings, should be stored and managed securely to prevent unauthorized access.

Azure Key Vault is a service that provides a secure and centralized location for managing secrets, keys, and certificates.

You can integrate Azure Key Vault into your IaC workflows by referencing secrets stored in Key Vault directly in your templates.

This ensures that sensitive information is not exposed in your templates or configurations.

Additionally, Azure Key Vault allows you to audit and monitor access to secrets, providing visibility into who accessed them and when.

Network security is a vital aspect of Azure IaC security.

Azure provides a range of tools and features to control and monitor network traffic.

Network Security Groups (NSGs) allow you to define inbound and outbound traffic rules to control the flow of data to and from virtual machines and other resources.

Using IaC templates, you can specify NSG rules that restrict network access based on your security requirements.

Azure Firewall is another option for securing your network, providing a managed firewall service that can be deployed and managed through IaC.

Additionally, Azure DDoS Protection can help safeguard your applications from distributed denial-of-service (DDoS) attacks by automatically detecting and mitigating threats.

Implementing these network security controls through IaC helps ensure that your Azure resources are protected from unauthorized access and threats.

Data encryption is a fundamental security measure in Azure IaC.

Azure offers encryption at rest and in transit for various services.

For example, Azure Disk Encryption can be used to encrypt virtual machine disks, while Azure Storage Service Encryption provides encryption for data stored in Azure Storage.

To implement encryption through IaC, you can include encryption settings and configurations in your templates.

This ensures that all data is encrypted according to your security requirements.

Another critical aspect of Azure IaC security is vulnerability management.

You should regularly assess and address vulnerabilities in your Azure resources to reduce the risk of security breaches.

Azure Security Center is a comprehensive solution that provides security monitoring, threat detection, and vulnerability assessment for your Azure environment.

You can use IaC templates to enable and configure Azure Security Center and its features, ensuring that security assessments and recommendations are consistently applied to your resources.

Identity and access management (IAM) is crucial for controlling and auditing access to Azure resources.

Azure Active Directory (Azure AD) is a central component for managing identities and access in Azure.

By integrating Azure AD into your IaC workflows, you can enforce secure identity management and authentication for users and applications.

Azure Multi-Factor Authentication (MFA) is an additional layer of security that can be enabled through IaC to require users to provide multiple forms of verification when signing in.

Auditing and monitoring are essential for detecting and responding to security incidents.

Azure Monitor provides a unified solution for collecting and analyzing telemetry data from Azure resources.

Through IaC, you can configure Azure Monitor settings, including log analytics, alerts, and dashboards, to ensure that you have visibility into the security of your Azure environment.

Security compliance is a critical consideration for organizations subject to regulatory requirements.

Azure Policy and Azure Blueprints, as mentioned earlier, can be used through IaC to enforce compliance standards and configurations.

You can create policy definitions and blueprints that align with regulatory frameworks and industry standards, ensuring that your Azure resources remain compliant.

To summarize, implementing security controls with Azure IaC is essential for safeguarding your cloud resources and maintaining a strong security posture.

By integrating RBAC, Azure Policy, Azure Key Vault, and other security features into your IaC workflows, you can enforce security policies, manage secrets securely, control network access, encrypt data, manage vulnerabilities, and maintain compliance.

By addressing security through IaC, you ensure that security measures are consistently applied across your Azure environment, reducing the risk of security breaches and data loss.

Chapter 6: Advanced Azure Networking with IaC

Compliance management and reporting are critical components of any organization's cloud governance strategy, particularly when utilizing Infrastructure as Code (IaC) in platforms like Azure.

Compliance refers to the adherence to regulatory requirements, industry standards, and internal policies that govern how an organization handles data and manages its infrastructure.

In the context of Azure IaC, compliance management involves ensuring that all deployed resources and configurations align with these rules and standards.

Organizations often need to meet various compliance standards, such as GDPR, HIPAA, PCI DSS, or ISO 27001, depending on their industry and geographic location.

Azure provides a robust set of tools and features to help organizations manage compliance effectively.

One such tool is Azure Policy, which allows organizations to define, enforce, and audit compliance policies across their Azure resources.

Using Azure Policy, you can create policy definitions that specify the rules and requirements that resources must adhere to.

These policies can cover a wide range of areas, from security and privacy to naming conventions and tagging standards.

When integrated with Azure IaC, policies can be applied automatically during resource deployment to ensure that configurations comply with organizational standards.

Organizations can also leverage the Azure Blueprints service to streamline compliance management further.

Azure Blueprints provides a way to package together various resources, such as policy assignments, role assignments, and resource templates, into a single reusable blueprint definition.

This enables organizations to enforce specific compliance requirements consistently across multiple environments, reducing the risk of configuration drift.

In addition to policy enforcement, compliance management often involves regular auditing and reporting.

Azure provides comprehensive auditing capabilities through Azure Monitor, which collects and stores telemetry data from Azure resources.

Organizations can use this data to track and monitor changes made to their resources and configurations.

Auditing logs can provide valuable insights into who performed specific actions, what changes were made, and when they occurred.

Azure Security Center is another powerful tool for compliance management and reporting.

It offers continuous security monitoring and threat detection, helping organizations identify and remediate security vulnerabilities and misconfigurations.

Security Center also provides compliance policies and recommendations based on industry standards and regulatory requirements, simplifying the compliance management process.

Through Azure IaC, organizations can automate the deployment and configuration of auditing and monitoring tools, ensuring that compliance reporting is consistently applied to all resources.

Compliance reporting is not only essential for internal governance but also for demonstrating adherence to external auditors and regulatory authorities.

Azure Policy and Azure Blueprints can generate compliance reports that show whether resources are meeting specific policy requirements.

These reports provide evidence of compliance and can be shared with auditors and stakeholders to demonstrate regulatory adherence.

Organizations may also need to perform custom compliance assessments to ensure that their Azure IaC configurations align with industry-specific standards.

Custom scripts and automation can be integrated into the IaC pipeline to perform these assessments regularly.

Once the compliance data is collected, organizations can generate compliance reports that summarize the status of resources and configurations.

These reports help organizations identify areas of non-compliance and take corrective actions to bring resources into compliance.

Additionally, organizations can use third-party compliance management solutions that integrate with Azure to provide advanced reporting and auditing capabilities.

These solutions offer predefined compliance checks, automated reporting, and dashboards to help organizations manage and demonstrate compliance more efficiently.

To maintain continuous compliance, organizations should establish a process for periodic reviews and updates of their Azure IaC templates and policies.

As new compliance standards or regulations emerge, organizations must adjust their policies and configurations accordingly.

Regularly reviewing and updating IaC templates and policies ensures that the Azure environment remains compliant with the latest requirements.

In summary, compliance management and reporting are essential aspects of Azure IaC governance.

By leveraging Azure Policy, Azure Blueprints, Azure Monitor, and Azure Security Center, organizations can enforce compliance policies, monitor configurations, and generate compliance reports automatically.

These tools, when integrated into the IaC workflow, help organizations demonstrate adherence to regulatory requirements and maintain a strong compliance posture in their Azure environment.

Configuring Azure networking for high availability is a fundamental aspect of building resilient and reliable applications in the cloud.

High availability ensures that your applications remain accessible and performant even in the face of failures or disruptions.

Azure provides a range of networking features and services that can be leveraged to achieve high availability.

One of the key considerations for high availability is the design of your virtual network (VNet).

Azure VNets allow you to create isolated network segments for your resources, and they serve as the foundation for your network architecture.

To achieve high availability, it's essential to design VNets with redundancy in mind.

Azure offers VNet peering, which enables you to connect VNets in the same region or across regions, creating a redundant network path for your resources.

This redundancy helps ensure that your applications remain accessible even if a portion of your network experiences issues.

Another critical aspect of high availability is the distribution of resources across multiple Azure availability zones.

Availability zones are physically separate data centers within an Azure region, each with its own power, cooling, and networking infrastructure.

By distributing resources across multiple availability zones, you reduce the risk of a single point of failure.

Azure Load Balancers play a vital role in achieving high availability for your applications.

Azure offers both Azure Standard Load Balancer and Azure Basic Load Balancer, each designed for specific use cases.

Standard Load Balancer provides a higher level of availability and includes features such as load balancing across availability zones, providing redundancy for your applications.

By configuring your application endpoints with Azure Load Balancer, you can distribute incoming traffic evenly, ensuring that your application remains accessible even if one of the backend instances fails.

Highly available network appliances, such as virtual network appliances and virtual firewalls, can be integrated into your Azure networking architecture to enhance security and redundancy.

These appliances can be deployed in an active-active or active-passive configuration, depending on your requirements.

In an active-active configuration, both instances of the appliance are actively processing traffic, providing load balancing and failover capabilities.

In an active-passive configuration, one instance remains active while the other acts as a standby, ready to take over in case of failure.

Azure also offers virtual network gateway redundancy for VPN and ExpressRoute connections.

By configuring gateway redundancy, you ensure that your network connectivity remains available even if one of the gateway instances experiences issues.

Azure Traffic Manager is another essential service for achieving high availability and load balancing.

Traffic Manager allows you to distribute incoming traffic across multiple endpoints, which can be Azure resources or external resources, based on various routing methods.

By configuring Traffic Manager with multiple endpoints in different regions or availability zones, you can ensure that your application remains available to users even if one region experiences a service disruption.

Azure Application Gateway is a layer 7 load balancer that provides advanced traffic management and security features.

It includes features such as SSL offloading, WAF (Web Application Firewall), and cookie-based session affinity.

Application Gateway can be configured with multiple instances and placed in different availability zones for high availability.

Ensuring the availability of your DNS (Domain Name System) is crucial for high availability.

Azure DNS is a reliable and scalable DNS hosting service that provides high availability for your domain names.

Azure DNS automatically replicates your DNS zones to multiple Azure name servers in different regions, ensuring redundancy and reliability.

Additionally, Azure Traffic Manager can be configured to use Azure DNS for routing traffic to the closest available endpoints, enhancing the availability of your applications.

Intraregion and interregion network redundancy are essential for achieving high availability.

Azure ExpressRoute is a dedicated network connection service that provides private and redundant connectivity between your on-premises data center and Azure.

By using ExpressRoute with multiple ExpressRoute circuits, you can ensure that your network connectivity to Azure remains available even if one circuit or connection experiences issues.

Azure Virtual WAN is a networking service that simplifies branch connectivity and provides global and local redundancy.

Virtual WAN allows you to connect multiple regions, on-premises locations, and remote users through a unified and scalable network infrastructure.

It provides automatic failover and built-in redundancy, ensuring that your network remains highly available.

Implementing Azure Backup for your virtual network resources is essential for high availability.

Azure Backup allows you to protect and recover virtual machines, virtual network appliances, and other resources.

By regularly backing up your critical network components, you can quickly restore them in the event of a failure or data loss, minimizing downtime.

Azure Monitor and Azure Security Center play a crucial role in maintaining high availability by providing continuous monitoring and threat detection.

Azure Monitor collects telemetry data from your resources, helping you identify performance issues and proactively address them.

Azure Security Center detects and alerts you to security threats, ensuring that your network remains secure and available.

In summary, configuring Azure networking for high availability involves designing redundant network architectures, distributing resources across availability zones, leveraging load balancers and traffic management services, implementing network appliance redundancy, and ensuring redundancy in network connections and DNS.

By carefully planning and implementing these strategies, you can achieve high availability for your Azure applications and services, ensuring that they remain accessible and reliable even in the face of disruptions or failures.

Testing strategies for Azure Infrastructure as Code (IaC) are essential for ensuring the reliability, security, and performance of your cloud infrastructure.

Testing allows you to identify and address issues early in the development process, reducing the risk of problems occurring in production.

One of the fundamental aspects of testing Azure IaC is validating the correctness of your templates and configurations.

This involves ensuring that your templates accurately define the desired state of your infrastructure and that they are free of syntax errors.

Tools like Azure Resource Manager (ARM) Template Linter and HashiCorp's Terraform **plan** command can help you perform static analysis of your templates to catch issues before deployment.

However, static analysis alone is not sufficient to validate the actual behavior of your infrastructure.

Dynamic testing, such as deploying your templates in a non-production environment, is crucial for uncovering runtime issues.

This involves creating a replica of your production environment in a separate Azure subscription or resource group and deploying your IaC templates there.

By doing so, you can verify that your templates correctly create and configure resources as expected.

You should test your IaC templates with various combinations of parameters and configurations to ensure they are robust and adaptable to different scenarios.

Another important aspect of testing Azure IaC is assessing the security of your infrastructure.

Security testing involves evaluating your templates and configurations for vulnerabilities and misconfigurations.

Tools like Azure Security Center and third-party security scanners can help you identify potential security risks in your IaC templates.

They can detect issues such as open ports, insecure network configurations, and public access to sensitive resources.

It's essential to conduct regular security assessments to address vulnerabilities promptly and enhance the security posture of your Azure infrastructure.

Performance testing is another critical aspect of Azure IaC testing. Performance tests evaluate the responsiveness, scalability, and efficiency of your infrastructure under different workloads.

You can use load testing tools to simulate user traffic and measure the performance of your applications and resources.

These tests help you identify performance bottlenecks, resource limitations, and areas that require optimization.

By conducting performance testing, you can ensure that your Azure IaC can handle the expected load and deliver a responsive user experience.

Automated testing plays a significant role in maintaining the reliability and consistency of your Azure IaC.

Automated tests are scripts or programs that can be run automatically to verify the functionality and correctness of your infrastructure.

For example, you can use tools like Pester for testing Azure PowerShell scripts or Terratest for testing Terraform configurations.

These tools enable you to write tests that validate specific aspects of your infrastructure, such as resource existence, configuration, and behavior.

Automated tests should cover both positive scenarios (e.g., resource creation) and negative scenarios (e.g., resource deletion) to ensure that your IaC behaves as expected in various situations.

Integration testing is crucial when your Azure IaC interacts with other Azure services or external systems.

Integration tests validate the interactions and dependencies between different components of your infrastructure.

For example, if your IaC provisions virtual machines that communicate with Azure databases, integration tests can verify that the VMs can successfully connect to and interact with the databases.

By conducting integration testing, you can identify issues related to connectivity, access controls, and data flow between different parts of your infrastructure.

Regression testing is an ongoing process that helps ensure that changes to your IaC templates do not introduce new issues or regressions.

Whenever you make updates to your templates or configurations, you should re-run your test suite to verify that existing functionality remains intact.

Regression testing helps catch unintended side effects of changes and provides confidence that your infrastructure still behaves correctly after updates.

To support effective testing, it's essential to establish a comprehensive test environment that closely resembles your production environment.

This includes replicating the network architecture, resource dependencies, and configurations of your production environment.

Having a well-defined test environment allows you to conduct tests in a controlled and representative environment, increasing the reliability of your test results.

Continuous integration (CI) and continuous delivery (CD) pipelines play a significant role in automating testing processes for Azure IaC.

In a CI/CD pipeline, automated tests can be integrated into the deployment workflow, ensuring that tests are executed whenever changes are made to your IaC templates.

This helps catch issues early in the development process and promotes a culture of testing and validation.

Monitoring and observability are essential for ongoing testing and validation of Azure IaC.

By implementing monitoring and logging solutions, you can gain insights into the behavior and performance of your infrastructure in real-time.

Azure Monitor, Azure Application Insights, and Azure Log Analytics are valuable tools for collecting and analyzing telemetry data from your resources.

Monitoring solutions help you detect anomalies, troubleshoot issues, and gather data for further testing and validation.

In summary, testing strategies for Azure Infrastructure as Code encompass various aspects, including correctness, security, performance, automation, integration, regression, and monitoring.

By adopting a comprehensive approach to testing, you can ensure that your Azure IaC remains reliable, secure, and performant throughout its lifecycle.

Testing should be an integral part of your Azure IaC development and deployment processes, enabling you to deliver high-quality cloud infrastructure that meets your organization's requirements and expectations.

Validation and error handling techniques are essential components of any software development process, ensuring that applications behave correctly and gracefully handle unexpected situations.

In the context of software development, validation refers to the process of checking data and inputs to ensure that they meet certain criteria or constraints.

Effective validation helps prevent data errors, improve data quality, and enhance the overall reliability of an application.

One common validation technique is input validation, which involves checking user inputs, such as form data, to ensure that they are within acceptable ranges and formats.

For example, a web application might validate user-provided email addresses to ensure they follow the correct format.

Input validation can help prevent common security vulnerabilities like SQL injection and cross-site scripting (XSS) attacks.

Error handling, on the other hand, involves dealing with unexpected or exceptional situations that may arise during the execution of an application.

Errors can occur due to various reasons, such as incorrect input data, network issues, or hardware failures.

Proper error handling ensures that an application can gracefully recover from errors, provide meaningful feedback to users, and maintain its stability.

One fundamental error handling technique is exception handling, which involves capturing and managing exceptions or errors that occur during program execution.

In many programming languages, exceptions are used to represent abnormal conditions, and developers can write code to handle these exceptions gracefully.

For example, if a file cannot be found when an application attempts to open it, an exception can be raised, and the application can provide a user-friendly error message instead of crashing.

Validation and error handling are closely related, as validation often leads to error handling when invalid data or conditions are encountered.

For example, during input validation, if a user enters an invalid date format, the application may raise an exception or generate an error message to inform the user of the problem.

Effective validation and error handling require a structured approach, starting with defining clear validation rules and error-handling strategies.

Validation rules should be well-documented and cover all possible scenarios, ensuring that data is checked comprehensively.

Developers should also consider both positive and negative test cases during validation, verifying that the application behaves correctly in various situations.

Input validation rules should be enforced both on the client side (e.g., in web forms using JavaScript) and on the server side to provide an additional layer of security.

When it comes to error handling, developers should follow best practices to create robust and maintainable code.

Error messages should be informative but not reveal sensitive information about the system's internals.

Instead of generic error messages like "An error occurred," specific messages that indicate the nature of the problem can be more helpful to users and support teams.

Logging is a critical aspect of error handling, as it allows developers to record information about errors for troubleshooting and debugging purposes.

Logs should capture details such as the error type, timestamp, user context, and a description of what happened leading up to the error.

A well-structured log can be invaluable for diagnosing issues in a production environment.

In addition to handling runtime errors, it's essential to validate data and inputs as early as possible in the application's workflow.

For instance, validating user inputs at the point of entry (e.g., web form submission) can prevent invalid data from propagating through the system and causing errors later on.

Validation should also be performed before persisting data in databases to ensure data consistency and integrity.

Error handling should include mechanisms for notifying system administrators or support teams when critical errors occur.

For example, in web applications, sending error notifications via email or integrating with error tracking tools can help ensure that issues are addressed promptly.

Validation and error handling should be an ongoing part of the development process, and developers should continuously review and update validation rules and error-handling strategies as the application evolves.

Automated testing, including unit tests, integration tests, and end-to-end tests, can help ensure that validation and error-handling code functions correctly and consistently.

During testing, developers can intentionally inject invalid data and unexpected conditions to verify that the application responds appropriately.

Code reviews and peer assessments can also be beneficial in identifying potential validation and error handling issues, as different perspectives can lead to more robust solutions.

In summary, validation and error handling techniques are crucial for building reliable and secure software applications.

Validation helps ensure data quality and security, while error handling allows applications to gracefully recover from unexpected situations.

Developers should follow best practices for defining validation rules, handling errors, and logging information for troubleshooting.

Continuous testing and code reviews help maintain the effectiveness of validation and error-handling code throughout the application's lifecycle.

By paying careful attention to validation and error handling, developers can create more robust and user-friendly applications that provide a better overall experience for users and administrators.

Chapter 8: Scaling and Optimization Strategies for Azure

Scaling your Azure resources dynamically is a fundamental aspect of cloud computing, allowing you to adapt to changing workloads and optimize resource usage.

Dynamic scaling enables your applications to handle increased traffic and demand without manual intervention, ensuring a seamless user experience.

Azure provides several services and techniques that empower you to scale your resources both vertically and horizontally based on your application's needs.

Vertical scaling, often referred to as scaling up or scaling in, involves increasing the capacity of individual resources, such as virtual machines (VMs) or database servers.

This approach is suitable when your application requires more processing power, memory, or storage.

Azure Virtual Machines support vertical scaling by allowing you to resize VMs to higher-tier configurations with more CPU and memory resources.

You can scale VMs vertically to accommodate increased workloads, and Azure provides options for manual and automatic scaling.

Azure SQL Database also supports vertical scaling by enabling you to change the performance tier to handle more significant database workloads.

For example, you can upgrade from a basic performance tier to a premium tier to gain access to more resources and improve database performance.

Horizontal scaling, also known as scaling out, involves adding more instances of a resource, such as VMs or web servers, to distribute the workload.

This approach is suitable for applications that need to handle a high volume of requests or concurrent users.

Azure provides several services that support horizontal scaling, including Azure Virtual Machine Scale Sets, Azure App Service, and Azure Kubernetes Service (AKS).

Azure Virtual Machine Scale Sets allow you to deploy and manage a set of identical VMs that can automatically scale based on demand.

You can define scaling rules that determine when new VM instances are added or removed from the set.

For web applications, Azure App Service offers built-in auto-scaling capabilities that can adjust the number of application instances based on metrics like CPU usage, memory consumption, and request throughput.

Azure Kubernetes Service (AKS) enables you to deploy containerized applications using Kubernetes orchestration, providing dynamic scaling for containers.

Kubernetes allows you to define replica sets and horizontal pod autoscalers to automatically adjust the number of container instances based on resource utilization.

Azure Functions and Azure Logic Apps provide serverless computing options that automatically scale to handle incoming events and triggers.

Azure Functions can execute code in response to events, such as HTTP requests or messages from Azure Event Grid or Azure Service Bus.

Azure Logic Apps allow you to create workflows that connect various services and systems, automatically scaling to handle the execution of workflows triggered by events.

To implement dynamic scaling effectively, it's essential to define clear scaling criteria and thresholds based on your application's performance metrics.

These criteria can include metrics like CPU usage, memory utilization, request latency, or queue depth.

Azure provides built-in monitoring and metrics collection through Azure Monitor, which allows you to create alerts and triggers for scaling actions based on specific conditions.

For example, you can configure an Azure Monitor alert to trigger an automatic scaling action when CPU usage exceeds a certain threshold for a specified duration.

Automation is a key component of dynamic scaling, as it allows you to respond to changes in resource demand quickly.

Azure offers automation tools like Azure Logic Apps, Azure Functions, and Azure Automation that can execute predefined scaling actions in response to alerts or triggers.

These tools enable you to create custom scaling logic to meet the specific requirements of your application.

Auto-scaling can be configured to scale both out and in, automatically adding or removing resources as needed.

Additionally, Azure allows you to define cooling periods and other policies to avoid excessive scaling operations triggered by short-term spikes in resource usage.

Testing and validation are critical aspects of implementing dynamic scaling to ensure that your scaling rules and configurations work as intended.

You should conduct load testing and performance testing to simulate different traffic patterns and assess how your application and resources respond to dynamic scaling.

By evaluating the results of these tests, you can fine-tune your scaling criteria and adjust scaling thresholds to optimize resource allocation.

Azure provides tools like Azure DevTest Labs and Azure Load Testing that can help you conduct realistic load tests and assess the performance of your applications under various conditions.

While dynamic scaling offers numerous benefits for managing resource allocation and improving application performance, it's essential to consider cost implications.

Scaling resources dynamically can increase your Azure usage costs, as additional resources are provisioned to meet demand.

To manage costs effectively, you can set budget limits, monitor spending, and use Azure Cost Management and Billing to gain visibility into your resource consumption.

Additionally, Azure offers cost-saving options like reserved instances, which provide discounts for long-term VM commitments, and auto-pause for databases and data warehouses, which can reduce costs during periods of inactivity.

In summary, scaling your Azure resources dynamically is a powerful strategy for optimizing resource utilization, improving application performance, and ensuring a seamless user experience.

Azure provides a range of services and tools to support both vertical and horizontal scaling, allowing you to respond to changing workloads and demand effectively.

By defining clear scaling criteria, automating scaling actions, conducting testing and validation, and considering cost implications, you can leverage dynamic scaling to build scalable and cost-effective applications in the Azure cloud.

Azure resource optimization best practices are essential for organizations seeking to maximize the value of their cloud investments while ensuring efficient resource utilization.

Resource optimization encompasses a set of strategies and techniques that help organizations minimize costs, improve performance, and enhance overall operational efficiency in their Azure environments.

One fundamental aspect of resource optimization is the continuous monitoring and analysis of resource usage patterns.

By regularly reviewing Azure resource usage data, organizations can gain insights into how their resources are being utilized and identify opportunities for optimization.

Azure provides tools like Azure Monitor and Azure Cost Management and Billing to help organizations track and analyze resource usage, enabling informed decision-making.

Organizations should establish clear policies and governance frameworks to govern resource provisioning and management in Azure.

These policies should define resource allocation limits, naming conventions, access controls, and resource tagging standards to ensure consistency and control.

By implementing resource governance practices, organizations can prevent resource sprawl, reduce operational risks, and maintain compliance with internal and external regulations.

Rightsizing resources is a crucial aspect of Azure resource optimization.

Rightsizing involves ensuring that Azure resources, such as virtual machines (VMs) and databases, are appropriately sized to match the actual workload requirements.

Organizations should regularly assess the performance and utilization of their resources and adjust resource sizes accordingly.

Azure provides tools like Azure Advisor and Azure VM Resize Recommendations to help organizations identify underutilized or oversized resources and make informed resizing decisions.

Another key optimization technique is the use of reserved instances (RIs) for virtual machines and other services.

Reserved instances allow organizations to commit to specific resource configurations for a predetermined period, typically one or three years, in exchange for significant cost savings compared to pay-as-you-go pricing.

By strategically purchasing RIs for their workloads, organizations can reduce their Azure spending while maintaining resource availability.

Resource consolidation is another optimization strategy that organizations can leverage to reduce costs and improve resource utilization.

Resource consolidation involves combining multiple workloads onto fewer resources or services to eliminate redundancy and reduce the overall number of resources in use.

This can be achieved through techniques like virtual machine scale sets, containerization, and serverless computing, which enable organizations to optimize resource usage by sharing resources efficiently.

Azure offers a variety of options for optimizing storage costs.

One common practice is tiered storage, which involves storing data in different storage tiers based on its access patterns and requirements.

Azure Blob Storage, for example, offers hot, cool, and archive storage tiers with varying prices, making it cost-effective for organizations to store data based on its access frequency.

Organizations should regularly review their storage usage and migrate data to appropriate storage tiers to optimize costs.

Automation is a powerful tool for Azure resource optimization.

By automating resource provisioning, scaling, and management tasks, organizations can reduce operational overhead and ensure that resources are provisioned and de-provisioned efficiently based on workload demands.

Azure offers automation capabilities through Azure Resource Manager templates, Azure DevOps, and tools like Azure Logic Apps and Azure Functions.

Resource tagging is a fundamental practice for resource organization and cost allocation.

By applying tags to Azure resources, organizations can categorize resources based on attributes such as environment, department, project, or owner.

Resource tagging helps organizations track costs and allocate expenses accurately, enabling better cost management and accountability.

Cost allocation and chargeback mechanisms should be established to align Azure costs with business units, departments, or projects.

This ensures that the cost of using Azure resources is transparent and accountable to the appropriate stakeholders.

Azure Cost Management and Billing provides capabilities for cost allocation and can integrate with Azure Active Directory for user access control.

Organizations should regularly review and optimize their Azure resource configurations.

Over time, workloads and resource requirements may change, making it necessary to adjust resource configurations to align with current needs.

This includes reviewing virtual machine configurations, network settings, security rules, and other resource attributes to ensure they are still appropriate.

Resource configuration management tools like Azure Automation Desired State Configuration (DSC) can help organizations enforce consistent and compliant resource configurations.

Resource cleanup and decommissioning practices are essential for Azure resource optimization.

Organizations should regularly identify and decommission resources that are no longer needed or in use.

This includes de-provisioning VMs, deleting unused storage accounts, and retiring obsolete databases.

Azure Policy and Azure Automation can help organizations automate resource cleanup and enforce resource lifecycle management.

Cost tracking and reporting are integral to resource optimization efforts.

Organizations should leverage Azure Cost Management and Billing to track and report on Azure spending, usage trends, and cost-saving opportunities.

Regularly reviewing cost reports and dashboards can help organizations identify areas where cost optimization efforts can be focused for maximum impact.

Lastly, organizations should promote a culture of resource optimization and cost consciousness among their teams.

By fostering awareness of resource costs and the impact of resource usage on the organization's bottom line, organizations can encourage employees to make resource-efficient choices and contribute to overall cost optimization efforts.

In summary, Azure resource optimization best practices are crucial for organizations seeking to achieve cost-effective and efficient Azure deployments.

These practices involve continuous monitoring, governance, rightsizing, reserved instances, resource consolidation, storage optimization, automation, tagging, cost allocation, configuration management, resource cleanup, and a culture of cost consciousness.

By implementing these strategies and techniques, organizations can achieve better cost control, improve resource utilization, and maximize the value of their Azure investments.

Chapter 9: Implementing Continuous Integration and Deployment (CI/CD) in Azure

Azure CI/CD pipelines for Infrastructure as Code (IaC) play a pivotal role in modern software development and cloud operations.

These pipelines automate the process of building, testing, and deploying infrastructure, allowing organizations to achieve rapid and reliable deployments.

Azure provides a robust set of tools and services to facilitate the implementation of CI/CD pipelines for IaC.

One of the core concepts of CI/CD is continuous integration, which involves frequently merging code changes into a shared repository and automatically verifying the integrity of the codebase.

In the context of IaC, continuous integration extends to the code that defines infrastructure resources, such as Azure Resource Manager (ARM) templates or Terraform configurations.

Azure DevOps Services, a cloud-hosted DevOps platform, offers features for source code version control, including Git repositories, where IaC code can be stored and managed.

Developers working on IaC can use Git to track changes, collaborate, and ensure that code is continuously integrated into a central repository.

Azure DevOps also provides features for defining build pipelines, which are responsible for building IaC code, running validation tests, and producing deployment artifacts.

Build pipelines can be configured to trigger automatically when changes are pushed to the source code repository.

For instance, when a developer commits changes to an Azure Resource Manager template, a build pipeline can be initiated to validate the template's syntax and structure.

This early feedback loop helps catch issues in IaC code before deployment, reducing the risk of errors in the infrastructure.

Azure DevOps supports the use of agent pools, which are virtual machines that execute the build and test tasks defined in the pipeline.

These agent pools can be customized to include specific tools, libraries, and configurations required for building and validating IaC code.

In addition to Azure DevOps, Azure provides Azure Pipeline as a dedicated CI/CD service that can be used independently or integrated into other DevOps platforms.

Azure Pipelines allows organizations to define multi-stage workflows for building and deploying IaC code to Azure environments.

These pipelines can include tasks like linting IaC code, running unit tests, and validating compliance with organizational policies.

Once IaC code passes all validation checks in the build pipeline, it can proceed to the deployment phase.

Continuous deployment (CD) is the next critical aspect of CI/CD pipelines for IaC.

Azure Pipelines and Azure DevOps offer release pipelines, which automate the deployment of IaC resources to Azure environments.

Release pipelines consist of environments that represent different deployment stages, such as development, staging, and production.

Each environment can have specific deployment tasks and approval gates to control the release process.

Azure Resource Manager (ARM) templates, Terraform configurations, or other IaC code artifacts are typically stored in version-controlled repositories and linked to the release pipeline.

When a new version of IaC code is ready for deployment, it can be triggered to move through the defined stages of the release pipeline.

For instance, in a development environment, IaC code may be deployed automatically upon successful validation.

In contrast, the staging environment may require manual approval before deploying changes to production.

Infrastructure validation is an integral part of the CD process for IaC.

Before deploying changes, organizations can incorporate policy-based compliance checks to ensure that the IaC code adheres to security, governance, and compliance standards.

Azure Policy and Azure Security Center provide tools and capabilities to enforce and validate resource configurations against predefined policies.

These checks help mitigate potential security risks and compliance violations.

In the CD pipeline, deployment tasks typically involve using tools like Azure CLI, PowerShell, or Terraform to apply the IaC code and create or update Azure resources.

Once the deployment is complete, post-deployment validation tests can be executed to confirm that the infrastructure is in the desired state.

Testing can include verifying resource connectivity, evaluating performance, and running integration tests on deployed services.

Continuous monitoring and feedback are essential components of Azure CI/CD pipelines for IaC.

Azure Monitor and Application Insights can provide real-time telemetry data and insights into the performance and health of deployed resources.

Monitoring allows organizations to detect issues promptly, troubleshoot problems, and gather data for future optimizations.

Feedback mechanisms can trigger automated rollback procedures in case of deployment failures or performance degradation, ensuring that the infrastructure remains stable and resilient.

Rollback strategies are a critical consideration in CI/CD pipelines for IaC.

They enable organizations to revert to a known-good state if issues arise during deployment.

Azure DevOps and Azure Pipelines support rollbacks by allowing organizations to define automated procedures to reverse changes in case of deployment failures.

These procedures may involve applying a previous version of IaC code or invoking Azure CLI commands to undo specific resource modifications.

Additionally, organizations should establish a robust change management process that includes change tracking, documentation, and auditing.

This process ensures that all changes to IaC code are well-documented, reviewed, and approved before they are promoted to production environments.

Azure DevOps and Azure Pipelines can help organizations enforce these processes by integrating with change management and issue tracking systems.

Finally, organizations should continuously evaluate and refine their CI/CD pipelines for IaC.

As infrastructure requirements evolve and new Azure services become available, pipelines should be updated to reflect these changes.

Regularly reviewing and optimizing the CI/CD process helps organizations maintain agility, reliability, and efficiency in managing their Azure infrastructure.

In summary, Azure CI/CD pipelines for IaC are instrumental in streamlining the deployment of infrastructure resources on the Azure platform.

These pipelines leverage continuous integration and continuous deployment principles, integrating source code management, build processes, validation checks, and automated deployment procedures.

By implementing these pipelines effectively, organizations can accelerate the delivery of infrastructure changes, improve reliability, and ensure that their Azure environments remain secure and compliant with policies and standards. Automated testing and deployment workflows are crucial components of modern software development and infrastructure management.

These workflows streamline the process of delivering software updates, changes, and infrastructure configurations while maintaining reliability and minimizing human error.

Automation is essential for ensuring that new code changes and infrastructure configurations are thoroughly tested and deployed without manual intervention.

Automated testing allows organizations to validate that the code or infrastructure changes meet quality, security, and performance criteria.

In the context of software development, automated testing encompasses various types of tests, such as unit tests, integration tests, and end-to-end tests.

For infrastructure as code (IaC), automated testing focuses on verifying that infrastructure configurations are correct and comply with organizational policies and best practices.

Automated testing of IaC involves tools and frameworks that can evaluate configuration files, templates, or scripts to identify potential issues before deployment.

Continuous Integration (CI) is a fundamental concept in automated testing and deployment workflows.

CI involves automatically building, testing, and validating code changes or infrastructure configurations whenever new code is committed to a version control repository.

CI pipelines are responsible for running automated tests and checks to ensure that the code or IaC changes do not introduce regressions or issues.

GitHub Actions, Azure DevOps Pipelines, Jenkins, and GitLab CI/CD are popular CI/CD platforms that facilitate the automation of testing and deployment workflows.

In a typical CI/CD workflow, code changes are committed to a version control system like Git.

Whenever a commit is made, the CI/CD pipeline is triggered to initiate the build and test processes.

For software development, the pipeline may include steps to compile code, run unit tests, and package the application.

For IaC, the pipeline may validate that the infrastructure code is syntactically correct, adhere to naming conventions, and conform to security and compliance policies.

Automated testing plays a pivotal role in providing rapid feedback to developers and infrastructure engineers.

When a code change or infrastructure configuration fails automated tests, the CI/CD pipeline alerts the team, making it possible to address issues early in the development or deployment process.

Integration tests in the CI/CD pipeline ensure that different components of the software or infrastructure work together as expected.

For IaC, integration tests may involve validating that various resources interact correctly and that dependencies are properly configured.

End-to-end tests for software applications simulate real-world user interactions, while for IaC, they may involve deploying the entire infrastructure stack in a test environment and validating its functionality.

Automated testing is not limited to functional testing; it also encompasses security and compliance checks.

Security testing tools, such as static code analysis and vulnerability scanners, can be integrated into the CI/CD pipeline to identify security weaknesses or vulnerabilities in code or infrastructure configurations.

Compliance checks help ensure that the code or infrastructure adheres to industry-specific regulations and internal policies.

Once automated tests have been executed successfully, the CI/CD pipeline proceeds to the deployment phase.

Automated deployment aims to deliver code changes or infrastructure configurations to a target environment, such as a staging or production environment, without manual intervention.

Deployment automation reduces the risk of human error and ensures consistency in the deployment process.

Infrastructure as code (IaC) benefits significantly from automated deployment workflows.

IaC tools like Terraform, Azure Resource Manager (ARM) templates, and AWS CloudFormation support automated deployments.

These tools use declarative configuration files that specify the desired state of infrastructure.

The CI/CD pipeline triggers the IaC tool to apply the changes defined in the configuration files to the target environment.

For software applications, containerization and orchestration technologies like Docker and Kubernetes are commonly used for automated deployments.

Containers encapsulate the application and its dependencies, ensuring consistency between development, testing, and production environments.

Kubernetes orchestrates the deployment, scaling, and management of containerized applications, automating many operational tasks.

Infrastructure provisioning tools like Ansible and Puppet automate the configuration and setup of servers and networking components.

Infrastructure as Code (IaC) allows organizations to define and manage infrastructure resources programmatically.

IaC templates describe the desired state of infrastructure resources, such as virtual machines, storage, and networking, using code.

This code can be version-controlled, reviewed, and tested, just like application code.

Automated testing and deployment workflows for IaC templates ensure that infrastructure changes are predictable, repeatable, and error-free.

Rollback strategies are an important aspect of automated deployment workflows.

In the event of a deployment failure or unforeseen issues, organizations need a mechanism to revert to a known-good state.

Automated deployments should incorporate procedures to roll back changes and restore the previous state of the infrastructure or application.

For IaC, this may involve applying a previous version of the configuration files or using the "destroy" capability of IaC tools to remove the problematic resources.

Automated testing and deployment workflows also support blue-green deployments and canary releases.

Blue-green deployments involve maintaining two identical environments: one with the current production version (blue) and one with the new version (green).

Automated testing ensures that the green environment is functioning correctly before traffic is switched to it.

Canary releases involve gradually deploying changes to a subset of users or resources to minimize risk.

Automated testing and monitoring help determine if the new version performs as expected, and if issues arise, automated rollback mechanisms can be triggered.

Continuous monitoring and feedback loops are essential components of automated testing and deployment workflows.

Monitoring tools provide real-time insights into the performance and health of deployed applications and infrastructure.

Metrics, logs, and alerts help detect issues promptly and enable teams to respond quickly to incidents.

Feedback loops from monitoring systems can trigger automated actions, such as scaling resources up or down in response to changing demand.

Regularly reviewing and optimizing automated testing and deployment workflows is crucial.

As software and infrastructure evolve, workflows should adapt to accommodate new technologies, best practices, and organizational requirements.

Feedback from monitoring and incident response should inform ongoing improvements to the automation process.

Collaboration between development, operations, and security teams is essential to ensure that automated testing and deployment workflows meet all requirements and align with the organization's goals.

In summary, automated testing and deployment workflows are indispensable for modern software development and infrastructure management.

They facilitate the rapid and reliable delivery of code changes and infrastructure configurations while maintaining high-quality standards.

Automation reduces human error, provides rapid feedback, supports rollbacks, enables blue-green deployments and canary releases, and ensures continuous monitoring and optimization. By implementing robust automated workflows, organizations can streamline their development and operations processes, enhance reliability, and respond more effectively to changing business needs.

Chapter 10: Real-world Azure IaC Best Practices and Case Studies

In this case study, we'll explore the deployment of a scalable web application using Infrastructure as Code (IaC) principles and cloud services.

Imagine a scenario where a startup company is launching a new web application that's expected to experience rapid growth in user traffic.

To meet the scalability and availability requirements, the team decides to leverage cloud resources and implement IaC.

The first step in this case study is to define the architecture of the web application and its infrastructure requirements.

The application consists of a front-end component hosted on a web server, a back-end API server, and a database.

For scalability, the team plans to use a load balancer to distribute incoming traffic across multiple instances of the front-end and back-end servers.

To achieve this, they will utilize a cloud provider's load balancing service.

With the architecture in mind, the team starts by selecting a cloud provider to host their application.

In this case, they opt for Amazon Web Services (AWS) due to its robust set of cloud services and global presence.

The next step is to set up the development environment and tools required for IaC.

The team chooses Terraform, an open-source IaC tool, to define and manage their infrastructure.

They install Terraform on their local development machines and set up version control for their IaC code using Git.

With Terraform in place, they can begin defining the infrastructure resources required for their web application.

They start by creating Terraform configuration files that describe the cloud resources, such as virtual machines, databases, and networking components.

The configuration files are written in HashiCorp Configuration Language (HCL), a language specifically designed for defining infrastructure as code.

The team divides the infrastructure definition into modules, making it more manageable and reusable.

For example, they create separate Terraform modules for the front-end servers, back-end servers, database, and load balancer.

Each module encapsulates the configuration details and dependencies for a specific resource type.

Once the Terraform configuration files are ready, the team initializes their Terraform workspace by running the "terraform init" command.

This step downloads the necessary provider plugins and prepares the environment for managing infrastructure.

Next, they create a Terraform execution plan using the "terraform plan" command.

The plan outlines the changes that Terraform will make to the cloud infrastructure to bring it in line with the desired state defined in the configuration files.

The team reviews the plan to ensure that it matches their expectations and doesn't introduce any unexpected changes.

With confidence in the plan, they execute it by running "terraform apply."

Terraform communicates with the AWS API to create the defined resources, such as virtual machines, databases, and load balancers.

The deployment process is automated and reproducible, ensuring consistency across different environments.

As part of their IaC best practices, the team tags their resources with metadata, such as environment, owner, and purpose, to enhance resource management and visibility.

Once the infrastructure is provisioned, the team deploys their web application code to the newly created virtual machines.

They use a version control system, such as Git, to manage the application codebase.

Continuous integration and continuous deployment (CI/CD) pipelines are set up to automate the testing and deployment of application updates.

This ensures that code changes are thoroughly tested before being deployed to production.

To further enhance security, the team configures security groups, network ACLs, and IAM (Identity and Access Management) policies to control access to their resources and enforce least privilege access principles.

They also implement logging and monitoring solutions to gain insights into the performance and health of their infrastructure.

AWS CloudWatch is used to collect and visualize metrics, while CloudTrail logs provide an audit trail of API activity.

Additionally, the team sets up alerts to receive notifications in case of unexpected incidents or resource scaling events.

As the web application gains popularity and user traffic increases, the team monitors the performance and scalability of their infrastructure.

Using the insights from monitoring data, they can make informed decisions about scaling resources up or down to accommodate changing demands.

When traffic surges, the auto-scaling feature of the load balancer automatically adds more instances of the web servers to handle the increased load.

This dynamic scaling ensures that the application remains responsive and available during peak usage periods.

With IaC in place, the team can easily replicate their infrastructure in multiple regions to achieve high availability and disaster recovery capabilities.

They use Terraform workspaces to manage different environments, such as development, staging, and production, with separate configurations.

This separation of environments ensures that changes are tested thoroughly before being promoted to production.

In summary, this case study demonstrates the effective use of Infrastructure as Code (IaC) principles and cloud services to deploy a scalable and highly available web application.

By defining their infrastructure as code, leveraging a cloud provider's resources, and implementing automation and best practices, the team can easily manage and scale their application infrastructure as it grows to meet user demand.

IaC, combined with continuous integration and continuous deployment (CI/CD) pipelines, provides the agility and reliability needed to succeed in a competitive and fast-paced digital landscape.

In this case study, we'll delve into the deployment of a data analytics platform in Microsoft Azure, highlighting the utilization of Infrastructure as Code (IaC) principles and Azure services.

Imagine a scenario where a data-driven organization aims to establish a robust data analytics platform to process and derive insights from large volumes of data.

To accomplish this, the organization decides to leverage the scalability and analytical capabilities of Azure's cloud services while embracing IaC for infrastructure management.

The initial step in this case study involves defining the architecture and requirements of the data analytics platform.

The platform is designed to ingest, process, and analyze various types of data, including structured, semi-structured, and unstructured data sources.

To accommodate the diverse data processing needs, the architecture includes Azure Data Lake Storage, Azure Databricks, and Azure Synapse Analytics (formerly known as SQL Data Warehouse).

To ensure data security and compliance, the organization integrates Azure Active Directory for identity and access management and Azure Security Center for threat protection.

With the architecture outlined, the organization chooses Microsoft Azure as the cloud provider due to its comprehensive set of data analytics services and strong security features.

The next crucial step is to set up the development environment and tools required for implementing IaC in Azure.

For this purpose, the organization selects Azure Resource Manager (ARM) templates as the IaC solution and installs the

Azure CLI (Command Line Interface) on local development machines.

They also adopt Git for version control to track changes in their IaC code effectively.

Having the IaC toolchain in place, the organization proceeds to define the infrastructure using ARM templates, a JSON-based language for describing Azure resources and their configurations.

They organize the templates into logical modules, each responsible for provisioning specific resources, such as data lakes, data pipelines, and analytics clusters.

Modularization allows for easier management and reusability of infrastructure definitions.

To ensure consistency and predictability in deployments, the organization adheres to IaC best practices, maintaining separate templates for each environment, including development, testing, and production.

To further enhance collaboration and maintain a history of changes, they leverage Git branches for managing different environment configurations.

Once the ARM templates are created, the organization initializes their Azure environment using Azure CLI commands to set up the necessary Azure resources, including resource groups and storage accounts.

With the environment prepared, they execute the ARM templates using the "az deployment group create" command, which deploys the infrastructure defined in the templates to Azure.

This automation ensures that the deployment process is both repeatable and consistent across environments.

In line with IaC principles, the organization tags Azure resources with metadata, such as environment, owner, and cost center, to improve resource management and cost tracking.

The tagging strategy also supports governance and compliance requirements.

After provisioning the infrastructure, the organization focuses on deploying data analytics workloads to the Azure platform.

They utilize Azure Data Factory to create data pipelines that orchestrate data movement and transformation tasks.

Azure Databricks serves as the analytics engine, enabling data engineers and data scientists to collaborate on data processing and machine learning tasks.

Azure Synapse Analytics is employed for data warehousing and querying to derive actionable insights from the processed data.

As part of the IaC strategy, the organization integrates Azure DevOps for continuous integration and continuous deployment (CI/CD) pipelines to automate the deployment of data analytics workloads.

These pipelines automate the testing, validation, and deployment of data processing workflows, ensuring the reliability of the platform.

Security is a paramount concern, and the organization implements role-based access control (RBAC) and Azure Policies to restrict access and enforce compliance with security standards.

Azure Key Vault is used to manage and safeguard secrets and keys used by the data analytics platform.

Auditing and monitoring are essential components of the platform's security posture.

Azure Monitor, along with Azure Security Center, provides continuous monitoring, alerting, and threat detection capabilities.

To further strengthen data security, data encryption is applied at rest and in transit using Azure-native encryption mechanisms.

As the data analytics platform matures, the organization closely monitors its performance, resource utilization, and costs.

Azure Monitor and Azure Cost Management enable the organization to gain insights into the platform's health and resource consumption.

Monitoring dashboards and alerts are configured to proactively identify and address issues.

To ensure cost efficiency, the organization regularly reviews resource utilization and adjusts resource provisioning to match actual workloads.

As data volumes increase or decrease, they scale resources up or down dynamically to optimize costs while meeting performance requirements.

High availability and disaster recovery considerations are also essential aspects of the platform's operation.

The organization replicates data across Azure regions to achieve data redundancy and failover capabilities.

They implement Azure Site Recovery to ensure business continuity in case of regional outages.

In summary, this case study highlights the successful deployment of a data analytics platform in Microsoft Azure, emphasizing the adoption of Infrastructure as Code (IaC) principles and Azure services.

By defining their infrastructure as code, automating deployments, and integrating security, monitoring, and cost management, the organization can effectively process and analyze vast amounts of data while maintaining scalability, reliability, and security.

The implementation of IaC and CI/CD pipelines streamlines the management of the platform, ensuring consistency and facilitating rapid updates and improvements.

In a data-driven world, such a platform enables organizations to derive valuable insights and make informed decisions to drive business success.

Book 4
Kubernetes Infrastructure as Code
Expert Strategies and Beyond

ROB BOTWRIGHT

Chapter 1: Introduction to Kubernetes and Infrastructure as Code (IaC)

Kubernetes, often abbreviated as K8s, is an open-source container orchestration platform that simplifies the management of containerized applications.

At its core, Kubernetes provides a framework for automating the deployment, scaling, and management of containerized workloads.

It was originally developed by Google and later donated to the Cloud Native Computing Foundation (CNCF), which oversees its development.

Kubernetes is designed to work with container runtimes like Docker and containerd, allowing users to package their applications and dependencies into lightweight containers.

Containers are a portable and consistent way to package and run applications, making them ideal for cloud-native and microservices architectures.

Kubernetes abstracts away the underlying infrastructure, enabling developers to focus on application logic rather than infrastructure management.

One of the fundamental concepts in Kubernetes is the "Pod."

A Pod is the smallest deployable unit in Kubernetes and represents a single instance of a running process in a cluster.

Pods can contain one or more containers that share the same network namespace and storage volumes.

This allows containers within the same Pod to communicate with each other using localhost, simplifying inter-container communication.

Pods are designed to be ephemeral, meaning they can be easily created, destroyed, and replaced.

Kubernetes takes care of distributing Pods across the cluster, ensuring high availability and efficient resource utilization.

To manage the deployment of Pods, Kubernetes introduces the concept of a "Controller."

Controllers are responsible for maintaining the desired state of a set of Pods and ensuring that the desired number of replicas is running at all times.

One common type of controller is the "Deployment," which allows users to define a desired state, such as the number of replicas and the container image to use.

Kubernetes automatically reconciles the desired state with the actual state, making adjustments as necessary.

Another crucial component in Kubernetes is the "Service."

A Service defines a set of Pods and a policy for accessing them.

Services provide network abstraction, allowing clients to connect to Pods using a stable IP address and DNS name, even as Pods are created or replaced.

This abstraction enables load balancing and service discovery within the cluster.

Kubernetes also supports "Ingress Controllers," which allow external access to services within the cluster.

Ingress Controllers provide features like HTTP routing, SSL termination, and path-based routing to route external traffic to the appropriate services.

Kubernetes offers a powerful way to manage configuration data through "ConfigMaps" and "Secrets."

ConfigMaps allow you to decouple configuration data from the application code, making it easier to change configuration without modifying the application itself.

Secrets are used to store sensitive information, such as API keys or passwords, securely.

Kubernetes ensures that ConfigMaps and Secrets are mounted as files or environment variables in containers, keeping sensitive data safe.

Another essential feature in Kubernetes is "Volume" support.

Volumes provide a way to persist data beyond the lifecycle of a Pod.

Kubernetes supports various types of volumes, including local storage, network storage, and cloud storage providers like AWS EBS or Azure Disk.

Persistent Volumes (PVs) and Persistent Volume Claims (PVCs) are used to manage storage resources and bind them to Pods.

Kubernetes offers a declarative approach to defining the desired state of the cluster using "YAML" or "JSON" configuration files.

Users describe the desired state of resources like Pods, Services, and Deployments in these files, and Kubernetes reconciles the actual state to match the desired state.

This declarative approach is crucial for infrastructure as code and automation.

Kubernetes also includes a robust set of "Labels" and "Annotations" for metadata management.

Labels are key-value pairs that can be attached to resources, allowing users to organize and categorize resources for various purposes, such as deployment strategies and monitoring.

Annotations are used to attach additional metadata to resources for documentation and other informational purposes.

Kubernetes provides "Namespaces" as a way to create isolated environments within a cluster.

Namespaces enable multi-tenancy by partitioning a cluster into multiple virtual clusters, each with its own set of resources and policies.

This isolation is valuable for organizations running multiple applications or teams within the same cluster.

Kubernetes supports "Horizontal Pod Autoscaling" to automatically adjust the number of replicas based on resource utilization or custom metrics.

Autoscaling ensures that applications can handle varying workloads efficiently.

Kubernetes also integrates with a wide range of cloud providers and storage solutions, making it adaptable to different infrastructure environments.

One of Kubernetes' strengths is its vibrant ecosystem of extensions and add-ons.

The Kubernetes community maintains a marketplace of extensions, including monitoring tools like Prometheus, logging solutions like Fluentd, and networking plugins like Calico and Cilium.

These extensions enhance Kubernetes' capabilities and cater to specific use cases.

To manage and interact with Kubernetes clusters, users typically employ a "kubectl" command-line tool.

Kubectl allows users to create, inspect, and modify resources in a Kubernetes cluster.

It communicates with the Kubernetes API server to perform operations on the cluster.

Kubernetes is designed to be highly available and fault-tolerant.

It achieves this by running multiple control plane components (such as the API server, controller manager, and scheduler) across multiple nodes in the cluster.

This redundancy ensures that the control plane remains operational even if some nodes fail.

Kubernetes also supports "etcd" as the distributed data store for storing configuration data and cluster state.

Etcd is designed for high availability and consistency, making it a reliable foundation for Kubernetes.

Kubernetes is suitable for a wide range of applications and use cases.

It excels in scenarios where applications need to scale dynamically, require high availability, or leverage microservices architectures.

Many organizations have adopted Kubernetes to streamline their application deployment, increase resource utilization, and simplify infrastructure management.

As you delve deeper into Kubernetes, you'll explore more advanced topics like "StatefulSets" for managing stateful applications, "Custom Resource Definitions" (CRDs) for extending Kubernetes with custom resources, and "Operators" for automating complex operational tasks.

In summary, Kubernetes is a powerful container orchestration platform that empowers organizations to manage containerized workloads efficiently.

Its declarative configuration, extensive ecosystem, and robust automation capabilities make it a valuable tool for building, deploying, and scaling containerized applications in a cloud-native world.

Implementing Infrastructure as Code (IaC) with Kubernetes offers a plethora of benefits that significantly enhance the management and operation of containerized workloads.

One of the primary advantages of using IaC with Kubernetes is the automation of infrastructure provisioning and management.

By defining infrastructure as code, organizations can automate the deployment of Kubernetes clusters and related resources, reducing manual intervention and the risk of human error.

This automation leads to faster and more reliable infrastructure setup, a crucial factor in today's fast-paced development environments.

With IaC and Kubernetes, infrastructure can be treated as code, versioned, and stored in source control repositories, providing a historical record of changes and enabling collaboration among team members.

This versioning and source control approach enhances transparency and accountability in infrastructure management.

IaC allows for the codification of infrastructure best practices and standards, ensuring that infrastructure is consistently provisioned and configured according to predefined guidelines.

This consistency helps maintain a secure and compliant infrastructure environment.

Kubernetes, as a container orchestration platform, is known for its ability to scale applications horizontally and automatically.

By combining IaC with Kubernetes, organizations can dynamically scale their infrastructure to handle varying workloads efficiently.

This scalability ensures that applications remain responsive and available during peak usage periods.

Infrastructure as Code with Kubernetes promotes infrastructure immutability, where infrastructure components are treated as disposable and replaceable.

When changes are required, new infrastructure is provisioned with the desired configuration, and the old infrastructure is decommissioned.

This immutability simplifies troubleshooting, as issues can often be resolved by replacing problematic components rather than attempting to repair them.

IaC with Kubernetes enables organizations to embrace a DevOps culture by fostering collaboration between development and operations teams.

Developers can define infrastructure requirements using code, and operations teams can manage the underlying infrastructure more effectively through automation.

This collaboration accelerates the delivery of applications and reduces friction between teams.

Another notable benefit of IaC with Kubernetes is the ability to version infrastructure configurations and roll back to previous states if needed.

This versioning provides a safety net in case of unexpected issues during infrastructure updates or changes.

Infrastructure changes can be thoroughly tested in a staging environment before being applied to production, reducing the risk of disruptions.

Kubernetes is renowned for its self-healing capabilities, such as automatic container rescheduling and node replacement.

When combined with IaC, these self-healing mechanisms ensure that infrastructure is continuously monitored and maintained according to the desired state.

This proactive approach minimizes downtime and improves system reliability.

IaC with Kubernetes simplifies disaster recovery by enabling the recreation of entire environments, including clusters, in a consistent and repeatable manner.

In the event of a catastrophic failure, organizations can quickly redeploy infrastructure to recover critical services.

The declarative nature of IaC and Kubernetes allows organizations to define infrastructure requirements using code that describes the desired state of resources.

Kubernetes continuously monitors the actual state and automatically reconciles it with the declared state.

This self-regulation ensures that infrastructure remains in the intended configuration, reducing configuration drift.

Kubernetes' support for container orchestration simplifies the deployment and scaling of microservices-based applications.

IaC complements this by automating the setup of the underlying infrastructure and networking required for microservices.

The combination of IaC and Kubernetes fosters a culture of experimentation and innovation by allowing teams to rapidly prototype and deploy new infrastructure configurations.

This agility is essential for staying competitive and adapting to changing business requirements.

IaC with Kubernetes facilitates infrastructure testing by providing the ability to create and destroy infrastructure quickly.

This enables organizations to validate changes, assess the impact of new configurations, and conduct thorough testing before deploying changes to production.

Kubernetes' extensibility allows organizations to integrate various tools and services into their infrastructure automation workflows.

IaC can be extended to include custom automation scripts and third-party tools, enabling a tailored approach to infrastructure management.

IaC with Kubernetes promotes cost optimization by allowing organizations to define infrastructure resources based on actual usage and requirements.

Resources can be dynamically scaled up or down, optimizing resource allocation and reducing infrastructure costs.

Kubernetes' support for multi-cloud and hybrid cloud deployments aligns well with the flexibility and portability provided by IaC.

Organizations can define infrastructure configurations that are cloud-agnostic, making it easier to migrate workloads between cloud providers or maintain hybrid environments.

IaC with Kubernetes simplifies security and compliance by codifying security policies and compliance standards into infrastructure definitions.

Organizations can enforce security controls and compliance requirements consistently across all environments.

Kubernetes' role-based access control (RBAC) and pod security policies enhance security, and IaC helps ensure that these security measures are applied consistently.

Implementing IaC with Kubernetes introduces a learning curve, as it requires teams to become proficient in both Kubernetes and IaC concepts and tools.

Additionally, organizations must invest in the development of infrastructure code and automation scripts.

However, these initial challenges are offset by the long-term benefits of increased efficiency, reliability, and agility.

The synergy between IaC and Kubernetes empowers organizations to modernize their infrastructure operations, accelerate application development, and meet the demands of a dynamic and competitive business landscape.

Ultimately, the adoption of IaC with Kubernetes positions organizations for greater success in their cloud-native journey.

Chapter 2: Setting Up Your Kubernetes Cluster for IaC

Preparing your Kubernetes environment is a critical step in the journey to effectively manage containerized workloads using Kubernetes.

This preparation involves several key considerations and actions that will set the stage for successful Kubernetes deployment and operation.

Before diving into Kubernetes, it's essential to assess your organization's readiness for containerization and orchestration.

This assessment includes evaluating your team's skillset, existing infrastructure, and the suitability of your applications for containerization.

Identify the applications that can benefit from containerization and assess the level of effort required to containerize them.

Additionally, ensure that your team has the necessary knowledge and expertise in container technology, Docker, and Kubernetes.

Training and upskilling your team may be necessary to ensure a smooth transition to Kubernetes.

Selecting the right infrastructure for your Kubernetes cluster is a crucial decision.

You can choose to deploy Kubernetes on various infrastructure providers, including public cloud platforms like AWS, Azure, or GCP, on-premises data centers, or hybrid environments.

Consider factors such as cost, scalability, and data residency requirements when making this decision.

Additionally, evaluate the networking capabilities of your chosen infrastructure to ensure it can support Kubernetes networking requirements.

Kubernetes relies on a highly available and performant network to function correctly.

One of the prerequisites for Kubernetes deployment is the installation of a container runtime, such as Docker, on your target nodes.

Ensure that all nodes in your cluster have the container runtime installed and configured correctly.

The container runtime is responsible for running and managing containers, which are the building blocks of your Kubernetes workloads.

Another essential component to prepare is the container image registry.

This is where you'll store and manage container images used by your applications.

Popular container image registries include Docker Hub, Google Container Registry, Amazon Elastic Container Registry (ECR), and Azure Container Registry.

Choose a registry that aligns with your infrastructure and security requirements, and ensure it is accessible to your Kubernetes nodes.

To manage and interact with your Kubernetes cluster, you'll need to install the Kubernetes command-line tool, **kubectl**, on your local machine.

kubectl allows you to interact with the cluster's API server, create and manage resources, and troubleshoot issues.

Ensure that you have the correct version of **kubectl** that matches the Kubernetes cluster version you plan to deploy.

Kubernetes relies on a distributed key-value store called **etcd** for storing cluster state and configuration data.

Plan the deployment and configuration of **etcd** to ensure it is highly available and resilient.

etcd is a critical component of your Kubernetes control plane, so it should be treated with the utmost care.

One of the key decisions to make when preparing your Kubernetes environment is choosing the Kubernetes distribution or platform that best suits your needs.

Popular Kubernetes distributions include vanilla Kubernetes, managed Kubernetes services from cloud providers (e.g., Amazon EKS, Azure AKS, Google GKE), and Kubernetes distributions like OpenShift.

Evaluate the features, support, and management capabilities offered by different distributions to make an informed choice.

Kubernetes relies on DNS for service discovery and communication between Pods.

Ensure that your cluster has a DNS service configured and that DNS resolution is functioning correctly.

This is vital for allowing Pods and services to communicate with each other using domain names.

When setting up your Kubernetes environment, define resource quotas and limits to manage the allocation of compute, memory, and storage resources to Pods and containers.

Resource quotas help prevent resource exhaustion and ensure fair resource sharing among applications.

Implementing resource quotas also aids in capacity planning and resource optimization.

An essential part of preparing your Kubernetes environment is securing it.

Kubernetes includes various security features and best practices to protect your cluster.

Implement role-based access control (RBAC) to define and enforce who can access and modify resources in the cluster.

Configure network policies to control communication between Pods and limit exposure to potential security threats.

Use Kubernetes secrets and ConfigMaps to manage sensitive information, such as passwords and API keys, securely.

Additionally, regularly apply security patches and updates to your Kubernetes nodes, as vulnerabilities may be discovered and patched over time.

To effectively monitor and troubleshoot your Kubernetes environment, set up logging and monitoring solutions.

Tools like Prometheus, Grafana, and Fluentd are commonly used for collecting metrics, monitoring cluster health, and aggregating logs.

These tools provide insights into the performance and reliability of your Kubernetes workloads.

Implement backup and disaster recovery strategies for your Kubernetes environment.

Ensure that you have reliable backup mechanisms in place to protect critical cluster data and configurations.

Consider using tools like Velero (formerly Heptio Ark) to automate backup and recovery tasks.

Plan for disaster recovery scenarios and test your recovery procedures regularly.

As part of your Kubernetes environment preparation, establish a comprehensive backup and version control system for your Kubernetes configuration files.

Store your Kubernetes resource definitions (e.g., Deployments, Services, ConfigMaps) in a version control system like Git.

This practice allows you to track changes, collaborate with team members, and roll back to previous configurations if issues arise.

Implement a robust CI/CD pipeline to automate the deployment and updates of your Kubernetes applications.

CI/CD pipelines ensure that code changes are tested, built, and deployed consistently across different environments.

Tools like Jenkins, GitLab CI/CD, and Travis CI can be integrated with Kubernetes for automated deployment.

Document your Kubernetes environment thoroughly.

Create documentation that includes cluster architecture, networking details, security policies, and procedures for scaling, upgrading, and troubleshooting.

This documentation is invaluable for onboarding new team members and ensuring that everyone understands how to operate the Kubernetes environment.

Perform thorough testing and validation of your Kubernetes environment before deploying production workloads.

Conduct tests to ensure that Pods are scheduled correctly, networking is functioning as expected, and resource limits and quotas are enforced.

Testing helps identify and address potential issues before they impact production systems.

Finally, consider implementing an incident response plan for handling unexpected issues or outages in your Kubernetes environment.

Define roles and responsibilities, communication channels, and escalation procedures to ensure a coordinated response to incidents.

Regularly review and update the incident response plan to reflect changes in your environment.

In summary, preparing your Kubernetes environment is a crucial step in successfully adopting container orchestration and managing containerized workloads efficiently.

By addressing infrastructure, security, monitoring, and automation considerations, you can create a stable and resilient Kubernetes environment that meets your organization's needs and supports your application deployment goals.

Configuring and setting up a Kubernetes cluster is a pivotal phase in harnessing the power of container orchestration for deploying, managing, and scaling containerized applications.

Kubernetes is designed to be versatile, but its flexibility also means there are multiple configurations to choose from.

To configure and set up a Kubernetes cluster effectively, you must first decide whether you want to create a single-node cluster for development and testing or a multi-node cluster for production use.

A single-node cluster is a straightforward option for experimentation and learning, but it lacks the fault tolerance and scalability benefits of a multi-node cluster.

For a production environment, a multi-node cluster is the recommended choice as it provides high availability and the ability to scale applications horizontally.

When creating a multi-node Kubernetes cluster, you need to decide whether you want to set up your own infrastructure on-premises or use a cloud-based solution like Amazon Web Services (AWS), Microsoft Azure, or Google Cloud Platform (GCP).

Each option has its advantages and trade-offs, such as control over hardware in an on-premises setup versus the convenience of managed services in a cloud-based setup.

Once you've made the infrastructure choice, you'll need to provision the virtual or physical machines that will serve as your Kubernetes nodes.

It's essential to ensure that these nodes meet the minimum system requirements, such as CPU, memory, and storage, to run Kubernetes effectively.

In a cloud-based environment, you can use services like AWS EC2 instances or Azure Virtual Machines to create the nodes.

In an on-premises setup, you'll need to provision the hardware and install the required operating system on each node.

Kubernetes relies on a consistent and reliable network connection between nodes, so configuring network connectivity is crucial.

Ensure that each node can communicate with every other node in the cluster over the network.

You should also set up network routing to allow communication between Pods running on different nodes.

Kubernetes requires that all nodes have unique hostnames and fully qualified domain names (FQDNs) for proper identification.

It's crucial to configure DNS resolution so that nodes can resolve each other's hostnames and FQDNs.

You can achieve this by setting up a Domain Name System (DNS) server within your cluster or integrating with an external DNS service.

Before you can set up the Kubernetes control plane and worker nodes, you need to install a container runtime on each node.

Docker is a popular choice, but other container runtimes like containerd or CRI-O are also supported.

Ensure that the container runtime is properly installed, configured, and functional on all nodes.

With the container runtime in place, you can proceed to install the Kubernetes control plane components, including the API server, etcd, controller manager, and scheduler.

These components are essential for managing the overall state of the cluster and scheduling workloads.

Configuration files for these components, such as kube-apiserver.yaml and kube-controller-manager.yaml, should be customized to match your cluster's requirements.

As part of the control plane setup, you must configure and secure the Kubernetes API server, which serves as the entry point for interacting with the cluster.

Use Transport Layer Security (TLS) certificates to encrypt communication with the API server, and enable authentication and authorization mechanisms like role-based access control (RBAC) to control access to cluster resources.

The etcd cluster stores the configuration data and state of the Kubernetes cluster.

It's essential to configure etcd for high availability and reliability to prevent data loss and maintain cluster consistency.

Implementing regular backups and monitoring of the etcd cluster is also critical to ensure its health.

The kube-controller-manager and kube-scheduler components are responsible for maintaining the desired state of the cluster and scheduling workloads, respectively.

Customize their configurations to align with your cluster's specific requirements and policies.

To manage Kubernetes cluster resources effectively, you must configure storage and network solutions that meet the needs of your workloads.

Persistent storage solutions like NFS, GlusterFS, or cloud-based storage services should be integrated into the cluster to provide storage volumes for Pods.

Network overlays like Calico, Flannel, or Cilium can be used to set up network policies and ensure secure communication between Pods.

A critical aspect of cluster setup is configuring the Kubernetes networking model, which defines how Pods can communicate with each other and external services.

Kubernetes supports various networking models, such as host-based routing, overlay networks, and Software-Defined Networking (SDN).

Select the networking model that aligns with your cluster's requirements and configure it accordingly.

In a multi-node Kubernetes cluster, you must implement load balancing to distribute incoming traffic evenly across multiple Pods.

Load balancers like AWS Elastic Load Balancing (ELB) or Azure Load Balancer can be used to expose services externally and route traffic to the appropriate Pods.

Internal load balancing solutions can also be set up to balance traffic within the cluster.

When setting up your Kubernetes cluster, it's essential to configure authentication and authorization to control who can access the cluster and what actions they can perform.

Role-based access control (RBAC) is a powerful tool for managing permissions and should be configured to align with your organization's security policies.

Additionally, configure identity providers like OpenID Connect (OIDC) or LDAP to allow users to authenticate securely.

Secrets management is a crucial part of cluster configuration.

Kubernetes allows you to store sensitive information like passwords, API keys, and certificates securely using secrets.

Configure secret management policies and practices to ensure that sensitive data is protected and accessible only to authorized applications and users.

Monitoring and observability are essential components of cluster setup.

Implement monitoring tools like Prometheus and Grafana to collect and visualize metrics from your cluster.

Set up alerts and notifications to proactively identify and address issues.

Logging solutions like Fluentd or Elasticsearch can help you gather and analyze logs from Pods and cluster components.

Security is paramount in Kubernetes cluster configuration.

Regularly apply security patches and updates to all nodes, containers, and components.

Implement best practices for securing the control plane, nodes, and workloads.

Configure network policies to restrict communication between Pods, limiting exposure to potential security threats.

Security scanning and vulnerability assessment tools can help identify and remediate security weaknesses.

Backup and disaster recovery planning should be an integral part of your Kubernetes cluster configuration.

Regularly back up critical cluster data, including etcd data, configurations, and secrets.

Test your backup and recovery procedures to ensure they can restore the cluster to a known good state in case of data loss or failure.

Kubernetes clusters should be highly available and fault-tolerant.

Distribute control plane components across multiple nodes to prevent a single point of failure.

Implement automated failover and recovery mechanisms to maintain cluster uptime.

Capacity planning is essential to ensure that your Kubernetes cluster can handle the expected workload.

Monitor resource utilization and performance metrics to identify bottlenecks and scale the cluster as needed.

Implement autoscaling policies to adjust the number of nodes and Pods dynamically based on demand.

Documentation is a critical part of cluster setup.

Create comprehensive documentation that includes cluster architecture, configuration details, security policies, and operational procedures.

This documentation is invaluable for onboarding new team members and ensuring consistent management of the cluster.

Testing is a crucial step in the configuration and setup of your Kubernetes cluster.

Conduct thorough testing to validate that all components, configurations, and policies work as expected.

Test various failure scenarios, such as node failures, network disruptions, and application faults, to ensure resilience.

In summary, configuring and setting up a Kubernetes cluster requires careful planning, attention to detail, and adherence to best practices.

By following these steps and considerations, you can create a well-configured and robust Kubernetes cluster that meets the needs of your containerized applications and workloads.

Deconstructing the architecture of Kubernetes provides valuable insights into how this container orchestration platform functions at its core.

At its heart, Kubernetes is designed to manage the deployment, scaling, and operation of containerized applications.

To understand its architecture, we'll break it down into its fundamental components and explore how they interact.

The key building blocks of Kubernetes include the control plane, worker nodes, and the etcd data store.

The control plane is responsible for the overall management and coordination of the cluster.

It consists of several components, including the API server, etcd, the scheduler, and the controller manager.

The API server serves as the front-end for Kubernetes and exposes the Kubernetes API.

It is the primary entry point for users and external systems to interact with the cluster.

The API server processes incoming requests, validates them, and updates the corresponding objects in etcd.

Etcd is a distributed key-value store that acts as the cluster's brain.

It stores all the configuration data and state information for the entire cluster.

This includes information about Pods, Services, ConfigMaps, and more.

The scheduler is responsible for placing workloads (Pods) onto nodes in the cluster.

It makes decisions based on factors like resource availability, affinity and anti-affinity rules, and user-defined constraints.

The controller manager includes a set of controllers that regulate the state of the cluster.

These controllers ensure that the desired state, as defined in the cluster's configuration, is maintained.

For example, the Replication Controller ensures that the specified number of Pod replicas is running, while the Node Controller monitors the health of nodes.

Worker nodes are the worker machines in the Kubernetes cluster. They are responsible for running containers and managing the workload.

Each worker node runs several components, including the Kubelet, Kube Proxy, and the container runtime.

The Kubelet is an agent that runs on each node and communicates with the control plane.

It ensures that containers are running in a Pod as expected, pulling images from a container registry when necessary.

Kube Proxy is responsible for network connectivity within the cluster.

It maintains network rules on nodes to enable communication between Pods and external traffic.

The container runtime is the software responsible for running containers.

Docker is a popular choice for this role, although other runtimes like containerd and CRI-O are also supported.

Together, these components make it possible to deploy and manage containerized applications in a distributed and resilient manner.

Beyond these core components, Kubernetes also relies on various services and plugins to extend its capabilities.

Networking is a crucial aspect of Kubernetes, and it offers a pluggable networking model.

Networking solutions like Calico, Flannel, and Weave can be integrated to provide network connectivity and isolation between Pods.

Kubernetes also supports service discovery and load balancing through the Service abstraction.

Services allow Pods to communicate with each other, regardless of their location within the cluster.

Load balancing is handled automatically by distributing traffic to healthy Pods.

Storage is another important consideration in Kubernetes architecture.

Persistent Volumes (PVs) and Persistent Volume Claims (PVCs) enable storage resources to be dynamically allocated to Pods.

This allows applications to access and use data that persists across Pod restarts and rescheduling.

Security is a top priority in Kubernetes, and it offers several layers of security mechanisms.

Role-Based Access Control (RBAC) allows fine-grained control over who can access and manipulate resources in the cluster.

Secrets and ConfigMaps enable the secure management of sensitive data and configuration parameters.

Pod Security Policies (PSPs) provide a way to define and enforce security policies for Pods.

Monitoring and observability are critical for maintaining the health and performance of a Kubernetes cluster.

Prometheus, Grafana, and other monitoring tools can be integrated to collect and visualize metrics.

Logging solutions like Fluentd and Elasticsearch help aggregate and analyze logs from Pods and system components.

Kubernetes can also integrate with external identity providers for authentication.

This is achieved through mechanisms like OpenID Connect (OIDC) and LDAP integration.

Kubernetes' extensibility allows users to add custom resources and controllers to meet specific requirements.

Custom Resource Definitions (CRDs) enable the creation of custom resources, which can be managed by custom controllers.

These controllers can automate tasks and enforce policies specific to an organization's needs.

Kubernetes' architecture is designed to be highly scalable and resilient.

It can handle large clusters with thousands of nodes and tens of thousands of Pods.

Horizontal Pod Autoscaling (HPA) and Cluster Autoscaler allow the cluster to adapt to varying workloads by dynamically scaling resources.

High availability is achieved through redundancy in the control plane components and worker nodes.

In the event of a failure, Kubernetes automatically reschedules Pods to healthy nodes.

In summary, Kubernetes' architecture is a sophisticated system of components that work together to manage containerized workloads in a flexible, scalable, and resilient manner.

Understanding these components and their interactions is essential for effectively deploying and managing applications in a Kubernetes cluster.

In the world of container orchestration, Kubernetes stands out as a powerful and versatile platform, and to harness its full potential, it's crucial to grasp its key components and concepts.

At the core of Kubernetes is the notion of a "cluster," which is a collection of nodes that work together to run containerized applications.

These nodes can be physical machines or virtual machines, and they are the foundation upon which Kubernetes operates.

Within a Kubernetes cluster, nodes can be categorized into two main types: control plane nodes and worker nodes.

Control plane nodes are responsible for managing the overall state of the cluster and making decisions about which containers should run on which nodes.

Worker nodes, on the other hand, are where the actual containers run and execute the workloads.

One of the central components of the control plane is the API server, which acts as the front-end to the Kubernetes control plane.

The API server serves as the interface through which users, administrators, and components interact with the cluster.

It accepts commands and configuration data, processes these requests, and communicates with the underlying cluster to ensure that the desired state is maintained.

Etcd is another crucial component of the control plane, serving as the cluster's distributed key-value store.

Etcd stores all the configuration data and state information for the entire cluster, ensuring that the cluster can recover from failures and maintain consistency.

The scheduler is responsible for deciding which nodes should run the containers, based on factors such as resource availability, quality of service requirements, and user-defined constraints.

Controllers, such as the Replication Controller and the StatefulSet Controller, are responsible for maintaining the desired state of the system.

These controllers ensure that the right number of Pod replicas are running and manage how they scale, replicate, and recover in response to failures.

Pods are the smallest deployable units in Kubernetes and represent a single instance of a running process in the cluster.

A Pod can contain one or more containers, which share the same network namespace, storage, and configuration.

Pods are often used to co-locate tightly coupled containers that need to share resources and communicate with each other.

Services provide an abstraction for networking in Kubernetes and enable communication between groups of Pods.

A Service defines a set of Pods using label selectors and ensures that requests to the Service are load-balanced to one of the selected Pods.

Services can be used for exposing applications to the internet, load balancing traffic, and providing stable network endpoints.

Labels and selectors are fundamental to Kubernetes, as they enable the grouping and selection of resources.

Labels are key-value pairs that can be attached to resources like Pods and Services, and selectors allow you to filter resources based on these labels.

Labels and selectors are used throughout Kubernetes to organize, manage, and interact with resources.

ConfigMaps and Secrets are used for storing configuration data and sensitive information, respectively.

ConfigMaps allow you to decouple configuration from your application code, making it easier to update and manage configuration settings.

Secrets, on the other hand, are used for sensitive data like passwords and API keys, and they are stored in a more secure manner.

Namespaces provide a way to partition a Kubernetes cluster into multiple virtual clusters, each with its own resources and policies.

Namespaces help in organizing and isolating workloads, especially in multi-tenant environments.

Resource Quotas and LimitRanges are used to enforce constraints on resource usage within a namespace.

Resource Quotas limit the total amount of resources that can be consumed by Pods and Services, while LimitRanges set constraints on individual containers within Pods.

Persistent Volumes (PVs) and Persistent Volume Claims (PVCs) enable the management of storage resources in Kubernetes.

PVs represent physical storage resources, while PVCs are requests for storage by Pods.

PVCs allow Pods to request storage without needing to know the underlying storage details, making it easier to manage storage across the cluster.

Kubernetes offers a variety of networking models, and one of the most common is the Service abstraction, which provides a stable network endpoint for accessing a set of Pods.

Ingress Controllers extend the capabilities of Services by providing HTTP and HTTPS routing, load balancing, and SSL/TLS termination.

Network Policies define how Pods can communicate with each other and control traffic between different parts of the cluster.

By enforcing network policies, you can segment and secure communication within the cluster.

Kubernetes offers several strategies for deploying and scaling applications.

Horizontal Pod Autoscaling (HPA) automatically adjusts the number of replicas of a Deployment or ReplicaSet based on CPU or custom metrics.

Vertical Pod Autoscaling (VPA) adjusts the CPU and memory requests of Pods to optimize resource usage.

Kubernetes also supports rolling updates and rollbacks for Deployments, allowing for seamless updates of application versions.

DaemonSets ensure that a Pod runs on every node in the cluster, which can be useful for tasks like log collection or monitoring.

StatefulSets are used for managing stateful applications, ensuring stable network identities and ordered pod startup and termination.

CronJobs enable the scheduling of jobs at specified intervals, making it easy to automate periodic tasks.

Chapter 4: Managing Kubernetes Resources with IaC

Resource management is a critical aspect of Kubernetes, as it ensures that containers and Pods have access to the necessary compute resources while optimizing cluster utilization.

In Kubernetes, each node in the cluster has a finite amount of CPU and memory capacity that can be allocated to Pods.

To efficiently manage these resources, Kubernetes relies on two main concepts: resource requests and resource limits.

Resource requests are used to specify the amount of CPU and memory that a container or Pod needs to run.

By defining resource requests, Kubernetes scheduler can make informed decisions about where to place Pods based on the available resources on nodes.

Resource limits, on the other hand, define the maximum amount of CPU and memory that a container or Pod can consume.

Resource limits act as a safeguard to prevent containers from using excessive resources and impacting the performance of other workloads on the same node.

When a container exceeds its resource limits, Kubernetes takes action to address the issue, which may involve throttling or terminating the offending container.

Pods can have different resource requests and limits for CPU and memory, allowing for fine-grained control over resource allocation.

For example, you can specify that a certain Pod requires 0.5 CPU cores and 512 MiB of memory for its normal operation.

Additionally, you can set resource limits to ensure that the Pod does not consume more than 1 CPU core and 1 GiB of memory.

Kubernetes uses the CFS (Completely Fair Scheduler) for CPU resource management.

The CFS ensures that CPU time is fairly distributed among Pods and containers.

It employs the concept of CPU shares to allocate CPU time based on the relative weight of Pods' resource requests.

CPU shares are calculated as a fraction of the total available CPU time, and Pods with higher shares get more CPU time.

Memory management in Kubernetes is handled differently from CPU management.

Kubernetes uses the Linux kernel's memory management mechanisms, including cgroups and namespaces, to enforce memory resource limits.

Containers are isolated from each other, and their memory usage is controlled within the defined limits.

When a container exceeds its memory limit, the Linux Out of Memory (OOM) killer may terminate the container to prevent the entire node from becoming unresponsive due to memory exhaustion.

It's important to note that resource management in Kubernetes is not just about setting requests and limits.

It also involves monitoring and optimizing resource utilization across the cluster.

Kubernetes provides various tools and metrics for tracking resource usage, including the Kubernetes Metrics Server, which collects resource utilization data from nodes and Pods.

With this data, administrators and operators can identify underutilized or overutilized nodes and make informed decisions about scaling and resource allocation.

Horizontal Pod Autoscaling (HPA) is a feature in Kubernetes that automatically adjusts the number of Pod replicas based on CPU or custom metrics.

HPA allows you to scale your application up or down dynamically in response to changes in resource demand.

For example, if a web application experiences a sudden increase in traffic, HPA can automatically add more Pod replicas to handle the load.

Conversely, when traffic decreases, HPA can scale down the number of replicas to save resources.

Resource management is not only about allocating and monitoring CPU and memory but also about optimizing storage resources.

Kubernetes provides Persistent Volumes (PVs) and Persistent Volume Claims (PVCs) to manage storage resources.

PVs represent physical storage resources, such as disks or network-attached storage, while PVCs are requests for storage by Pods.

By defining PVCs and binding them to PVs, you can ensure that your Pods have access to the required storage while abstracting away the underlying storage details.

Kubernetes supports various storage backends, including local storage, cloud-based storage, and network-attached storage, allowing you to choose the best storage solution for your needs.

In addition to resource requests and limits, Kubernetes provides mechanisms for controlling the quality of service (QoS) for Pods.

Pods are categorized into three QoS classes: Guaranteed, Burstable, and BestEffort.

Guaranteed Pods have both CPU and memory requests and limits set, ensuring that they are guaranteed the resources they need.

Burstable Pods have CPU requests and limits but no memory limits, allowing them to use additional memory when available.

BestEffort Pods have no resource requests or limits, relying on the unused resources of the node.

Understanding resource management in Kubernetes is essential for maintaining the stability and performance of your containerized applications.

By carefully defining resource requests and limits, monitoring resource utilization, and implementing horizontal autoscaling, you can optimize resource allocation and ensure efficient resource utilization across your Kubernetes cluster.

Writing your first Infrastructure as Code (IaC) code for Kubernetes is an exciting step in your journey to managing containerized applications with precision and consistency.

Kubernetes, as a powerful container orchestration platform, allows you to define your desired infrastructure and application configurations in code, making it reproducible, version-controlled, and easily manageable.

To begin writing Kubernetes IaC code, you'll need to understand and use YAML files extensively.

YAML (YAML Ain't Markup Language) is a human-readable data serialization format that Kubernetes uses for configuration files.

In Kubernetes, YAML files describe the desired state of your resources, such as Pods, Services, and Deployments.

Your first step is to create a basic Kubernetes YAML file for defining a simple Pod.

A Pod is the smallest deployable unit in Kubernetes, representing a single instance of a running process in the cluster.

To create a Pod YAML file, start by specifying the Kubernetes API version, which indicates the version of the Kubernetes API you're using.

Next, define the kind of resource you're creating, which, in this case, is a "Pod."

Now, you can set the metadata for your Pod, including its name and labels.

Labels are key-value pairs that help you organize and categorize your resources.

For instance, you can add a label like "app: web" to indicate that this Pod is part of a web application.

Moving on, you'll define the specification for the containers running within the Pod.

Containers are specified under the "containers" field, and you can specify the container's name, image, and ports.

The "image" field should point to the Docker image you want to run in the container.

For example, you might use the image "nginx" for a simple web server.

Additionally, you can define the container's resource requests and limits for CPU and memory.

Resource requests specify the minimum resources that the container should have, while resource limits set an upper bound on resource consumption.

These resource settings help Kubernetes schedule and manage your containers effectively.

Once you've created your Pod YAML file, you can apply it to your Kubernetes cluster using the "kubectl apply" command.

This command sends the configuration to the cluster's API server, which then creates the Pod according to your specifications.

After applying the Pod configuration, you can use "kubectl get pods" to check the status of your Pod.

The output will show you the Pod's name, status, and other relevant information.

If everything is configured correctly, you should see your Pod in the "Running" state.

Now that you've successfully deployed your first Kubernetes Pod using IaC, you can take your learning a step further by exploring more complex configurations.

Kubernetes offers a wide range of resource types and features for managing your containerized applications effectively.

For instance, you can create Services to provide networking and load balancing for your Pods.

Services allow external clients to access your application without needing to know the specific Pod that serves the request.

To define a Service in YAML, you'll specify its API version, kind (Service), metadata, and specifications, including the type (ClusterIP, NodePort, LoadBalancer), selector to identify the Pods it should route traffic to, and the port mappings.

You can also create Deployments, which provide declarative updates to applications.

Deployments manage ReplicaSets, ensuring that the desired number of replicas (Pods) are running at all times.

By defining a Deployment, you can easily scale your application up or down, roll out updates, and roll back to previous versions if needed.

Kubernetes also supports ConfigMaps and Secrets, which allow you to decouple configuration data from your application code.

You can store configuration settings, API keys, and secrets separately from your application containers, making it easier to manage and update configurations without changing the container images.

To use ConfigMaps and Secrets in your IaC code, you'll create separate YAML files for these resources and reference them in your Pod or Deployment configurations.

In addition to defining resources individually, Kubernetes IaC allows you to create complex application stacks and dependencies.

You can use Helm, a package manager for Kubernetes, to manage charts (packages of pre-configured Kubernetes resources) and deploy entire applications as a single unit.

Helm simplifies the process of managing complex applications by providing templating, dependency management, and versioning.

To get started with Helm, you'll create Helm charts that define the structure and configuration of your applications.

These charts can be version-controlled and shared with others, making it easy to collaborate on Kubernetes projects.

As you gain more experience with Kubernetes IaC, you'll discover the power of custom resource definitions (CRDs) and operators.

CRDs enable you to extend Kubernetes with custom resources, while operators automate the management of those resources.

For example, you can create a custom resource definition for a database and then use an operator to automatically provision and manage database instances based on custom configurations.

This advanced level of IaC customization can significantly enhance your ability to manage complex applications and services in Kubernetes.

As you continue to explore Kubernetes IaC, you'll encounter other concepts and tools, such as Helm charts, Kubernetes namespaces for resource isolation, and RBAC (Role-Based Access Control) for fine-grained access control.

With each step, you'll become more proficient in managing containerized applications and infrastructure using Kubernetes IaC, unlocking the full potential of this powerful container orchestration platform.

Chapter 5: Advanced Kubernetes IaC Techniques

In the world of container orchestration, Kubernetes stands out as a powerful platform for managing resources, applications, and services with precision and efficiency.

As you advance in your journey of Kubernetes resource management, it's essential to explore advanced strategies that can help you optimize, scale, and fine-tune your cluster.

One of the critical considerations in Kubernetes is resource allocation, and advanced resource management techniques can significantly impact the performance and cost efficiency of your applications.

To achieve optimal resource allocation, you can leverage Kubernetes Horizontal Pod Autoscaling (HPA).

HPA allows your application to automatically adjust the number of Pod replicas based on resource utilization metrics, such as CPU or custom metrics.

This means that when your application experiences increased traffic or resource demands, HPA can dynamically scale up the number of Pods to meet those demands.

Conversely, during periods of lower demand, HPA can scale down, saving resources and cost.

Configuring HPA involves defining scaling rules, target metrics, and thresholds to trigger scaling events.

For instance, you can set up HPA to maintain an average CPU utilization of 70% across your Pods, ensuring that your application scales efficiently to handle traffic spikes.

Kubernetes also offers Vertical Pod Autoscaling (VPA), which optimizes resource allocation at the container level.

VPA can automatically adjust resource requests and limits for individual containers based on their actual resource usage.

By doing so, VPA ensures that each container gets the resources it needs without over-provisioning.

For example, if a container consistently uses less CPU than its request, VPA can lower the resource request to save CPU for other containers.

On the other hand, if a container frequently hits its resource limits, VPA can increase the resource request to prevent resource starvation.

Another advanced strategy for managing Kubernetes resources is Pod Priority and Preemption.

Pod Priority allows you to assign different priority levels to Pods, indicating their relative importance within the cluster.

Higher-priority Pods are scheduled before lower-priority Pods when resources become scarce.

This can be crucial for ensuring that mission-critical workloads always get the resources they need, even in resource-constrained situations.

You can define Pod Priority classes and assign them to your Pods in the PodSpec.

Additionally, Kubernetes offers PodDisruptionBudgets (PDBs) to control the disruption of Pods during events like node maintenance or scale-downs.

PDBs allow you to specify the minimum number of Pods that must remain available within a certain priority class, ensuring the stability of your applications during disruptions.

Resource Quotas are another advanced feature that helps you enforce resource limits at the namespace level.

With Resource Quotas, you can define constraints on CPU, memory, and other resources to prevent over-provisioning and resource contention within a namespace.

This is particularly valuable in multi-tenant Kubernetes clusters where you want to ensure fair resource allocation among different teams or projects.

Kubernetes Resource Quotas also enable you to specify a "hard" limit, which cannot be exceeded, and a "soft" limit, which triggers warnings but does not block resource allocation.

To create Resource Quotas, you define them within the desired namespace, specifying the limits for each resource type.

When the combined resource usage of all Pods in the namespace approaches the specified limits, Kubernetes enforces the quotas by rejecting new Pod creations that would exceed the limits.

While Kubernetes offers powerful tools for resource management, monitoring and observability are equally crucial for maintaining the health and performance of your cluster.

Advanced monitoring strategies involve the use of tools like Prometheus and Grafana to collect, store, and visualize cluster metrics.

Prometheus, as a popular open-source monitoring solution, can scrape metrics from Kubernetes components, applications, and services.

It allows you to create custom queries and alerts to track resource usage, performance bottlenecks, and potential issues.

Grafana complements Prometheus by providing interactive and customizable dashboards for visualizing metrics and creating alerts.

Together, Prometheus and Grafana offer deep insights into your cluster's resource utilization, enabling proactive resource management and troubleshooting.

Another advanced monitoring technique is the use of Kubernetes Custom Metrics.

Custom Metrics enable you to define your own application-specific metrics and use them for autoscaling or alerting.

You can collect custom metrics using tools like the Prometheus Adapter, which converts Prometheus metrics into custom metrics that Kubernetes can understand.

By scaling your applications based on custom metrics like request latency or queue depth, you can ensure that your resources are allocated efficiently according to your application's unique needs.

Advanced resource management in Kubernetes also involves optimizing the cluster's network and storage resources.

For networking, Kubernetes Network Policies allow you to define fine-grained rules for controlling the flow of traffic between Pods.

By setting up Network Policies, you can isolate applications, control access, and enhance security within your cluster.

Network Policies can be complex, as they involve defining rules based on Pod selectors and specifying ingress and egress traffic.

However, they are a powerful tool for advanced network resource management.

When it comes to storage, Kubernetes offers advanced storage management features like Persistent Volume (PV) resizing and dynamic provisioning.

PV resizing allows you to adjust the size of existing PVs dynamically, accommodating changing storage requirements.

Dynamic provisioning, on the other hand, automatically creates PVs as needed, reducing the manual overhead of managing storage resources.

By using advanced storage features, you can ensure that your applications always have access to the right amount of storage without over-provisioning.

Resource management in Kubernetes is a continuous process of optimization and adaptation to changing demands and requirements.

As you delve into advanced strategies and features, it's essential to strike a balance between resource allocation, monitoring, and observability.

By leveraging tools and techniques like HPA, VPA, Pod Priority, and advanced monitoring, you can fine-tune your Kubernetes cluster to deliver optimal performance, scalability, and cost efficiency for your applications and services.

Chapter 6: Kubernetes Security and Compliance with IaC

Implementing security best practices in Kubernetes Infrastructure as Code (IaC) is paramount to ensure the safety and integrity of your containerized applications and the underlying infrastructure. Kubernetes, known for its flexibility and scalability, offers a robust framework for deploying and managing container workloads, but with this power comes the responsibility to address security concerns.

One of the fundamental security principles in Kubernetes is the principle of least privilege.

This principle dictates that each component, user, or process should only have the minimum level of access necessary to perform its functions.

In Kubernetes, this translates to limiting the permissions and privileges assigned to Pods, containers, and service accounts.

To enforce the principle of least privilege, Kubernetes provides Role-Based Access Control (RBAC).

RBAC allows you to define fine-grained access policies for various resources within your cluster.

By carefully configuring RBAC roles and role bindings, you can ensure that users and Pods have precisely the permissions they need and nothing more.

This granular control is essential for reducing the attack surface and minimizing the potential impact of security breaches.

Another critical aspect of security in Kubernetes IaC is container image security.

Container images serve as the building blocks of Kubernetes workloads, and ensuring their integrity is vital.

To enhance container image security, it's essential to follow best practices when creating, distributing, and deploying container images.

One key practice is regularly scanning container images for vulnerabilities and ensuring they are up to date.

Vulnerability scanning tools can help you identify known security issues within your container images and take corrective actions.

Additionally, consider signing and verifying container images using cryptographic signatures to guarantee their authenticity and prevent tampering.

In Kubernetes, you can use tools like Notary or Docker Content Trust for image signing.

When deploying container images, Kubernetes offers the PodSecurityPolicy (PSP) resource, which allows you to define security policies that Pods must adhere to.

PSPs enforce constraints on various aspects of Pod execution, such as running with a specific user or group, using only allowed host namespaces, and limiting container capabilities.

By creating and implementing PSPs, you can mitigate the risks associated with running containers in your cluster.

Another security best practice in Kubernetes IaC is network segmentation.

In a Kubernetes cluster, network segmentation involves isolating workloads and controlling communication between Pods.

This isolation helps prevent lateral movement by attackers and limits the potential impact of security breaches.

You can achieve network segmentation in Kubernetes by using Network Policies.

Network Policies define rules for traffic flow between Pods based on their labels and namespaces.

By specifying which Pods can communicate with each other and on which ports, you can establish strict network security boundaries.

Furthermore, consider implementing a Service Mesh like Istio or Linkerd for enhanced network security and observability.

Service Meshes provide advanced traffic management, encryption, and authentication capabilities that can bolster the security of your Kubernetes applications.

Secrets management is another vital aspect of security in Kubernetes IaC.

Applications often require sensitive information, such as API keys, database passwords, or TLS certificates, to operate.

Kubernetes Secrets allow you to store and manage this sensitive data securely.

When using Secrets, ensure that you follow best practices, such as avoiding hardcoding secrets in IaC manifests and rotating them regularly.

Tools like HashiCorp Vault or Kubernetes-native solutions like Sealed Secrets can enhance secrets management and encryption.

Additionally, consider implementing encryption at rest and in transit for your Kubernetes cluster.

Encrypting data at rest protects information stored on disks, while encryption in transit safeguards data as it moves between nodes and services.

Kubernetes provides mechanisms for enabling both types of encryption, such as Transparent Data Encryption (TDE) for data at rest and Transport Layer Security (TLS) for data in transit.

Auditing and monitoring are crucial for detecting and responding to security incidents in Kubernetes IaC.

Enable auditing in your cluster to capture detailed logs of API server requests and responses.

Kubernetes audit logs can provide valuable insights into unauthorized access attempts and unusual behavior.

To analyze and alert on these logs effectively, integrate your Kubernetes cluster with a robust monitoring and logging solution like Prometheus and Grafana or ELK Stack.

These tools can help you set up alerting rules, visualize metrics, and investigate security incidents.

Regularly reviewing and analyzing audit logs is a proactive measure that can help you identify and respond to security threats promptly.

Another security best practice in Kubernetes IaC is to keep your cluster and its components up to date.

Kubernetes releases regular updates, including security patches and bug fixes.

It's crucial to have a well-defined update and patch management process in place to ensure that your cluster remains secure.

Use automated deployment pipelines to streamline the process of applying updates and patches to your cluster.

Additionally, consider implementing a robust backup and disaster recovery strategy for your Kubernetes IaC.

Backing up critical cluster configurations, application data, and secrets ensures that you can recover from unexpected incidents or security breaches.

Regularly test your backup and restore procedures to validate their effectiveness.

Lastly, security is an ongoing process, and it's essential to stay informed about the latest security threats and vulnerabilities in the Kubernetes ecosystem.

Subscribe to security mailing lists, follow security best practices, and participate in the Kubernetes community to stay up to date with security updates and recommendations.

In summary, implementing security best practices in Kubernetes IaC is essential to protect your applications and data from potential threats.

By following the principle of least privilege, securing container images, implementing network segmentation, managing secrets, enabling auditing and monitoring, staying up to date, and having a robust backup and disaster recovery strategy, you can create a secure Kubernetes environment for your workloads.

Compliance as Code (CaC) is an emerging practice in the realm of Kubernetes Infrastructure as Code (IaC), focusing on ensuring that your Kubernetes cluster and workloads adhere to regulatory requirements and industry standards.

Kubernetes, with its dynamic and ever-changing nature, presents unique challenges when it comes to compliance.

To address these challenges, organizations are turning to CaC to automate the enforcement and validation of compliance controls.

One of the primary drivers for adopting Compliance as Code in Kubernetes is the need to meet specific regulatory standards, such as GDPR, HIPAA, or PCI DSS, which mandate stringent data protection and security measures.

By codifying compliance requirements, organizations can automate the auditing and validation of their Kubernetes configurations to ensure they align with these standards.

Additionally, CaC helps organizations maintain an audit trail of their compliance efforts, making it easier to demonstrate compliance to auditors and regulators.

In Kubernetes, CaC is often implemented using tools like Open Policy Agent (OPA) and Gatekeeper.

OPA is a policy enforcement engine that allows you to define and enforce policies as code.

You can create policies that specify the desired configuration for your Kubernetes resources, such as Pods, Services, and ConfigMaps.

Gatekeeper, built on top of OPA, provides a Kubernetes-native way to enforce these policies during resource creation and updates.

By integrating Gatekeeper into your Kubernetes clusters, you can prevent non-compliant resources from being deployed.

A fundamental concept in Compliance as Code is the use of policy-as-code.

This means translating compliance requirements and best practices into machine-readable policies that can be evaluated automatically.

For example, you can create policies that ensure all containers in a Pod run with non root users, enforce resource limits, and prohibit the use of insecure container images.

These policies act as guardrails, guiding developers and operators to adhere to best practices and compliance standards.

Another key aspect of Compliance as Code is continuous compliance monitoring.

Rather than relying solely on periodic manual audits, organizations can use automated tools to continuously assess their Kubernetes clusters for compliance violations.

This proactive approach helps identify and rectify non-compliance issues in real-time, reducing the risk of security breaches and compliance failures.

Automated compliance checks can include validating that encryption is enabled for communication within the cluster, verifying that access controls are correctly configured, and ensuring that containers use trusted base images.

Kubernetes also provides native features that support compliance efforts, such as PodSecurityPolicies (PSPs) and Network Policies.

PSPs allow you to define and enforce security policies for Pods, ensuring they adhere to security best practices.

You can specify which users and groups are allowed to run Pods, control the use of host namespaces, and limit the capabilities of containers.

Network Policies, on the other hand, enable you to define rules for network traffic between Pods, helping you enforce network segmentation and control communication.

By leveraging these built-in Kubernetes features in conjunction with Compliance as Code tools, organizations can strengthen their overall security posture.

Another advantage of Compliance as Code is the ability to create custom policies tailored to your organization's specific compliance requirements.

While many off-the-shelf policies are available, organizations can develop policies that align with their unique needs and industry regulations.

Custom policies can cover areas such as data encryption, secrets management, and specific container image scanning requirements.

Additionally, organizations can use CaC to automate the validation of compliance controls related to configuration drift.

Configuration drift occurs when the desired state of resources diverges from their actual state over time due to manual changes or misconfigurations.

CaC tools can continuously compare the current configuration of Kubernetes resources against the defined policies and alert administrators to any discrepancies.

This real-time feedback loop helps maintain the desired state and reduce the risk of drift-induced compliance issues.

Furthermore, Compliance as Code is not limited to enforcing compliance controls during resource creation but can also be used for post-deployment auditing and continuous assessment.

By regularly auditing your Kubernetes clusters, you can identify and remediate compliance violations promptly.

Continuous assessment ensures that your cluster remains compliant even as configurations change over time.

In summary, Compliance as Code is a valuable practice for organizations leveraging Kubernetes Infrastructure as Code.

It helps organizations codify compliance requirements, enforce policies, and continuously monitor and assess their Kubernetes clusters for compliance violations.

By combining Compliance as Code tools with Kubernetes-native features like PSPs and Network Policies, organizations can establish robust compliance controls and maintain a strong security posture in their containerized environments.

Chapter 7: Infrastructure Testing and Validation in Kubernetes

Testing Kubernetes Infrastructure as Code (IaC) is a critical aspect of ensuring the reliability and correctness of your Kubernetes cluster configurations and applications.

Kubernetes IaC testing encompasses a range of strategies and techniques aimed at identifying issues early in the development lifecycle and preventing problems in production environments.

One of the fundamental strategies for testing Kubernetes IaC is unit testing.

Unit testing involves evaluating individual components or resources within your Kubernetes configurations in isolation.

For example, you can write unit tests to validate that a particular Pod configuration adheres to security best practices or that a Service is exposed on the correct port.

Unit tests help catch configuration errors and misalignments with best practices at an early stage, making it easier to address them before they propagate to higher-level configurations.

Another important testing strategy is integration testing.

Integration testing involves evaluating how different Kubernetes resources and components work together as a cohesive system.

This type of testing can uncover issues related to resource dependencies, network communication, and compatibility between different resource types.

For example, you can perform integration tests to ensure that Pods can communicate with the associated Services or to verify that ConfigMaps are correctly mounted in Pods.

Integration tests help validate the overall behavior of your Kubernetes cluster and the interactions between its components.

End-to-end (E2E) testing is another crucial strategy for testing Kubernetes IaC.

E2E tests simulate real-world scenarios and interactions with your applications running in Kubernetes.

These tests often involve deploying a complete application stack, interacting with it, and verifying the expected behavior.

For instance, you can create E2E tests that deploy a web application, interact with it using automated browser testing tools, and check for correct functionality.

E2E tests are essential for verifying that your Kubernetes IaC not only deploys resources correctly but also delivers the expected functionality to users.

Kubernetes provides a framework for running E2E tests, known as Kubernetes E2E testing or "KubeConformance."

KubeConformance allows you to define and execute tests that validate your Kubernetes cluster's conformance to Kubernetes specifications and behaviors.

Another aspect of testing Kubernetes IaC is performance testing.

Performance testing evaluates how your Kubernetes applications and configurations perform under various loads and conditions.

It helps identify potential bottlenecks, scalability issues, and resource utilization problems.

Performance tests can be categorized into several types, including load testing, stress testing, and capacity testing.

Load testing assesses how your applications and clusters handle increasing loads, stress testing pushes systems to their limits to identify breaking points, and capacity testing determines the cluster's resource limits.

These tests help ensure that your Kubernetes IaC can meet performance expectations and scale effectively.

Security testing is an integral part of testing Kubernetes IaC.

Security testing aims to identify vulnerabilities, misconfigurations, and security weaknesses within your Kubernetes configurations.

Common security testing practices include vulnerability scanning of container images, penetration testing of Kubernetes clusters, and static analysis of IaC code for security issues.

Security tests are essential for identifying and mitigating security risks before they can be exploited by attackers.

Additionally, automated testing is a key strategy for Kubernetes IaC.

Automated testing encompasses unit tests, integration tests, and E2E tests that can be run automatically as part of your CI/CD (Continuous Integration/Continuous Deployment) pipeline.

Automated tests ensure that changes to your IaC code are thoroughly validated before they are deployed to production clusters, reducing the risk of introducing errors.

Continuous testing throughout the development lifecycle helps catch issues early, leading to more reliable and secure Kubernetes IaC.

Furthermore, infrastructure validation is a crucial strategy for testing Kubernetes IaC.

Infrastructure validation involves regularly validating your Kubernetes clusters' configurations against predefined policies, best practices, and security standards.

Tools like Open Policy Agent (OPA) and Gatekeeper allow you to codify and enforce policies as code.

These policies can define rules for Kubernetes resources, network policies, and security settings.

By validating your IaC against these policies, you can ensure that your clusters adhere to compliance requirements and internal standards.

Lastly, chaos engineering is an advanced testing strategy for Kubernetes IaC.

Chaos engineering involves intentionally injecting failures and disruptions into your Kubernetes clusters to assess their resilience and fault tolerance.

Tools like Chaos Mesh and LitmusChaos provide frameworks for conducting chaos experiments in Kubernetes environments.

Chaos engineering helps you identify weaknesses in your configurations and applications, allowing you to implement improvements that enhance your cluster's reliability.

In summary, testing Kubernetes IaC is a multifaceted process that encompasses unit testing, integration testing, E2E testing, performance testing, security testing, automation, infrastructure validation, and chaos engineering.

By adopting a comprehensive testing strategy, organizations can ensure the reliability, security, and performance of their Kubernetes clusters and applications, ultimately delivering a better user experience and reducing the risk of downtime and security breaches.

Validation and error handling are critical aspects of Kubernetes Infrastructure as Code (IaC) that ensure the reliability, stability, and security of your Kubernetes clusters and applications.

In the context of Kubernetes IaC, validation refers to the process of confirming that your configurations and deployments adhere to predefined criteria and standards.

Effective validation helps prevent misconfigurations and errors from propagating to production environments, reducing the risk of outages and security vulnerabilities.

Error handling, on the other hand, involves managing and responding to unexpected issues and failures that can occur during the lifecycle of your Kubernetes resources.

Both validation and error handling are essential for maintaining the robustness and resilience of your Kubernetes IaC.

One fundamental aspect of validation in Kubernetes IaC is validating the syntax and structure of your configuration files.

This initial validation step ensures that your YAML or JSON configuration files are well-formed and free of syntax errors.

Tools like **kubectl**, **kubectl apply**, and **kubeval** can be used to check the validity of your configuration files before applying them to your cluster.

Validation at this stage helps catch basic errors early in the development process.

Beyond syntax validation, Kubernetes provides built-in resource schema validation.

Resource schemas define the structure and constraints for Kubernetes resource objects, specifying the allowed fields, data types, and default values.

When you apply a configuration to your cluster, Kubernetes validates whether the resource objects match their corresponding schemas.

This validation helps ensure that your resource objects adhere to Kubernetes specifications, reducing the likelihood of runtime errors.

Resource schema validation can catch issues such as missing required fields, incorrect data types, and invalid values.

However, it's essential to note that schema validation alone may not cover all aspects of your application logic and desired state.

To address this, Kubernetes provides a mechanism for custom resource validation using ValidatingAdmissionWebhooks.

ValidatingAdmissionWebhooks allow you to define custom validation rules and logic for your resources.

You can create webhooks that intercept resource creation and updates, perform custom validations, and reject or modify resources that do not meet your criteria.

These webhooks enable you to implement application-specific validation checks, ensuring that your IaC aligns with your business logic.

Another aspect of validation involves verifying that your Kubernetes resources conform to best practices and compliance standards.

This validation can encompass checks for security policies, network policies, resource quotas, and naming conventions.

Tools like Open Policy Agent (OPA) and Gatekeeper provide a framework for defining and enforcing policies as code.

These policies can be used to validate that your resources meet your organization's standards and industry regulations.

For instance, you can create policies that enforce the use of non-root user accounts, require specific labels on resources, or prohibit the use of insecure container images.

The implementation of these policies ensures that your IaC configurations align with security and compliance requirements.

In addition to policy validation, Kubernetes also supports resource-specific validation using admission controllers.

Admission controllers are extensions in the Kubernetes API server that intercept requests to the API server and can perform validation and mutation operations.

You can develop custom admission controllers to validate resources based on your specific requirements.

For example, you can create an admission controller that checks whether a Pod specification includes resource requests and limits.

If these resource requirements are missing, the admission controller can reject the Pod creation request.

In terms of error handling, Kubernetes provides mechanisms for capturing and responding to errors that occur during resource creation and management.

When an error occurs, Kubernetes generates events that provide details about the issue.

You can use the **kubectl describe** command or query the Kubernetes API to access these events and diagnose problems.

Common errors include resource constraints, such as insufficient CPU or memory, conflicts with existing resources, and issues related to network configurations.

To handle errors effectively, it's essential to implement appropriate error-handling strategies in your IaC.

One common approach is to use Kubernetes probes, such as liveness probes and readiness probes, to detect and respond to errors in your application containers.

Liveness probes check whether a container is still running, while readiness probes determine whether a container is ready to accept traffic.

By configuring these probes, you can ensure that Kubernetes automatically restarts containers that encounter errors or delays in starting up.

Another error-handling strategy involves implementing retry mechanisms in your application code and Kubernetes resources.

For example, you can configure your Deployment resources to retry failed container creations or updates, allowing Kubernetes to make multiple attempts to achieve the desired state.

Additionally, Kubernetes supports error handling through resource-specific configurations.

For instance, you can define a **PodDisruptionBudget** resource to control how many Pods of a certain application can be disrupted simultaneously during maintenance or failures.

By setting resource-specific error-handling policies, you can mitigate the impact of disruptions and errors on your applications' availability.

In summary, validation and error handling are integral components of Kubernetes Infrastructure as Code that contribute to the stability, security, and reliability of your clusters and applications.

Validation involves syntactical checks, schema validation, custom policy validation, and compliance checks to ensure that your IaC adheres to standards and best practices.

Error handling encompasses mechanisms to detect, diagnose, and respond to errors during resource creation and management, including the use of probes, retries, and resource-specific configurations.

By implementing robust validation and error-handling strategies, you can maintain a resilient Kubernetes infrastructure and minimize the impact of unexpected issues on your applications.

Chapter 8: Scaling and Optimization Strategies for Kubernetes

Scaling Kubernetes resources is a fundamental aspect of managing and optimizing your containerized applications and infrastructure in a dynamic and efficient manner.

The ability to scale resources, both vertically and horizontally, allows you to adapt to changing workloads, increase application availability, and optimize resource utilization.

Vertical scaling, often referred to as "scaling up," involves increasing the capacity of individual Pods or containers by adding more CPU, memory, or other resources.

This approach is suitable for applications that have performance bottlenecks and can benefit from additional resources to handle increased loads.

Horizontal scaling, on the other hand, is known as "scaling out" and involves adding more instances of the same resource, such as Pods or nodes, to distribute the workload and improve redundancy.

Horizontal scaling is particularly valuable for applications that need to handle variable workloads, providing elasticity and resilience.

One of the primary mechanisms for scaling Kubernetes resources is by adjusting the number of replicas for a particular resource, such as a Deployment or StatefulSet.

Replica scaling allows you to control the number of identical Pods running your application.

For example, you can scale a Deployment from two replicas to five replicas to handle increased user traffic.

Horizontal Pod Autoscaling (HPA) is a Kubernetes feature that automates the scaling process based on CPU utilization or custom metrics.

HPA continuously monitors resource usage and can automatically increase or decrease the number of replicas to maintain desired resource utilization levels.

This ensures that your applications can efficiently allocate resources based on demand, optimizing cost and performance.

Vertical scaling, in contrast, involves modifying the resource requests and limits for individual Pods.

Resource requests indicate the minimum amount of CPU and memory that a Pod requires, while limits specify the maximum amount of resources a Pod can consume.

By adjusting these parameters, you can control how Pods are scheduled on nodes and how resources are allocated.

Vertical scaling is essential for optimizing resource utilization and ensuring that applications receive the necessary resources to perform effectively.

However, it's essential to monitor resource utilization and fine-tune resource requests and limits to strike the right balance between performance and efficiency.

Another aspect of scaling Kubernetes resources is node scaling, which involves adjusting the number of nodes in your cluster.

Node scaling is crucial for accommodating changes in workload and ensuring that your cluster has sufficient capacity to run your applications.

You can manually add or remove nodes from your cluster as needed, or you can use auto-scaling groups provided by cloud providers to automate this process.

Auto-scaling groups monitor cluster resource utilization and automatically adjust the number of nodes based on predefined policies.

This ensures that your cluster can handle varying workloads without manual intervention.

In addition to adjusting replica counts and node scaling, Kubernetes also provides the concept of cluster auto-scaling.

Cluster auto-scaling enables your cluster to automatically adjust its size by adding or removing nodes based on resource demand.

This capability is particularly valuable for optimizing cost and ensuring that your cluster is neither underutilized nor over-provisioned.

Horizontal scaling and vertical scaling can be combined to achieve a balanced and efficient resource allocation strategy.

For example, you can use horizontal scaling to handle spikes in user traffic by adding more replicas and vertical scaling to optimize the resource utilization of individual Pods.

Furthermore, Kubernetes supports advanced scaling strategies such as pod anti-affinity and node affinity.

Pod anti-affinity ensures that Pods belonging to the same service or application are spread across different nodes, increasing availability and fault tolerance.

Node affinity, on the other hand, allows you to specify preferences for scheduling Pods on nodes based on labels or node characteristics.

These strategies can be used to enhance the resiliency and efficiency of your Kubernetes workloads.

Scaling Kubernetes resources also involves considerations for managing storage and network resources.

For storage, you can utilize Kubernetes Persistent Volumes (PVs) and Persistent Volume Claims (PVCs) to ensure that your applications have access to the necessary storage capacity.

Scaling storage resources often involves dynamically provisioning PVs and PVCs as needed to accommodate growing data requirements.

When it comes to network scaling, Kubernetes provides Network Policies that allow you to define rules for controlling network traffic between Pods and services.

These policies help you segment and secure network traffic within your cluster, ensuring that resources are efficiently used while maintaining security and compliance.

In summary, scaling Kubernetes resources is a multifaceted process that encompasses both horizontal and vertical scaling, node scaling, and advanced strategies like pod anti-affinity and node affinity.

Effective resource scaling enables you to optimize application performance, handle variable workloads, and minimize resource wastage, ultimately ensuring that your Kubernetes infrastructure is cost-effective and resilient.

Optimization techniques for Kubernetes clusters are essential for ensuring that your containerized applications run efficiently, cost-effectively, and with minimal resource waste.

These techniques encompass various strategies and best practices aimed at improving the performance, scalability, and resource utilization of your Kubernetes infrastructure.

One key aspect of optimizing Kubernetes clusters is managing resource allocation effectively.

Kubernetes allows you to define resource requests and limits for Pods, specifying how much CPU and memory each Pod should have access to.

Setting appropriate resource requests and limits ensures that Pods receive the necessary resources without over-provisioning, which can lead to wasted resources and increased costs.

To optimize resource allocation, you can monitor resource utilization using Kubernetes metrics and adjust resource requests and limits based on real-time data.

Scaling your application horizontally by adding more replicas or instances of your Pods can also help distribute the workload and improve resource utilization.

Another important optimization technique involves optimizing the deployment and orchestration of your Pods and services.

Kubernetes provides several strategies for optimizing Pod scheduling, such as node affinity and pod anti-affinity rules.

Node affinity allows you to influence which nodes Pods are scheduled on, while pod anti-affinity ensures that Pods from the same service or application are spread across different nodes, improving fault tolerance and availability.

These strategies help distribute workloads evenly across nodes and prevent resource contention.

Efficient networking is another crucial aspect of Kubernetes cluster optimization.

By configuring network policies and service mesh solutions, you can control and secure the flow of traffic between Pods and services, reducing unnecessary network overhead and ensuring that communication is efficient.

Optimizing container images is another effective technique for improving Kubernetes cluster performance.

Using minimal and well-optimized container images reduces the resource footprint of your Pods and speeds up container image pull times.

Additionally, regularly scanning container images for vulnerabilities and updating them can enhance security and maintain the overall health of your cluster.

Effective cluster monitoring and logging are essential for optimizing Kubernetes clusters.

Implementing monitoring tools like Prometheus and Grafana allows you to collect and visualize cluster metrics, helping you identify performance bottlenecks and resource constraints.

Logging solutions like Elasticsearch and Fluentd enable you to centralize and analyze logs for troubleshooting and performance optimization.

Auto-scaling is a valuable optimization technique that automates the process of adjusting the number of Pods or nodes in your Kubernetes cluster based on predefined metrics and policies.

Horizontal Pod Autoscaling (HPA) automatically scales the number of replicas for a Deployment or StatefulSet based on CPU or custom metrics, ensuring that your application can handle varying workloads efficiently.

Cluster auto-scaling, provided by cloud providers, automatically adjusts the number of nodes in your cluster based on resource demand, optimizing cost and resource utilization.

Regularly updating and patching your Kubernetes cluster components, including the control plane and worker nodes, is critical for security and performance optimization.

Ensuring that you are using the latest stable releases and security patches helps protect your cluster from vulnerabilities and keeps it running smoothly.

Using container runtime security tools like PodSecurityPolicies (PSPs) and admission controllers can help enforce security policies and limit the risk of malicious or insecure containers impacting cluster performance.

Kubernetes also supports the use of custom resource quotas and limits to prevent resource hogging by Pods and services, ensuring fair resource distribution within the cluster.

To further optimize Kubernetes clusters, consider leveraging Kubernetes-native storage solutions like Persistent Volumes (PVs) and Persistent Volume Claims (PVCs) to efficiently manage storage resources.

By dynamically provisioning and reclaiming storage as needed, you can prevent resource waste and reduce storage costs.

Implementing CI/CD pipelines and GitOps practices streamlines the deployment and management of applications in Kubernetes clusters, promoting automation, version control, and consistency.

Using Helm charts and Git repositories for managing application configurations simplifies application deployment and maintenance, enhancing cluster optimization.

Optimization also involves capacity planning, where you analyze your workloads and resource usage trends to ensure that your cluster can handle expected growth without resource exhaustion.

Regularly reviewing and optimizing your Kubernetes cluster's architecture and configuration settings, such as resource quotas and resource limits, helps ensure efficient resource utilization.

To optimize cluster performance, regularly monitor and analyze application performance metrics, resource utilization, and error rates using tools like Kubernetes Dashboard, Prometheus, and Grafana.

By proactively addressing performance bottlenecks and resource constraints, you can fine-tune your cluster for optimal operation.

Lastly, consider implementing auto-scaling for your Kubernetes cluster nodes, allowing the cluster to dynamically adjust its size based on resource demand.

This can help optimize costs by ensuring that you have the right amount of compute capacity to meet your application's needs without over-provisioning.

In summary, optimization techniques for Kubernetes clusters encompass a range of strategies and best practices aimed at improving resource allocation, orchestration, networking, container images, monitoring, security, and scalability.

By applying these techniques, you can ensure that your Kubernetes clusters operate efficiently, cost-effectively, and with optimal performance, supporting your containerized applications effectively.

Chapter 9: CI/CD Pipelines for Kubernetes IaC

Implementing Continuous Integration and Continuous Deployment (CI/CD) for Kubernetes Infrastructure as Code (IaC) projects is crucial for streamlining the development and deployment of containerized applications in Kubernetes clusters.

CI/CD pipelines automate the build, test, and deployment processes, enabling developers to deliver code changes more rapidly and reliably.

By integrating CI/CD into your Kubernetes IaC projects, you can achieve greater efficiency, consistency, and agility in managing your infrastructure and applications.

The first step in implementing CI/CD for Kubernetes IaC projects is setting up a version control system (VCS) such as Git to manage your project's source code and infrastructure definitions.

Using a VCS allows you to track changes, collaborate with team members, and maintain a history of your project's codebase, making it a fundamental component of CI/CD workflows.

Once your codebase is in a VCS, you can establish automated build and test processes triggered by code changes.

These processes involve compiling code, running unit tests, and performing other quality checks to ensure that changes are valid and do not introduce regressions.

For Kubernetes IaC projects, this involves validating your infrastructure configurations and code to catch errors early in the development cycle.

CI/CD tools like Jenkins, Travis CI, GitLab CI/CD, and CircleCI can be integrated with your VCS to create pipelines that automate these build and test stages.

Using Kubernetes-specific tools like kubectl and kustomize, you can define and manage your cluster's infrastructure declaratively, specifying the desired state of your resources.

Infrastructure configurations, such as Deployments, Services, ConfigMaps, and PersistentVolumeClaims, are stored in version-controlled YAML files.

These files serve as the single source of truth for your infrastructure, and changes to them trigger the CI/CD pipeline.

Incorporating automated testing into your CI/CD pipeline is essential for ensuring that your Kubernetes IaC configurations are valid and will function as expected when deployed to a cluster.

Testing can include static analysis of YAML files, linting, validation against best practices, and functional testing to verify that resources can be created and interact as intended.

By including these tests in your pipeline, you can prevent misconfigurations and reduce the likelihood of issues in production environments.

Containerization plays a significant role in Kubernetes IaC projects, as applications are typically packaged as Docker containers.

Therefore, your CI/CD pipeline should also include container image building and testing steps.

You can use tools like Docker, Buildah, or Kaniko to build container images from your application code and dependencies.

After building the images, they can be pushed to a container registry like Docker Hub, Google Container Registry, or Amazon Elastic Container Registry (ECR) for distribution and deployment.

To ensure that container images are free from vulnerabilities and meet security standards, you should integrate container scanning and security testing into your CI/CD pipeline.

Tools like Clair, Trivy, and Anchore can analyze images for known vulnerabilities and compliance issues, providing insights and recommendations for remediation.

Once your Kubernetes IaC project's code and container images have passed all tests and security checks, you can proceed to the deployment stage of your CI/CD pipeline.

In Kubernetes, deploying infrastructure and applications is typically done using declarative configurations, which specify the desired state of resources in the cluster.

Tools like kubectl, Helm, and kustomize allow you to apply these configurations to your Kubernetes cluster.

However, it's important to manage deployments carefully to avoid disruptions and maintain high availability.

One common practice is to use rolling updates, which gradually replace old versions of Pods with new ones while monitoring the deployment's progress.

Rolling back to a previous version is also possible in case of issues.

To implement CI/CD for Kubernetes IaC projects effectively, it's important to adopt GitOps practices.

GitOps is a methodology that uses Git repositories as the source of truth for both code and infrastructure configurations.

With GitOps, changes to your infrastructure are made through pull requests and are reviewed and approved in the same way as code changes.

Tools like ArgoCD and Flux can automatically synchronize your Kubernetes cluster with the Git repository, ensuring that the desired state of the infrastructure is always maintained.

Using GitOps, you can achieve greater visibility, traceability, and control over changes to your Kubernetes cluster, enhancing security and compliance.

Secret management is another crucial aspect of CI/CD for Kubernetes IaC projects.

Sensitive information, such as API keys, passwords, and certificates, should not be stored in version-controlled files.

Instead, you can use Kubernetes Secrets or external secrets management tools like HashiCorp Vault or AWS Secrets Manager to store and manage sensitive data.

Integrating secrets management into your CI/CD pipeline allows you to securely inject secrets into your application Pods at deployment time.

This ensures that sensitive information is kept confidential and that secrets can be rotated and managed effectively.

Monitoring and observability are essential components of CI/CD for Kubernetes IaC projects.

By incorporating monitoring tools like Prometheus and Grafana into your pipeline, you can collect and visualize metrics, logs, and alerts from your Kubernetes cluster.

This enables you to proactively detect and respond to issues, track performance, and ensure the health of your infrastructure and applications.

Automated testing and deployment are critical aspects of managing Kubernetes clusters efficiently and ensuring the reliability of containerized applications in production environments.

Kubernetes has gained popularity due to its ability to orchestrate containerized workloads at scale, but it also introduces complexity in managing and monitoring these workloads.

To maintain the desired state of your Kubernetes resources and ensure they work as expected, you need a robust automated testing and deployment strategy.

In Kubernetes, you describe the desired state of your resources using declarative configuration files, such as YAML manifests.

These configuration files define the structure, properties, and relationships of resources like Pods, Services, Deployments, ConfigMaps, and more.

Automated testing in Kubernetes involves verifying that these configurations are correct, adhere to best practices, and do not introduce security vulnerabilities or compliance issues.

One common type of automated testing for Kubernetes configurations is static analysis.

Static analysis tools examine your YAML files for syntax errors, formatting issues, and potential problems with resource definitions.

These tools can catch mistakes early in the development process, preventing issues from propagating to production.

Linters and validators like kubeval, kube-score, and kube-linter are examples of static analysis tools that can be integrated into your CI/CD pipeline to automate this testing.

In addition to static analysis, automated testing for Kubernetes configurations can include dynamic checks that verify the functional correctness of your resources.

Functional testing involves validating that your resources can be created, updated, and deleted as expected, and that they interact correctly with other resources.

For example, you might want to ensure that a Deployment scales the desired number of replicas, or that a Service can route traffic to the correct Pods.

Functional testing tools, such as Kyverno and Open Policy Agent (OPA), enable you to define policies that enforce resource behavior and characteristics.

These policies are evaluated against your configurations to ensure compliance with your intended use cases.

Security is a paramount concern in Kubernetes, and automated security testing is a crucial part of your CI/CD pipeline.

Container images used in Kubernetes are often the target of security vulnerabilities.

To address this, you can integrate container scanning tools into your CI/CD workflow to automatically check for known vulnerabilities in your images.

Tools like Trivy, Clair, and Anchore scan container images for vulnerabilities and generate reports that help you identify and remediate security issues.

By automating container image scanning, you can ensure that only secure and trusted images are deployed to your Kubernetes cluster.

In addition to image scanning, you should also automate the validation of Kubernetes security configurations.

Kubernetes has a wide range of security settings that can be customized to protect your cluster and workloads.

Automated security testing tools can assess your cluster's security posture, identify misconfigurations, and suggest remediation steps.

Tools like kube-bench and kube-hunter are designed to automate security audits and penetration testing of Kubernetes clusters.

By including these security checks in your CI/CD pipeline, you can continuously monitor and improve the security of your Kubernetes infrastructure.

Once your automated testing processes are in place, the next step is to automate the deployment of your Kubernetes resources.

Continuous Deployment (CD) pipelines enable you to automate the deployment process, ensuring that changes to your configurations are automatically applied to your Kubernetes cluster.

CD pipelines can be triggered by changes to your codebase, configuration files, or container images, ensuring that updates are deployed consistently and without manual intervention.

To implement automated deployments in Kubernetes, you can use tools like kubectl, Helm, and kustomize, which enable you to manage resource configurations and apply changes declaratively.

Kubectl, the Kubernetes command-line tool, allows you to apply configuration changes directly to your cluster.

Helm is a package manager for Kubernetes that simplifies the management of resource configurations using templates and releases.

Kustomize provides a way to customize and manage Kubernetes resource definitions using overlays and patches.

When automating deployments, it's essential to follow best practices to ensure reliability and minimize disruptions.

One common practice is to use rolling updates, which gradually replace old versions of Pods with new ones to maintain high availability.

Rolling back to a previous version is also possible in case of issues, allowing you to quickly recover from deployment failures.

Another best practice is to use GitOps principles to manage deployments declaratively using version-controlled Git repositories as the source of truth.

Tools like ArgoCD and Flux can automate the synchronization of your Kubernetes cluster with your Git repository, ensuring that the desired state is maintained.

By adopting GitOps, you gain visibility, traceability, and control over changes to your cluster, enhancing security and compliance.

Secret management is a crucial consideration when automating deployments in Kubernetes.

Sensitive information such as API tokens, database passwords, and encryption keys should be kept secure and not exposed in configuration files or container images.

Kubernetes provides Secret objects for managing sensitive data, and you can use external secrets management solutions like

HashiCorp Vault or Kubernetes Secrets Store CSI Driver to centralize and secure secrets.

Integrating secret management into your CI/CD pipeline allows you to securely inject secrets into your application Pods at deployment time.

This ensures that sensitive information remains confidential and can be rotated and managed effectively.

Monitoring and observability are essential components of automated testing and deployment in Kubernetes.

Automated testing and deployment workflows should include monitoring tools like Prometheus and Grafana to collect and visualize metrics, logs, and alerts from your cluster.

These tools enable you to proactively detect and respond to issues, track performance, and ensure the health of your infrastructure and applications.

Automated testing in production-like environments is a critical part of your CI/CD pipeline.

Production-like environments closely resemble your production cluster and provide a controlled environment for testing changes before deploying them to production.

By automating the creation and teardown of these environments, you can validate configurations, perform end-to-end testing, and catch potential issues early in the development cycle.

Tools like Kubernetes namespaces and tools like kind (Kubernetes in Docker) or Minikube are valuable for creating isolated environments that mimic your production cluster.

Automating the deployment of applications in these environments and running comprehensive tests helps ensure that your changes will perform as expected when deployed to your production cluster.

In summary, automated testing and deployment in Kubernetes are essential for maintaining the reliability and security of your containerized applications and infrastructure.

By integrating automated testing for configurations and container images into your CI/CD pipeline, you can catch issues early and ensure that your Kubernetes resources are compliant and secure.

Automating deployments using best practices like rolling updates, GitOps, and secret management streamlines the process of applying changes to your cluster.

Monitoring and observability tools provide visibility into your cluster's performance and health, helping you proactively address issues.

Finally, automating the creation of production-like environments for testing enables you to validate changes in a controlled setting, reducing the risk of issues in your production cluster.

Chapter 10: Real-world Kubernetes IaC Expert Strategies and Case Studies

In this case study, we will explore the deployment of highly available microservices on a Kubernetes cluster, highlighting the benefits and challenges of leveraging Kubernetes for such a scenario.

High availability (HA) is a critical requirement for modern applications, ensuring that they remain accessible and responsive even in the face of component failures or other issues.

Microservices architecture has gained popularity due to its ability to break down complex applications into smaller, more manageable services that can be developed and scaled independently.

However, as the number of microservices grows, managing their deployment, scaling, and availability becomes increasingly challenging.

Kubernetes provides a robust solution for addressing these challenges by offering a platform for orchestrating containerized microservices at scale.

To achieve high availability in a Kubernetes-based microservices environment, several key considerations and strategies must be employed.

One fundamental aspect is the distribution of microservices across multiple Kubernetes nodes to minimize the impact of node failures.

Kubernetes does this through its deployment of Pods, which are scheduled onto nodes in a way that ensures redundancy and resilience.

Load balancing is another critical component of achieving high availability.

In Kubernetes, Services provide a way to load balance traffic across multiple Pods, distributing requests evenly and redirecting traffic away from unhealthy or failed Pods.

Additionally, Kubernetes offers the concept of readiness and liveness probes, which allow you to define conditions that determine whether a Pod is considered healthy and ready to receive traffic.

By configuring these probes correctly, you can ensure that only healthy Pods serve incoming requests, improving the overall reliability of your microservices.

Stateless microservices are often easier to make highly available because they don't rely on local state that could be lost if a Pod fails.

Stateless microservices can be horizontally scaled by deploying multiple replicas, and traffic can be evenly distributed to these replicas using Kubernetes Services.

For stateful microservices, which require persistent data, Kubernetes offers solutions like StatefulSets and Persistent Volumes (PVs) to ensure data persistence and availability.

StatefulSets provide stable network identities for Pods and maintain a consistent order for Pod creation and scaling.

PVs allow you to attach persistent storage to Pods, ensuring that data remains available even if a Pod is rescheduled to a different node.

When designing a highly available microservices architecture in Kubernetes, it's crucial to consider the application's resilience to network failures.

Kubernetes provides features like Pod anti-affinity and node affinity rules that allow you to control how Pods are scheduled across nodes.

These rules can be used to ensure that critical microservices are not colocated on the same node, reducing the risk of simultaneous failures due to node issues.

In addition to managing microservices' availability within a single cluster, Kubernetes offers features for disaster recovery and multi-cluster management.

Kubernetes Federation and tools like ArgoCD can be used to deploy and manage microservices across multiple clusters, providing geographical redundancy and failover capabilities.

Implementing high availability in a Kubernetes-based microservices architecture also involves continuous monitoring and observability.

Kubernetes provides a wealth of metrics and logs that can be collected and analyzed to detect issues early and troubleshoot effectively.

Prometheus and Grafana are popular tools for monitoring Kubernetes clusters and microservices, offering real-time visibility into the health and performance of the system.

Kubernetes also integrates with container runtime monitoring solutions like cAdvisor and containerd to provide insights into resource usage and container behavior.

High availability is not only about ensuring that your microservices are available but also about automating recovery in case of failures.

Kubernetes provides tools like ReplicaSets, DaemonSets, and Deployments that allow you to define desired states for your microservices and automatically recover from failures by creating new Pods or rescheduling existing ones.

These automated recovery mechanisms reduce the need for manual intervention and help maintain a consistent level of availability.

In summary, Kubernetes offers a powerful platform for deploying highly available microservices, but achieving high availability requires careful planning and implementation.

Considerations such as distribution, load balancing, statefulness, network resilience, disaster recovery, and monitoring all play crucial roles in building a resilient microservices architecture on Kubernetes.

By leveraging Kubernetes' features and best practices, organizations can confidently deploy microservices that meet their high availability requirements and deliver reliable, responsive applications to their users.

In this case study, we will delve into the design and deployment of a Kubernetes-based big data processing platform, demonstrating how Kubernetes can efficiently manage the complexities of distributed data processing at scale.

Big data processing is a fundamental aspect of modern data-driven organizations, requiring the ability to ingest, process, and analyze large volumes of data from various sources.

Traditionally, big data platforms like Apache Hadoop and Apache Spark have been deployed on dedicated clusters, which can be costly to maintain and inflexible in terms of resource allocation.

Kubernetes offers a more flexible and cost-effective solution by allowing organizations to leverage containerization for their big data workloads.

One of the key benefits of using Kubernetes for big data processing is its ability to dynamically allocate and scale resources based on workload demand.

Kubernetes provides a range of resource management features, such as Horizontal Pod Autoscaling, that can automatically adjust the number of processing nodes to handle changing workloads.

For our case study, let's consider a scenario where an e-commerce company needs to process and analyze customer behavior data to gain insights for improving its services and marketing strategies.

The company collects data from various sources, including website logs, mobile app interactions, and transaction records, resulting in a significant volume of data that needs to be processed efficiently.

To address this challenge, the company decides to build a Kubernetes-based big data processing platform, which offers the following advantages:

First, Kubernetes simplifies the deployment and management of big data processing frameworks like Apache Spark, Apache Flink, and Apache Kafka.

These frameworks can be packaged as Docker containers and deployed as Kubernetes Pods, allowing for consistent deployment and easier maintenance.

Kubernetes also provides built-in features for managing stateful workloads, which is essential for many big data processing tasks that involve data persistence.

Persistent Volumes and StatefulSets in Kubernetes can be used to ensure that data remains available even if a processing node fails.

Furthermore, Kubernetes' ability to orchestrate microservices can be leveraged to create complex data pipelines where data is ingested, transformed, and analyzed using different processing frameworks.

Each component of the pipeline can be independently scaled, allowing for efficient resource utilization.

In our case study, the company designs its big data processing platform with multiple components, including data ingestion, data processing, and data storage.

For data ingestion, Kubernetes Jobs are used to periodically fetch data from various sources, such as log files and databases, and store it in a distributed file system like HDFS (Hadoop Distributed File System) running on Kubernetes.

Data processing is performed using Apache Spark, which is deployed as a Kubernetes StatefulSet.

The Spark cluster can scale horizontally by adding or removing worker nodes based on the workload.

Spark applications are submitted to the cluster using Kubernetes Jobs, which allows for the isolation and management of individual processing tasks.

Data storage is handled by distributed databases like Apache Cassandra, also deployed on Kubernetes using StatefulSets.

This ensures that data is stored reliably and can be accessed quickly by the processing components.

One of the critical aspects of big data processing is fault tolerance.

Kubernetes helps address this challenge by providing tools for monitoring and automatic recovery.

For example, if a Spark worker node fails, Kubernetes can automatically replace it with a new one, ensuring that processing tasks continue without interruption.

Additionally, Kubernetes monitoring and logging solutions, such as Prometheus and Fluentd, can be used to gain visibility into the health and performance of the big data platform.

These tools allow operators to proactively identify issues and optimize resource utilization.

Another advantage of deploying big data processing on Kubernetes is the ability to leverage cloud-native features.

Many cloud providers offer Kubernetes-managed services, such as Google Kubernetes Engine (GKE) and Amazon Elastic Kubernetes Service (EKS), which simplify cluster management and provide integration with cloud-specific services.

In our case study, the e-commerce company chooses to run its Kubernetes-based big data platform on a cloud provider's managed Kubernetes service to take advantage of scalability and integration with other cloud services.

In summary, this case study illustrates how Kubernetes can be utilized to build a scalable, cost-effective, and fault-tolerant big data processing platform.

By containerizing big data processing frameworks and leveraging Kubernetes' resource management, orchestration, and monitoring capabilities, organizations can efficiently process and analyze large volumes of data, gaining valuable insights for decision-making and business optimization.

Kubernetes' flexibility and cloud-native features make it a compelling choice for modern big data processing workloads, providing a competitive advantage in today's data-driven landscape.

Conclusion

In "IaC Mastery: Infrastructure as Code - Your All-in-One Guide to Terraform, AWS, Azure, and Kubernetes," we embarked on a comprehensive journey through the world of Infrastructure as Code (IaC), exploring the essential tools and strategies that empower modern cloud infrastructure management. This four-book bundle, comprising "Getting Started with IaC: A Beginner's Guide to Terraform," "Cloud Infrastructure Orchestration with AWS and IaC," "Azure IaC Mastery: Advanced Techniques and Best Practices," and "Kubernetes Infrastructure as Code: Expert Strategies and Beyond," has equipped readers with a wealth of knowledge and skills to excel in the field of IaC.

In the first book, "Getting Started with IaC: A Beginner's Guide to Terraform," we laid the foundation by introducing the fundamental concepts of IaC and immersing readers in the world of Terraform. From understanding the basics of Terraform to mastering its configuration and syntax, this book provided newcomers with a solid grasp of how to create, manage, and scale infrastructure as code.

With "Cloud Infrastructure Orchestration with AWS and IaC," the second book in the bundle, readers ventured into the realm of Amazon Web Services (AWS) and learned how to harness the power of IaC for AWS infrastructure management. From setting up an AWS environment for IaC to exploring advanced techniques, security, and compliance, this book enabled readers to orchestrate AWS resources efficiently and securely.

"Azure IaC Mastery: Advanced Techniques and Best Practices," the third book in the series, expanded our horizons into the Azure ecosystem. Readers delved into advanced IaC techniques specific to Azure, gaining insights into intricate networking, security, testing, and optimization strategies. This book elevated readers to a mastery level, equipping them with the expertise needed to excel in Azure infrastructure management.

The journey reached its zenith with "Kubernetes Infrastructure as Code: Expert Strategies and Beyond," the fourth and final book in the bundle. Here, readers explored the cutting-edge world of Kubernetes IaC, unraveling its intricacies, security measures, testing frameworks, and advanced strategies. Armed with this knowledge, readers became true experts in managing Kubernetes infrastructure as code.

Throughout this book bundle, we emphasized the importance of best practices, collaboration, version control, and continuous integration and deployment (CI/CD) in the IaC landscape. We explored real-world case studies that showcased the practical applications of IaC in various scenarios, highlighting its transformative power in modern IT operations.

As we conclude our journey through "IaC Mastery: Infrastructure as Code," it is our hope that readers have not only gained a deep understanding of Terraform, AWS, Azure, and Kubernetes but have also developed the skills and confidence to excel in their roles as cloud infrastructure professionals. In an ever-evolving technological landscape, embracing Infrastructure as Code is not just a choice but a necessity, and this book bundle has provided the knowledge and guidance needed to thrive in this exciting field.

Thank you for joining us on this educational journey, and we wish you continued success in your endeavors to master the art of Infrastructure as Code.

www.ingramcontent.com/pod-product-compliance
Lightning Source LLC
Chambersburg PA
CBHW071235050326
40690CB00011B/2121